DATE

FEDERAL CIVIL SERVICE JOBS

12th Edition

Hy Hammer

MACMILLAN • USA

Twelfth Edition

Macmillan General Reference
A Simon & Schuster Macmillan Company
1633 Broadway
New York, NY 10019-6785

Macmillan Publishing books may be purchased for business or sales promotional use. For information please write: Special Markets Department, Macmillan Publishing USA, 1633 Broadway, New York, NY 10019-6785.

An ARCO Book

Library of Congress Number: 97-81096

ISBN: 0-02-862506-4

Manufactured in the United States of America

10 9 8 7 6 5 4 3 2 1

CONTENTS

INTRODUCTION

The federal government is the employer of a far greater number of Americans than is any other employer. A large percentage of these government employees are members of the military, but there are also millions of civilian federal employees. Many civilian federal employees are employed through the Legislative Branch—the Congress itself, the General Accounting Office, the Government Printing Office, and the Library of Congress, for example—and through the Judicial Branch—the Supreme Court and the U.S. Court system. But by far the greatest number of federal civilian employees are employees of the Executive Branch, Executive Departments, and Independent Agencies such as the U.S. Postal Service, the General Services Administration, the Smithsonian, the Environmental Protection Agency, and the Office of Personnel Administration itself, to name only a few.

The Executive Branch includes the Office of the President, the departments with cabinet representation, and a number of independent agencies, commissions, and boards. This branch is responsible for such activities as administering federal laws, handling international relations, conserving natural resources, treating and rehabilitating disabled veterans, conducting scientific research, maintaining the flow of supplies to the armed forces, and administering other programs to promote the health and welfare of the people.

The federal government employs about three million white-collar workers. Entrance requirements for white-collar jobs vary widely. Entrants into professional occupations are required to have highly specialized knowledge in a specified field, as evidenced by completion of a prescribed college course of study. Occupations typical of this group are attorney, physicist, and engineer.

Entrants into administrative and managerial occupations usually are not required to have specialized knowledge but rather they must indicate, by graduation from a four-year college or by responsible job experience, that they have the potential for future development. The entrant usually begins at a trainee level and learns the duties of the job after being hired. Typical jobs in this group are budget analyst, claims examiner, purchasing officer, administrative assistant, and personnel officer.

Technician, clerical, and aide-assistant jobs have entry level positions that usually are filled by persons having a high school diploma or the equivalent. For many of these positions, no prior experience or training is required. The entry level position is usually that of trainee, where the duties of the job are learned and skill is improved. Persons with junior college or technical school training or those having specialized skills may enter these occupations at higher levels. Jobs typical of this group are engineering technician, supply clerk, clerk-typist, and nursing assistant.

Blue-collar jobs—service, craft, and manual labor—provide employment to over 600,000 workers. The majority of these workers are in establishments such as naval shipyards, arsenals, air bases, or army depots, or they work on construction, harbor, flood-control, irrigation, or reclamation projects.

The single largest group of blue-collar workers consists of mobile equipment operators and mechanics. Among these jobs are forklift operator, chauffeur, truck driver, and automobile mechanic. The next largest group is general laborers who perform a wide variety of manual jobs.

Many skilled occupations may be entered through apprenticeship programs. Experience normally is not required to qualify, but a test may be given to indicate whether an applicant has an aptitude for the occupation.

Federal employees are stationed in all parts of the United States and its territories and in many foreign countries. (Although most government departments and agencies have their headquarters in the Washington, D.C., metropolitan area, only 1 out of 11 federal workers was employed there at the beginning of this year.)

PART ONE

Working for the Federal Government

HOW TO GET A JOB IN THE FEDERAL GOVERNMENT

General Categories of Federal Jobs

Professional occupations are those requiring knowledge in a field, characteristically acquired through education or training equivalent to a bachelor's or higher degree, with major study in or pertinent to the specialized field, e.g., engineer, accountant, biologist, chemist.

Administrative occupations are those which require progressively responsible experience or college level general education, e.g., personnel specialist, administrative officer.

Technical occupations are those involving support of a professional or administrative field which is nonroutine in nature, e.g., computer technician, electronic technician.

Clerical occupations are those involving structured work in support of office, business, or fiscal operations, e.g., clerk-typist, mail and file clerk.

Other occupations are those that do not fall into the above categories, e.g., painters, carpenters, and laborers.

Specific Programs in the Federal Service

Part-time positions—16 to 32 hours per week—are available in agencies throughout the federal government. Flex time, job sharing, and nontraditional configurations of workday and workweek are also available in some positions. Make inquiries at the personnel office of the agency of your choice.

Summer employment opportunities for high school, college, law, medical, and dental students are available in limited numbers throughout the federal government. Applications are accepted for summer employment from December through April 15, and the jobs tend to run from mid-May through September 30. Hiring is done by the individual agencies. There are certain restrictions that limit summer employment in the same department or agency in which a parent is employed.

The student career experience is a work/study program for high school, vocational/ technical school, and college students who are enrolled in school at least half time. This program offers employment in positions directly related to the student's course of study. Positions in this program may lead to permanent employment with the agency upon the student's graduation from school. Students who are interested in a career experience should contact their high school counselors, college employment coordinators, or the agency at which they would like to work.

Student temporary employment is part-time employment for students which is not necessarily related to the careers for which they are preparing. This employment must end when the student is no longer enrolled in school at least half time. The procedure for locating and securing this employment is similar to that for the student career experience.

The PMI program for Presidential Management Interns is specifically targeted for graduate students in the last year of their graduate programs. Only graduate students who expect to receive their degrees by the next June should apply. These students enter the two-year PMI program at the GS-9 level and perform high level work in their chosen fields. At the end of the two years, PMIs may continue in regular federal employment at the GS-12 level. Students interested in this program must be nominated by the Dean of the college or university or by the chairman of their department or graduate program. With government cutbacks and downsizing, all student programs are limited.

Veterans are entitled to special consideration in hiring. In some cases, veterans are entitled to positions that are not open to the general public. In other instances, extra points are added to their exam scores, placing them at a competitive advantage. The Veterans Employment Coordinator of the agency can give more information.

Persons with physical disabilities should contact the Selective Placement Coordinator at the agency of interest for special placement assistance.

Alaska, Guam, Hawaii, Puerto Rico, and the Virgin Islands offer very limited federal employment possibilities. Residents of these localities will receive first consideration for employment in these areas. Other candidates will be considered only when there are no qualified residents available.

Postal Service hiring is very localized. Rather than making application to the Postal Service, interested persons should make inquiry and application at the post office branch in which they wish to be employed.

Where and How to Obtain Information

By far the easiest and most efficient way to get information about job openings throughout the country and to get application materials is to call the Career America Connection at (912) 757-3000. This is a toll call, but it is a 24-hour automated service, so you can hold down costs by calling at night or on the weekend. You will need a touch tone telephone to utilize the service. Allow yourself at least one-half hour to search job categories and geographical areas. The system is equipped to record your name and mailing address so that you can be sent announcements and required forms through the mail. If you have a computer with modem, you can access the same information from an OPM electronic bulletin board by dialing (912) 757-3100.

You might also look under the heading "U.S. Government" in the blue pages of your telephone directory for a listing for Office of Personnel Management or Federal Job Information Center. A telephone call to this number may give you automated information pertinent to your own area or may direct you to a location at which you can pick up printed materials or conduct a search on a computer touch screen.

Some state employment services maintain computer touch screens which contain listings of available federal jobs within the state. You might also check with your public library and, for postal employment, on your post office bulletin board. Announcement material should tell you how to proceed with making application for the position.

At one time, federal hiring was a centralized function of the Office of Personnel Management. This is no longer the case. All hiring is done by the individual agencies. If you know which agencies you wish to work for, you may contact them directly to learn what vacancies exist and the application procedures. At some agencies you may prepare an application to be kept on file for future vacancies. Other agencies accept applications only for current or projected openings. If a federal agency has offices in your area, you may find the telephone number under "U.S. Government" in the blue pages. If the agency has no office in your area, you may have to place a call to information in the District of Columbia, (202) 555-1212, to ask for the telephone number of the personnel office or employment office of the agency that you wish to reach. Calls to government offices must be made during business hours, so prepare your questions ahead of time to hold down your phone bill.

How to Apply

The announcement of the position for which you are applying will specify the form of application requested. For most federal jobs, you may submit either the Optional Application for Federal Employment (OF 612) or a resume which fulfills the requirements set forth in the pamphlet, Applying for a Federal Job (OF 510). The essence of each of these publications is reproduced below.

You will note that you are repeatedly cautioned not to send more backup material than is requested on the announcement. By the same token, be sure to include any backup material that is requested. Your application must be complete according to the requirements of the announcement, but must not be overwhelming. You want to command hiring attention by exactly conforming to requirements.

NEW ELECTRONIC OPTIONS

The most recent development in the federal employment picture is the construction of the Office of Personnel Management web site. You can access this site at its URL: www.usajobs.opm.gov/ At this site you can find explanations of federal job categories and specific job descriptions. You can then search geographically and alphabetically to find out which jobs have current openings and exactly where the openings are located. The listings, in turn, refer you to full vacancy announcements, including qualifications requirements and application procedures and deadlines. With adequate equipment you can download the announcement. Or you can then take notes from the information on your screen. Likewise, with sophisticated equipment you can download application forms or even apply electronically using your computer. Or, you can follow instructions for getting the proper forms by telephone or mail.

Optional Application for Federal Employment — OF 612

Form Approved
OMB No. 3206-0219

You may apply for most jobs with a resume, this form, or other written format. If your resume or application does not provide all the information requested on this form and in the job vacancy announcement, you may lose consideration for a job.

1 Job title in announcement	**2** Grade(s) applying for	**3** Announcement number

4 Last name	First and middle names	**5** Social Security Number

6 Mailing address		**7** Phone numbers (include area code)
City	State	ZIP Code	Daytime ( )
			Evening ( )

WORK EXPERIENCE

8 Describe your paid and nonpaid work experience related to the job for which you are applying. Do **not** attach job descriptions.

1) Job title (if Federal, include series and grade)

From (MM/YY)	To (MM/YY)	Salary $ per	Hours per week
Employer's name and address			Supervisor's name and phone number ( )

Describe your duties and accomplishments

2) Job title (if Federal, include series and grade)

From (MM/YY)	To (MM/YY)	Salary $ per	Hours per week
Employer's name and address			Supervisor's name and phone number ( )

Describe your duties and accomplishments

50612-101

NSN 7540-01-351-9178

Optional Form 612 (September 1994)
U.S. Office of Personnel Management

9 May we contact your current supervisor?

YES [　] 　NO [　] ➧ If we need to contact your current supervisor before making an offer, we will contact you first.

EDUCATION

10 Mark highest level completed. **Some HS** [　] 　**HS/GED** [　] 　**Associate** [　] 　**Bachelor** [　] 　**Master** [　] 　**Doctoral** [　]

11 Last high school (HS) or GED school. Give the school's name, city, State, ZIP Code (if known), and year diploma or GED received.

12 Colleges and universities attended. Do **not** attach a copy of your transcript unless requested.

Name				Total Credits Earned		Major(s)	Degree (if any)	– Year Received
				Semester	Quarter			
1) City		State	ZIP Code					
2)								
3)								

OTHER QUALIFICATIONS

13 **Job-related** training courses (give title and year). **Job-related** skills (other languages, computer software/hardware, tools, machinery, typing speed, etc.). **Job-related** certificates and licenses (current only). **Job-related** honors, awards, and special accomplishments (publications, memberships in professional/honor societies, leadership activities, public speaking, and performance awards). Give dates, but do **not** send documents unless requested.

GENERAL

14 Are you a U.S. citizen? 　　　　YES [　] 　NO [　] ➧ Give the country of your citizenship. _____

15 Do you claim veteran's preference? **NO** [　] 　**YES** [　] ➧ Mark your claim of 5 or 10 points below.

5 points [　] ➧ Attach your DD 214 or other proof. **10 points** [　] ➧ Attach an *Application for 10-Point Veterans' Preference* (SF 15) and proof required.

16 Were you ever a Federal civilian employee?

| | Series | Grade | From (MM/YY) | To (MM/YY) |

NO [　] 　YES [　] ➧ For highest civilian grade give:

17 Are you eligible for reinstatement based on career or career-conditional Federal status?

NO [　] 　YES [　] ➧ If requested, attach SF 50 proof.

APPLICANT CERTIFICATION

18 I **certify** that, to the best of my knowledge and belief, all of the information on and attached to this application is true, correct, complete and made in good faith. I **understand** that false or fraudulent information on or attached to this application may be grounds for not hiring me or for firing me after I begin work, and may be punishable by fine or imprisonment. I **understand** that any information I give may be investigated.

SIGNATURE　　　　　　　　　　　　　　　　　　　**DATE SIGNED**

APPLYING FOR A FEDERAL JOB—OF 510

HERE'S WHAT YOUR RESUME OR APPLICATION MUST CONTAIN
(in addition to specific information requested in the job vacancy announcement):

JOB INFORMATION

❏ Announcement number, and title and grade(s) of the job for which you are applying

PERSONAL INFORMATION

❏ Full name, mailing address (with ZIP code) and day and evening phone numbers (with area code)
❏ Social Security Number
❏ Country of citizenship (Most Federal jobs require United States citizenship.)
❏ Veterans' preference (See reverse.)
❏ Reinstatement eligibility (If requested, attach SF 50 proof of your career or career-conditional status.)
❏ Highest Federal civilian grade held (Also give job series and dates held.)

EDUCATION

❏ High school
 Name, city, and State (ZIP Code if known)
 Date of diploma or GED
❏ Colleges and universities
 Name, city, and State (ZIP Code if known)
 Majors
 Type and year of any degrees received
 (If no degree, show total credits earned and indicate whether semester or quarter hours.)
❏ Send a copy of your college transcript only if the job vacancy announcement requests it.

WORK EXPERIENCE

❏ Give the following information for your paid and nonpaid work experience related to the job for which you are applying (Do not send job descriptions.)
 Job title (include series and grade if Federal job)
 Duties and accomplishments
 Employer's name and address
 Supervisor's name and phone number
 Starting and ending dates (month and year)
 Hours per week
 Salary
❏ Indicate if we may contact your current supervisor

OTHER QUALIFICATIONS

❏ **Job-related** training *courses* (title and year)
❏ **Job-related** skills, for example, other languages, computer software/hardware, tools, machinery, typing speed
❏ **Job-related** certificates and licenses (current only)
❏ **Job-related** honors, awards, and special accomplishments, for example, publications, memberships in professional or honor societies, leadership activities, public speaking, and performance awards (Give dates but do not send documents unless requested.)

The Federal Government is an equal opportunity employer

Job Openings

For job information 24 hours a day, 7 days a week, call **912-757-3000,** the U.S. Office of Personnel Management (OPM) automated telephone system. Or, with a computer modem dial **912-757-3100** for job information from an OPM electronic bulletin board. You can also reach the board through the Internet (Telnet only) at FJOB.MAIL.OPM.GOV.

Applicants with Disabilities

You can find out about alternative formats by calling OPM. Select "Federal Employment Topics" and then "People with Disabilities." Or, dial our electronic bulletin board. If you have a hearing disability, call **TDD 912-744-2299.**

How to Apply

Review the list of openings, decide which jobs you are interested in, and follow the instructions given. **You may apply for most jobs with a resume, the *Optional Application for Federal Employment,* or any other written format you choose.** For jobs that are unique or filled through automated procedures, you will be given special forms to complete. (You can get an *Optional Application* by calling OPM or dialing our electronic bulletin board at the numbers given above.)

What to Include

Although the Federal Government does not require a standard application form for most jobs, we do need certain information to evaluate your qualifications and determine if you meet legal requirements for Federal employment. If your resume or application does not provide all the information requested in the job vacancy announcement and in this flyer, you may lose consideration for a job. Help speed the selection process by keeping your resume or application brief and by sending only the requested material. Type or print clearly in dark ink.

Veterans' Preference in Hiring

❑ If you served on active duty in the United States Military and were separated under honorable conditions, you may be eligible for veterans' preference. To receive preference if your service began after October 15, 1976, you must have a Campaign Badge, Expeditionary Medal, or a service-connected disability. For further details, call OPM at **912-757-3000.** Select "Federal Employment Topics" and then "Veterans." Or, dial our electronic bulletin board at **912-757-3100.**

❑ Veterans' preference is not a factor for Senior Executive Service jobs or when competition is limited to status candidates (current or former Federal career or career-conditional employees).

❑ To claim 5-point veterans' preference, attach a copy of your DD-214, *Certificate of Release or Discharge from Active Duty,* or other proof of eligibility.

❑ To claim 10-point veterans' preference, attach an SF 15, *Application for 10-Point Veterans' Preference,* plus the proof required by that form.

Other Important Information

❑ Before hiring, an agency will ask you to complete a *Declaration for Federal Employment* to determine your suitability for Federal employment and to authorize a background investigation. The agency will also ask you to sign and certify the accuracy of all the information in your application. **If you make a false statement in any part of your application, you may not be hired; you may be fired after you begin work; or you may be fined or jailed.**

❑ If you are a male over age 18 who was born after December 31, 1959, you must have registered with the Selective Service System (or have an exemption) to be eligible for a Federal job.

❑ The law prohibits public officials from appointing, promoting, or recommending their relatives.

❑ Federal annuitants (military and civilian) may have their salaries or annuities reduced. All employees must pay any valid delinquent debts or the agency may garnish their salary.

Working Conditions, Benefits, and Holidays

HOURS OF WORK

The usual government workweek is 40 hours. Most government employees work eight hours, five days a week, Monday through Friday, but, in some cases, the nature of the work may call for a different workweek. As in any other business, employees sometimes have to work overtime. If you are required to work overtime, you will either be paid for overtime or given time off to make up for the extra time you worked.

ADVANCEMENT

Most agencies fill vacancies by promoting their own employees whenever possible.

Federal employees receive on-the-job training. They may also participate in individual career development programs and receive job-related training in their own agency, in other agencies, or outside the government (for example, in industrial plants and universities). It is not always necessary to move to a new job in order to advance in grade. Sometimes an employee's work assignments change a great deal in the ordinary course of business. The job "grows." When that happens, it is time for a position classifier to study the job again. If he or she finds that the job should be put in a higher grade because of increased difficulty or responsibility of the duties, the change is made.

EFFICIENCY COUNTS

At intervals, employees are rated on their job performance. In most agencies, the ratings are "outstanding," "satisfactory," and "unsatisfactory."

Employees with "outstanding" ratings receive extra credit toward retention in case of layoffs. An employee whose rating is "unsatisfactory" may be dismissed or assigned to another position with duties he or she can be expected to learn to do satisfactorily.

INCENTIVE AWARDS

Government agencies encourage their employees to suggest better, simpler, or more economical ways of doing their jobs. They may give a cash award to an employee for a suggestion or invention that results in money savings or improved service. They may also reward outstanding job performance or other acts that are deserving of recognition.

VACATION AND SICK LEAVE

Most federal employees earn annual leave for vacation and other purposes, according to the number of years (civilian plus creditable military service) they have been in the federal service. They earn it at the rate of 13 days a year for the first 3 years of service and 20 days a year for the next 12 years of service. After 15 years, they earn 26 days of annual leave each year.

Sick leave is earned at the rate of 13 days a year. You can use this leave for illnesses serious enough to keep you away from your work and for appointments with a doctor, dentist, or optician. Sick leave that is not used can be saved for future use.

INJURY COMPENSATION

The government provides generous compensation benefits, including medical care, for employees who suffer injuries in the performance of official duty. Death benefits are also provided if an employee dies as a result of such injuries.

GROUP LIFE INSURANCE

As a federal employee, you may have low-cost term life insurance without taking a physical examination. Two kinds of insurance are provided: (1) life insurance, and (2) accidental death and dismemberment insurance.

HEALTH BENEFITS

The government sponsors a voluntary health insurance program for federal employees. The program offers a variety of plans to meet individual needs, including basic coverage and major medical protection against costly illnesses. The government contributes part of the cost of premiums, and the employee pays the balance through payroll deductions.

RETIREMENT

The Federal Employees Retirement System (FERS) offers very favorable terms for retirement. The government's share of the retirement package is generous, and the employee has opportunities to contribute to the program so as to create an even more comfortable retirement. The FERS retirement plan stands on three legs.

The first part of FERS is Social Security. All federal employees are members of the Social Security system. This means that employees pay a portion of each salary check toward social security insurance and another percentage toward Medicare. At retirement at age 62 or later, these employees are entitled to monthly Social Security benefits based upon number of quarters' contribution into the system and the level of those contributions. At age 65, these same employees, retired or not, are eligible for Medicare hospitalization insurance and can pay for low-cost Medicare Part B insurance toward other medical expenses. Employees pay 6.2% of their salaries into the Social Security system and 1.45% into the Medicare fund. The government matches these contributions, just as do all private employers.

The second part of FERS is the Basic Benefit Plan. Employees contribute .8% of their salaries into the retirement fund of the Basic Benefit Plan. An employee who has served for at least five years becomes eligible for retirement; that is, the employee vests in the retirement fund. If the vested employee leaves federal service before the age of 62, the employee has the option of withdrawing retirement funds or of leaving them with the government to be withdrawn as an annuity at retirement after age 62. In general, the basic retirement benefit is based on "high-3 average pay." This means that the highest salary earned in any three consecutive years is averaged; then 1% of this figure is multiplied by the number of years of service. Government retirement annuities are increased by regular Cost-of-Living Adjustments (COLAs). COLAs are based on the increase in the Consumer Price Index (CPI).

The third leg of FERS is the Thrift Savings Plan (TSP). TSP is similar to the 401(k) plans of workers in the private sector and to the 403(b) plans of persons employed by government entities other than the federal government. Under these plans, employees contribute towards their own retirement on a before-tax basis. This means that they do not pay income tax on the money they contribute to the plans. Rather, they pay tax upon the money they withdraw at retirement, at which time they are likely to be in a lower tax bracket. Funds contributed to the TSP are invested in common stock funds, government securities funds, and bond index funds as directed by the employee. These funds all yield dividends which are then reinvested through TSP. The income generated by these funds is also tax deferred until drawn out by the retiree as lump sum or as monthly payments.

Employees are not required to join TSP. Even if an employee chooses not to contribute, the government contributes 1% of the employee's salary toward TSP each pay period. The employee may contribute up to 10%. The government makes TSP contributions even more attractive by a matching program. For the first 3% of the employee's salary which he or she invests in TSP, the government matches dollar for dollar. The next 2% of the employee's investment is matched by the government at the rate of 50 cents on the dollar. No further contribution is matched, but the employee still receives the benefit of deferring tax on the contribution and on the interest earned.

HOLIDAYS

Government workers are entitled to the following ten regular holidays each year.

- New Year's Day, January 1
- Martin Luther King's Birthday, third Monday in January
- Presidents' Day, third Monday in February
- Memorial Day, last Monday in May
- Independence Day, July 4
- Labor Day, first Monday in September
- Columbus Day, second Monday in October
- Veterans Day, November 11
- Thanksgiving Day, fourth Thursday in November
- Christmas Day, December 25

When Inauguration Day falls on a regularly scheduled workday, employees in the Washington metropolitan area get an eleventh holiday.

GLOSSARY OF SELECTED FEDERAL PERSONNEL TERMS

Affirmative Action—A policy that requires Federal agencies to take positive steps to insure equal opportunity in employment, development, advancement, and treatment of all employees and applications for employment regardless of race, color, sex, religion, age, national origin, or physical or mental handicap. Affirmative Action also requires that specific actions be directed at the special problems and unique concerns in assuring equal employment opportunity for minorities and women.

Agency—Any department or independent establishment of the Federal Government, including a Government-owned or controlled corporation.

Application forms—Documents: Standard Form 171, Optional Application for Federal Employment—OF 612, or resume to specifications of OF 510 and supplementary forms completed by persons seeking Federal employment. The forms require information about the applicant's qualifications for the positions for which he or she is applying and about his or her suitability for Federal service.

Appointment—The process of selecting a person and assigning him or her to a position.

Appointment, career-conditional—The tenure of a permanent employee who has not yet completed three years of creditable, substantially continuous Federal service.

Appointment, competitive—Employment of a person after competition with others for the same position. Includes appointments from the register, some appointments from the applicant supply file, and most appointments under the Merit Promotion Program.

Appointment, noncompetitive—Employment without competing with others, in the sense that it is done without regard to OPM registers or the priorities of applicant supply files. Includes reinstatements, transfers, reassignments, demotions, and some promotions.

Career—Tenure of a permanent employee in the competitive service who has completed three years of substantially continuous creditable Federal service.

Competitive service—Federal positions normally filled through open competitive examination (hence the term "competitive service") under civil service rules and regulations. About 62 percent of all Federal positions are in the competive service.

Eligible—Any applicant for appointment or promotion who meets the minimum qualification requirements.

Entrance level position—A position in an occupation at the beginning level grade.

Examination—A means of measuring, in a practical and suitable manner, qualifications of applicants for employment in specific positions.

General Schedule (GS)—The graded pay system as presented by Chapter 51 of Title 5, United States Code, for classifying positions.

Grade—All classes of positions which, although different with respect to kind or subject matter of work, are sufficiently equivalent as to (1) level of difficulty and responsibility, and (2) level of qualification requirements of the work to warrant the inclusion of such classes of positions within one range of rates of basic compensation.

Job title—The formal name of a position as determined by official classification standards.

Journeyman level (full performance level)—The lowest level of a career ladder position at which an employee has learned the full range of duties in a specific occupation. All jobs below full performace level are developmental levels, through which each employee in the occupation may progress to full performance.

Leave, annual—Time allowed to employees for vacation and other absences for personal reasons.

Merit promotion program—The system under which agencies consider an employee for internal personnel actions on the basis of personal merit.

Personnel action—The process necessary to appoint, separate, reinstate, or make changes affecting an employee (e g., change in position, assignment, tenure, etc.).

Position classification—Analyzing and categorizing jobs by occupational group, series, class, and grade according to like duties, responsibilities, and qualification requirements.

Position description—An official written statement of the major duties, responsibilities, and supervisory relationships of a position.

Preference, Compensable Disability ("CP")—Ten-point preference awarded to a veteran separated under honorable conditions from active duty, who receives compensation of 10 percent or more for a service connected disability. Eligible "CP" veterans are placed at the top of civil service lists of eligibles for positions at GS-9 or higher.

Preference, 30 Percent or More, Disability ("CPS")—A disabled veteran whose disability is rated at 30 percent or more, entitled to special preference in appointment and during reduction in force.

Preference, Disability ("XP")—Ten-point preference in hiring for a veteran separated under honorable conditions from active duty and who has a service-connected disability or receives compensation, pension, or disability retirement from the VA or a uniformed service.

Preference, Mother ("XP")—Ten-point preference to which the mother of a deceased or disabled military veteran may be entitled.

Preference, Spouse ("XP")—Ten-point preference to which a disabled military veteran's spouse may be entitled.

Preference, Tentative ("TP")—Five-point veteran preference tentatively awarded an eligible who served on active duty during specified periods and was separated from military service under honorable conditions. It must be verified by the appointing officer.

Preference, Veteran—The statutory right to special advantage in appointment or separations; based on a person's discharge under honorable conditions from the armed forces, for a service connected disability. Not applicable to the Senior Executive Service.

Preference, Widow or Widower ("XP")—Ten point preference to which a military veteran's widow or widower may be entitled.

Probationary period—A trial period which is a condition of the initial competitive appointment. Provides the final indispensable test of ability, that of actual performance on the job.

Promotion—A change of an employee to a higher grade when both the old and new positions are under the same job classification system and pay schedule, or to a position with higher pay in a different job classification system and pay schedule.

Promotion, career—Promotion of an employee without current competition when: (1) he or she had earlier been competitively selected from a register or under competitive promotion procedures for an assignment intended as a matter of record to be preparation for the position being filled; or (2) the position is reconstituted at a higher grade because of additional duties and responsibilities.

Promotion, competitive—Selection of a current or former Federal civil service employee for a higher grade position, using procedures that compare the candidates on merit.

Register—A list of eligible applicants compiled in the order of their relative standing for referral to Federal jobs, after competitive civil service examination.

Senior Executive Service—A separate personnel system for persons who set policy and administer programs at the top levels of the government (equivalent to GS-16 through Executive Level IV.)

FEDERAL JOBS OVERSEAS

INTRODUCTION

United States citizens are employed by the Federal Government in Alaska, Hawaii, United States territories, and in foreign countries. They are found in almost every occupational field. They are construction and maintenance workers, doctors, nurses, teachers, technical experts, mining engineers, meteorologists, clerks, stenographers, typists, geologists, skilled tradesmen, social workers, agricultural marketing specialists, and agricultural and other economists.

Current needs of agencies with jobs to fill are generally limited to highly qualified and hard-to-find professional personnel, skilled technicians, and, in some cases, stenographers and clerical and administrative personnel. A few agencies are seeking experienced teachers, librarians, nurses, and medical personnel. However, a few vacancies occur in most fields from time to time because of normal turnover in personnel.

HOW JOBS ARE FILLED

In Alaska, Hawaii, and United States territories, most vacancies are filled by the appointment of local eligibles who qualify in competitive Civil Service examinations which are announced and held in the local area. Normally, there is a sufficient local labor market to fill the needs and examinations are not publicized outside the local areas. Some positions, however, may be filled by transferring career Government employees from the United States mainland.

When a vacancy is to be filled in a foreign country, determination is made whether to recruit from among persons in the area where the job is located or to seek qualified applicants residing in the United States. If the position is to be filled locally, the appointee may be a United States citizen residing or traveling in the area, the wife or dependent of a citizen employed or stationed in the area, or a foreign national.

In most instances where United States installations are established in foreign countries, either formal or informal agreements have been drawn up assuring the host government that local nationals will be employed wherever possible in order to be of maximum assistance to the economy of that country. Furthermore, it is almost always to the economic advantage of the United States to employ foreign nationals at local pay rates without responsibility for travel costs and overseas cost-of-living allowances. Positions held by foreign nationals are in the excepted service and are not subject to the competitive requirements of the Civil Service Act and Office of Personnel Management rules.

COMPETITIVE SERVICE POSITIONS

However, there are many thousands of technical, administrative, and supervisory positions in which United States citizens are employed in foreign countries. These positions are usually in the competitive service, and as vacancies occur they are filled in most cases by transferring career Government employees from the United States. This is the case in the Department of Defense, the largest employer of overseas personnel, and in most other agencies having overseas positions. When Government employees are not available for transfer overseas, and qualified United States citizens cannot be recruited locally, these vacancies are filled through the regular competitive examining process.

Approximately 30 examinations now open on a nationwide basis are being used, as recruiting needs require, to fill overseas positions. The examinations cover a variety of business and economics, engineering and scientific, medical, social and educational, and trades positions. Qualified persons interested in overseas assignments in these fields should establish eligibility under appropriate examinations. Applications and copies of examination announcements can be obtained from Federal Job Information Centers.

EXCEPTED SERVICE POSITIONS

Some positions are excepted from the competitive requirements of the Civil Service rules and regulations. Included in this group are positions in the Foreign Service of the Department of State, dependents' school teachers, positions in the attache offices, and most positions of clerk-translator, translator, and interpreter. Applications for these positions should be made directly to the agency in which employment is desired.

A description of the principal agencies which employ personnel outside the United States, with the addresses to which inquiries or applications should be sent, begins on page 17.

CONDITIONS OF EMPLOYMENT

PHYSICAL REQUIREMENTS

Applicants for most overseas positions must be able to pass rigid physical examinations, since employees may be required to serve under extremely difficult living conditions and, in some areas, at posts where complete medical facilities are not available. Physical standards are applied which are suitable for the location and occupation involved, and may include standards of mental and emotional stability and maturity.

Any physical defect which would make the employee a hazard to himself or to others, or prevent efficient performance of the duties of the position, is disqualifying. Conditions which require periodic medical care, hospitalization, special foods or medicine may be disqualifying for some areas.

Accompanying dependents may also be required to pass rigid physical examinations.

TOUR OF DUTY

Individuals selected in the United States for overseas employment generally are required to sign a transportation agreement for a definite period of service, which is usually for a minimum of 36 months. In certain areas the minimum period is 12 or 24 months.

INVESTIGATION

All appointments are subject to satisfactory security, character, and suitability investigations. Applicants considered for appointment are carefully screened, and only those possessing suitable qualifications are selected for overseas employment.

> Since most Federal jobs overseas are filled by local residents or by the transfer of people who already work for the Government, opportunities for appointment to an overseas position are extremely limited.

GENERAL INFORMATION

QUALIFICATIONS

Generally, the qualification requirements are the same as those established for like positions in the United States. Applicants may, however, be required to meet certain additional or higher standards. A foreign language capability, while not required in all, or even most, Federal jobs overseas, would obviously be a valuable qualification.

DEPENDENTS

For middle and upper-level positions in what may be broadly termed "professional occupations," most agencies permit employees to take their families with them. In certain other job categories, and in accordance with an established system of priorities, it is usually possible to arrange for dependents to follow from several months to a year after the employee has arrived at the overseas post.

For most clerical and secretarial positions abroad, agencies prefer single persons without dependents.

Appointments of both husband and wife are very infrequent, since there rarely are simultaneous vacancies in which their qualifications could be appropriately utilized at the same post. However, in foreign countries with a large American presence, both governmental and private-industrial, qualified U.S. citizens are sometimes needed for a variety of job openings. In the majority of cases, dependents of U.S. Government employees overseas are given priority consideration for such employment.

SALARY

Generally, overseas white-collar workers are paid the same base salaries as Federal employees in the United States occupying similar positions. In addition, where warranted by conditions at the post, they receive a post differential or cost-of-living allowance. In foreign areas, the wages of blue-collar workers are based upon continental United States rates plus, in some cases, a post differential or cost-of-living allowance; in United States areas overseas, their wages may be set in a similar way or they may be based on local rates.

QUARTERS ALLOWANCES

In foreign areas, employees are sometimes housed in Government quarters. If Government housing is not provided, a quarters allowance is paid which covers in large part the cost of rent and utilities. In most United States areas, Government quarters are not provided and no quarters allowance is paid.

FEDERAL EMPLOYMENT BENEFITS

In general, Federal employees are entitled to such liberal benefits as paid vacations, sick leave with pay, and retirement coverage. They are eligible for life insurance and health benefits partially financed by the Government. Employees serving overseas also normally receive special benefits such as free travel for themselves and their dependents, free transportation or storage for their household goods, and additional paid vacations with free travel to their homes in the United States between tours of duty. Also, the United States Government operates dependents' schools in many areas and provides educational opportunities for children which are comparable to those offered in the better schools in the United States.

VETERAN PREFERENCE

Veterans must be given consideration by appointing officers in the filling of overseas positions in accordance with the provisions of the Veterans' Preference Act.

AGENCIES EMPLOYING OVERSEAS PERSONNEL

This section indicates the kinds of positions for which these agencies may be recruiting and lists addresses to which inquiries about employment opportunities may be sent. (Persons who have never worked for the Government should also contact the Office of Personnel Management for information about competitive examinations.)

The largest employers of overseas personnel include the Departments of State, Army, Navy, Air Force, Interior, Commerce, and Agriculture, the International Communications Agency, the Agency for International Development, and the Panama Canal Company-Canal Zone Government.

DEPARTMENT OF AGRICULTURE

The Foreign Agricultural Service assigns agricultural attaches and secretaries to staff its offices at foreign posts. These personnel analyze and report on production, trade and consumption of agricultural commodities and work to develop foreign markets for U.S. farm products. Professional positions normally are filled by Department of Agriculture employees trained in agricultural marketing and agricultural economics. Secretarial positions are generally filled by transferring persons already employed by the Department of Agriculture; otherwise, vacancies are filled by appointment from the Office of Personnel Management's list of eligibles in the clerk-stenographer examination, followed by a training program in Washington, D.C. Additional information may be obtained from:

Recruitment Officer
Foreign Agricultural Service, USDA
FAS Personnel, Room 5627, South Bldg.
14th St. and Independence Ave., SW
Washington, DC 20250
(202) 720-5267

DEPARTMENT OF THE AIR FORCE

The Air Force uses the Department of Defense Overseas Employment Program (OEP) as the primary source of candidates in filling its overseas positions.

Although first consideration is given to qualified employees currently serving at Air Force installations in the United States, employees of other Federal agencies are also considered if sufficient well-qualified candidates are not available within the Air Force. Government employees or former employees having reinstatement eligibility and interested in registering in the OEP should contact the Civilian Personnel Officer at the nearest Department of Defense installation. When well-qualified employees are not available through the OEP, vacancies are filled from the appropriate Civil Service register through the regular competitive examining process.

DEPARTMENT OF THE ARMY

Civilian positions with the Army overseas are frequently filled through reassignment of current Army employees from the United States; however, employees of other Federal agencies, or former Federal service employees with reinstatement eligibility, may also submit applications. Administrative, technical and professional positions are those most often available. The U.S. Army Corps of Engineers accepts applications from career/career conditional employees with expertise in engineering design and construction. Department of the Army does not normally recruit for overseas positions in trades and crafts, equipment operation or general labor. These positions are normally filled by citizens of the host country or by private U.S. contractors. Clerical positions (including clerk typists/steno and secretarial) are also usually filled locally overseas. Dependents of military and civilian personnel stationed in the overseas area receive preferential consideration for these positions if qualified. Applications or inquiries regarding employment should be submitted to the appropriate recruiting office below:

Europe, Middle East and Africa:

> USAREUR Civilian Recruitment Office
> Attention: AEAGA-CRC
> APO New York 09403

Far East:

> Civilian Personnel Center, Hawaii
> WESTPAC Support Office
> P.O. BOX 50148
> Honolulu, Hawaii 96850

Alaska and Panama:

> Civilian Personnel Office
> HQ FORSCOM
> Attention: AFPR-CPS
> Fort McPherson, Georgia 30330

Army Corps of Engineers
Headquarters
U.S. Army Corps of Engineers
Room 5215
Washington, DC 20314-1000
Attn.: CEHR-E
(202) 761-1759

DEPARTMENT OF THE NAVY

Vacancies are principally filled through the assignment of well-qualified Navy and Marine Corps career employees desiring to serve overseas. Primary recruitment sources are Department of the Navy career programs and the Department of Defense Overseas Employment Program (OEP). When recruitment from other sources is necessary, it is mainly for positions in engineering, science, skilled trades, accounting and auditing, and administration.

For information about appointment or assignment to overseas positions, see the Civilian Personnel Officer at the nearest Navy or Marine Corps installation.

DEPARTMENT OF DEFENSE

Employment opportunities are available for educators with the Department of Defense Dependents Schools.

The Department of Defense maintains a school system from kindergarten through grade 12 for the dependent children of military and civilian personnel stationed abroad. School year salaries for educators are comparable to the average rates for similar positions in school systems in U.S. districts having a population of 100,000 or more. Transportation and housing allowances are provided. Qualification requirements include completion of a baccalaureate degree with a minimum of 18 semester hours in the field of professional education to include student teaching and 1 full school year of professional employment as a teacher within the past 5 years. For information about teaching positions overseas, write to:

Department of Defense Education Activity
Personnel Center
4040 North Fairfax Drive
Arlington, VA 22203-1634

U.S. DEPARTMENT OF COMMERCE

National Oceanic and Atmospheric Administration-Overseas positions are available for persons with meteorological or electronics backgrounds at weather stations maintained in Alaska, Puerto Rico, Mexico, Hawaii, Wake Island, Guam, Johnson Island, American Samoa, and the Trust Territories. Positions exist for persons with appropriate education or experience in geophysics at observatories located in Alaska, Hawaii, and American Samoa. There are a few positions available in the Antarctic for electronics engineers, technicians and physical scientists who have specialized experience in atmospheric research. Qualified persons interested in any of these positions should address inquiries to:

Human Resources Management Office, OA22
National Oceanic and Atmospheric Administration
1315 East-West Highway
Silver Spring, MD 21910
(301) 713-1534

DEPARTMENT OF TRANSPORTATION

Federal Highway Administration—Highway design, planning, construction, maintenance, and bridge engineers and specialists with experience in the administration and supervision of the operation and repair of highway construction equipment provide technical assistance to countries in connection with the Government's overseas technical aid program. Experienced persons interested in overseas employment should send inquiries to:

Federal Highway Administration
Attn.: Chief, Classification and Staffing Branch
400 7th St., NW
Room 4334
Washington, DC 20590
(202) 366-0541
(202) 366-9357 (Job Hotline)

DEPARTMENT OF THE INTERIOR

Most of the positions are in Alaska. Almost all of these positions have been brought into the competitive service. Vacancies occur from time to time in engineering, metallurgy, geology, forestry, and teaching (elementary) positions. The jobs are usually filled through competitive examinations announced by the Office of Personnel Management. For more information about employment opportunities, address inquiries to the Department of the Interior, Washington, D.C. 20240.

DEPARTMENT OF STATE

The Foreign Service of the United States, administered by the Department of State, recruits personnel for the career Foreign Service Officer Corps. Career Foreign Service Officers fill virtually all professional positions in the over 250 embassies and consulates maintained by the United States in more than 100 countries throughout the world. Officers serve primarily in one of the four functional specializations within the Department of State: Administration, consular affairs, economic/commercial, or political work. The Department of State is interested in personnel with training in diverse fields including political science, economics, public and business administration as well as experience in business, government and organizations involved in international activities. Appointments are made from among those who take competitive Foreign Service Officer examinations. Candidates for these examinations must be at least 21 years of age, except that candidates may apply at 20 years of age. Inquiries regarding these examinations should be addressed to:

Foreign Service
Recruitment Division - WWW
U.S. Department of State
P.O. Box 9317
Arlington, VA 22219
(703) 875-7490

There is a continuing need for secretaries, communications officers and communications technicians in the Foreign Service to staff the embassies and consulates throughout the world. Requests for information regarding opportunities and qualifications for employment in positions listed above should be addressed to:

Employment Information Office
U.S. Department of State
22nd and D Streets, NW
Room 2819
Washington, DC 20520
(202) 647-7284 (Personnel/vacancies)
(202) 647-7256 (TDD)

AGENCY FOR INTERNATIONAL DEVELOPMENT

The Agency for International Development (AID) is the principal administrator of U.S. economic and technical assistance to the developing countries of Africa, Asia, Latin America and the Near East.

To administer these development programs, AID relies upon a staff of highly skilled men and women with postgraduate degrees in a number of technical and professional disciplines. While employment opportunities vary from country to country and time to time, the most frequent needs are for agriculturists, public health physicians, economists, accountants, financial managers, auditors, contract specialists, family planning/population specialists, and nutritionists.

Many Foreign Service officers join AID in mid-level or senior-level positions. Others are recruited at the junior officer entry level as International Development Interns. The Interns are young men and women who have graduate degrees in the relevant disciplines and have had some working experience. Training is provided in Washington, D.C., and at overseas missions. Appropriate education and experience are the decisive criteria in the selection of candidates for both professional and intern positions. U.S. citizenship is a requirement.

Requests for information should be addressed to:
U.S. Agency for International Development
Office of Human Resources—Recruitment Branch
1550 Wilson Boulevard, Room 658A SA-36
Washington, DC 20523-3607

PANAMA CANAL COMMISSION

The efficient operation of the Panama Canal Commission is of vital importance to world trade. Applications are accepted from qualified ship pilots, towboat masters, towboat and dredge engineers and from most skilled craftsmen. Mail SF 171 or inquiries to U.S. Recruitment and Placement Assistance Section, Office of Personnel Administration, Panama Canal Commission, APO Miami 34011.

THE PEACE CORPS (ACTION)

The Peace Corps provides opportunities for skilled Americans to serve in developing nations overseas. Its purpose is threefold: to give help where help is needed, to promote a better understanding of the American abroad, and to sharpen the Americans' image of other peoples.

Tours of duty are approximately for 2 years including several months of training received before overseas departure. Volunteers receive a living allowance to provide for food, housing, clothing and incidentals, and a readjustment allowance.

While most of the volunteers work in educational and community development programs, there are positions available in more than 300 separate skill areas. A college degree is not required. Beyond teaching and community development, demands are greatest for volunteers experienced in the fields of public health, agriculture, home economics, mechanics, construction, and social work.

Applicants must be at least 18 years of age and American citizens. Although the minimum age for volunteers is 18, very few applicants under 20 have the skills and experience to qualify. Married couples are eligible if they have no dependents under 18. There is no upper age limit.

For further information on opportunities for service, and instructions for application, contact the Peace Corps office in your state or:
Peace Corps
1990 K Street NW
Washington, DC 20526
(800) 424-8580

INTERNATIONAL COMMUNICATIONS AGENCY
(Formerly USIA)

Generally, all but a few specialized positions are filled from within the ranks of ICA's career Foreign Service. Entry into the Foreign Service Information Officer corps is open to individuals over 21 years of age under the Junior Officer Program. Candidates must participate in a competitive process involving both comprehensive written and oral examinations. Information about the next examination can be obtained from the:

Foreign Service
Recruitment Division-WWW
U.S. Department of State
P.O. Box 9317
Arlington, VA 22219
(703) 875-7490

As needed, the Agency may recruit experienced professionals for information and cultural work overseas. They are appointed as Foreign Service Limited Reserve Officers for a maximum of 5 years. They are eligible to apply for career status (FSIO) after 3 years in the Limited Reserve.

Candidates for the Foreign Service must have a knowledge of American foreign policy and international relations, and a solid background in the historical, political, economic and cultural development of the United States. They must possess an ability to communicate convincingly and tactfully, both orally and in writing. A good working command of a foreign language and an ability to learn foreign languages are useful. Candidates must be willing to serve in any country and at any post.

Opportunities for serving overseas also exist for teaching English abroad. For information contact:

U.S. Information Agency
English Language Programs Division
301 4th Street SW, Room 304
Washington, DC 20547
(202) 619-5869

FEDERAL JOB INFORMATION CENTERS

The Office of Personnel Management offers Federal employment information through Federal Job Information Centers located in several major metropolitan areas across the country. They are listed under "U.S. Government" in the blue pages of local phone directories. In addition, Federal job opportunities are posted in local State Job Service (or State Employment Security) offices.

A call can save you time and unnecessary effort if you want to obtain application forms, announcements and other general types of information.

For specific information on possible openings in overseas areas, you should write:

For Pacific areas:

Honolulu Area Office
Office of Personnel Management
1000 Bishop Street, Suite 1500
Honolulu, Hawaii 96813

For Atlantic areas:

Washington Area Office
Office of Personnel Management
1900 E Street, N.W.
Washington, DC 20415

PATRONAGE AND "EXCEPTED" JOBS

Although the merit system for selecting employees is talked about a good deal, it is not practiced throughout the government. Patronage and political considerations control selection of certain public employees, particularly those in the more responsible and higher-paying positions. Patronage, or the spoils system, is not all bad. Employees and officials chosen by this method are frequently competent and often display a freshness of approach which some authorities maintain is not a common characteristic among competitive civil service employees.

The 14 percent of Federal positions that are excepted from Civil Service requirements number 347,800. Of these, 136,400 are excepted by statute and the remainder by action of the Office of Personnel Management (OPM). Some people believe that all of these are patronage positions; actually, relatively few are true patronage jobs. Except for the very top positions, the Federal Bureau of Investigation and the Central Intelligence Agency, for example, are not likely to be touched by the breath of patronage. In fact, the FBI and CIA, along with many other similarly sensitive agencies, subject their applicants to extremely rigorous competitive examination procedures.

And many thousands of temporary positions, and others filled for special duties outside the range of Civil Service requirements, must be maintained in order to uphold the continuity of government functions. It is often useful to "know someone" to get one of these jobs, but few of these jobs lead into a long-term government career. The great majority of responsible government careers, both those within the regular Civil Service and those excepted by statute, are obtained through a showing of competitive qualifications.

Examples of positions excepted by statute are those in the Foreign Service, on the Atomic Energy Commission, in the Library of Congress, and with the Tennessee Valley Authority. While hiring for these and many other independent government agencies and commissions is entirely outside the regular Civil Service system and is in no way under control of the OPM, it is equally removed from politics or patronage.

The recommendations of college deans, professors, and prominent public figures with "contacts" in Washington may be helpful; knowing an official in an agency is often useful, since he or she may bring the applicant to the attention of the agency chief. The job hopeful must then provide credentials and submit to inquiries and interviews to demonstrate suitability for the position under consideration.

Nevertheless, there are still left a considerable number of jobs under the spoils system. Several hundred top jobs are open whenever a new regime proceeds with its "housecleaning." A new cabinet is selected, along with Presidential assistants and various agency heads and subheads. The chiefs of commissions and boards are appointed to serve definite terms, but little difficulty is encountered by a new President who wishes to oust some of these individuals to make room for his own appointees. A quiet Presidential request for resignation will, of course, be honored.

The top patronage positions tend to go to persons known by or known to the President, but many other jobs do indeed get handed out to the party faithful—both to big contributors and to loyal workers of long standing. There are always more aspirants for a job than there are open positions, so even in patronage jobs, competence usually comes into play. The "down side" of holding a political appointment is that the appointee has no job security. Being outside of civil service selection means being outside of civil service protection as well. The patronage job holder holds his or her position at the pleasure of the President or of the agency head and can be replaced in the service of political expediency or simply on a whim. Furthermore, he or she is likely to lose the job at the change of administrations and is sure to be ousted with a change of parties in power. Appointments in the legislative branch of the Federal Government are not subject to Civil Service requirements. These appointments include all the workers in the Library of Congress, which hires directly, and the various aides—researchers, lawyers, secretaries, messengers, pages, clerks, and guards—to senators and congressmen. Those who want such jobs should get in touch with their representatives in Congress or talk to their political leaders.

Judicial positions in Federal courts are not under Civil Service. Candidates for judicial appointments, however, are subject first to scrutiny, appraisal, and rating by bar associations and judicial review committees and then to interrogation by the Senate Judiciary Committee. Finally, the full Senate must vote to give or to withhold its advice and consent.

RULE VI ("EXCEPTED" APPOINTMENTS)

There is a special rule concerning "excepted" appointments, that is, jobs which are not filled through the usual Civil Service methods. The rule sets down the kinds of positions which may be filled without examination. Rule VI states that certain positions shall be excepted from competitive service "because of their confidential or policy-making character, or because it is not practicable to make appointments through competitive examination." When it is decided (by the OPM) that a position should be "excepted," the title of that position is published in the Federal Register. At the end of each fiscal year the OPM submits to the White House a list of the jobs which have been thus freed of competitive requirements. An "excepted" position does not acquire competitive status.

Excepted positions (a long list of them) include all those which were excluded from competition by the original Civil Service Act of 1883, positions excepted by executive order of the President, positions which may be filled under personal service contract, and positions in government corporations. Veterans are entitled to preference in these positions, as in others, and each agency is supposed to set up proper standards for every excepted position, so that it is not filled by incompetents.

Positions excepted by action of the OPM are placed in 1 of 3 schedules—A, B, or C—after a study of all pertinent facts (such as the duties, pay, and location of the positions) has been made by OPM.

Schedule A is for positions for which it is not practicable to hold any examinations. Examples are: Chaplains, professional and technical experts for temporary consultation purposes, narcotics agents for undercover work, certain part-time positions at isolated localities, and many positions in foreign countries. There are 108,000 positions in this schedule.

Schedule B is for positions for which competitive examinations are impracticable but for which *non-competitive* examinations are given. Examples are positions assigned exclusively to Navy or Air Force Communications Intelligence activities. There are about 2,000 jobs in this schedule.

Schedule C is for positions whose occupants serve in a policy-determining capacity to the politically appointed heads of agencies or in a confidential capacity to them and their key officials. It was established to more clearly define the career service by setting apart from it positions properly in the political area. It contains key positions which should be filled by the administration in power with persons who will fully support its political aims and policies.

No examination is required for appointment to Schedule C jobs. Departments and agencies have authority to assign duties to any position. They may recommend to OPM that a position be placed in Schedule C if they feel the duties assigned are either policy determining or require the incumbent to serve in a confidential relationship to a key official.

VETERANS' PREFERENCE

A large system of special advantages is available to veterans who seek work with the government, and to those already in Federal jobs. These advantages extend from preferential treatment in getting jobs to preferential treatment if layoffs should occur. Certain disabled veterans' wives, veterans' widows, and veterans' mothers are included in this system of advantages.

Here, in capsule form, are the major privileges which veterans enjoy.

Disabled veterans have 10 points added to the grade they earn on a Civil Service exam. Thus if a disabled vet gets a mark of 70, he or she is granted an additional 10 points—bringing him up to 80 and much closer to the job he or she wants. Non-disabled veterans are granted five additional points.

On any examination, the veteran must make 70 before 5- or 10-point preference is added.

A Federal employee who left his position to enter the armed forces is entitled to his old job back (unless it was a temporary job) or a position of like status, pay, and seniority.

In all positions except scientific and professional positions in grade GS-9 or higher, disabled veterans with a compensable service-connected disability of 10 percent or more go to the top of the lists of those to be appointed.

No appointing officer may pass over a veteran on an Office of Personnel Management certificate of eligibles to appoint a non-veteran without giving his reasons in writing to the OPM.

In making temporary appointments for which no examination is needed, agencies must give consideration first to disabled veterans with a compensable service-connected disability of 10 percent or more, second to other disabled veterans and then to non-disabled veterans before any consideration is given to non-veterans.

When layoffs take place the veteran must be retained longer than the non-veteran. Under the Veteran's Preference Act, veterans who have satisfactory or better performance (efficiency) ratings are retained in preference to all non-veterans, irrespective of their efficiency ratings or length of service, who rate "in competition with them" for retention.

Other privileges are given the veteran. In most examinations, he is granted a waiver of height, weight, and age requirements. He gets credit for experience and training in the armed forces. Under certain conditions an examination already "closed" will be opened for him. His protections against dismissal extend to other disciplinary actions—suspension, furlough without pay, demotion, debarment from future employment. If a veteran, after getting his extra points on an exam, has the same grade as a non-veteran, he is entered ahead of the non-veteran as a job prospect. The veteran isn't required to meet the "members-of-family" rule—the rule that not more than two members of the family living under one roof may hold permanent Federal positions. Nor will he be denied employment in case his state is "over-quota" in the number of its residents in armed forces.

Since January 1979, veterans with service-connected disabilities of 30% or more have received additional benefits, including:
- appointment without competitive examination, with a right to be converted to career apointments, and
- retention rights over other preference eligibles in reductions in-force.

Veterans with disabilities of 30% or more also have the right to be notified in advance and respond to any decision in which:
- they are considered ineligible for a position due to physical requirements of the position;
- they would be passed over by an agency in the course of filling a position from a Civil Service certificate; or
- they are deemed ineligible for retention in a position during a reduction-in-force due to the physical requirements of the position.

On October 1, 1980, veterans' preference was eliminated for non-disabled military retirees who retire from the service at or above the rank of major or its equivalent.

JOBS FOR VETERANS ONLY

Appointments to certain positions are restricted to veteran-preference eligibles. Persons not entitled to preference may file for and compete in examinations for these positions, but their applications will not be rated or referred to agencies for appointment as long as sufficient veterans are available.

Restricted positions include guard, elevator operator, messenger, and custodian.

Restricted positions in the "guard" category include: air corps patrolman; patrolman; building guard; mint guard; private and special officer (Secret Service); chief guard-fire marshall; guard chauffeur; guard-fire-fighter; guard-fireman; guard laborer; guard (U. S. Engineer Department); lieutenant of the guard (Post Office Custodial Service); housemaster (U. S. Naval Academy); parking lot attendant; customs enforcement officer; chief, project police (Public Housing Administration); safety and security chief, Terre Haute Ordnance Depot, Indiana; shipkeeper; and security officer (Bureau of Immigration and Naturalization).

Restricted examinations for custodial positions include: janitor and assistant foreman of janitors; engineman-janitor, head charwoman, laborer, matron, and window cleaner, Post Office Custodial Service; caretaker of abandoned Federal reservation, Federal cemetery, or small military reservation; caretaker-mechanic at inactive military reservation; charman; charwoman; clean-up man, Ordnance Department of the Army; dam tender; fireman-laborer; foreman of laborers (when duties are custodial); headwaiter, kitchen helper, and waiter, Veterans Administration; hospital attendant; hospital servitor; housekeeper (custodial); laborer (custodial); lockman; lockmaster; maid (custodial); matron (custodial); mess attendant; restroom matron; shipkeeper (custodial), U. S. Maritime Commission Reserve Fleets; supervisor of hospital attendants; ward attendant; ward orderly; bridge tender; and maintenance foreman (housing).

Those for elevator operator include elevator starter, Post Office Custodial Service.

Restricted messenger positions do not include special delivery messenger at first-class post offices.

BACKGROUND OF VETERANS' PREFERENCE

It is estimated that about 65 percent of the total number of men working for the government as civilians are veterans of the wars in which the United States has engaged. Eight per cent of all women workers are either veterans themselves or the widows of veterans or the wives of disabled veterans, or the mothers of deceased or disabled veterans. This is the result of a conscious move on the part of the government to grant preference in Federal employment to veterans. Serious concern has been voiced in many quarters concerning the effect of this policy upon the efficiency of the government. It is pointed out that the concept of veterans' preference runs contrary to the concept of merit and fitness in government service; that a veteran has only barely to pass an examination to go to the top of the list, if he has a compensable service-connected disability of 10 percent or more (except for professional and scientific jobs in grade GS-9 or higher) even though others may be far better qualified; that the Federal establishment is tending to become overloaded with veterans; that opportunities for younger people and women in the Federal service are being reduced.

On the other hand it is argued that veterans have lost out in economic competition with those who stayed at home during the wars and that the government owes them an opportunity to make up for this loss; that the number of veterans is so great that the government can be assured of quality personnel; that the need to help the veteran is an overriding consideration; that to get a Federal job the veteran must meet certain minimum standards—and that these standards should be sufficiently high so that those who meet them are qualified for the positions. Moreover it is argued that the nation overwhelmingly desires a system of veterans' preference, although this argument has never been proved.

The policy of granting preference is not a new one. Even before the first Civil Service Act was passed in 1883, when all public jobs were dispensed on a patronage basis, Congress granted job preference to war veterans. The first such statute came one month before the end of the Civil War, in March 1865, giving preference to qualified persons discharged from the armed forces because of disabilities incurred while in service.

During the next half century, Congress increased this preference so that veterans, along with their widows and orphans, received preferential treatment in the matter of discharge when a cut in personnel became necessary. After World War I, Congress granted preference in appointment to jobs in Washington to veterans and veterans' widows and also extended this preference to cover the wives of disabled veterans who could not qualify for appointment because of their disability. Each war has meant increased preference for veterans.

The present system of preference applies to veterans of all wars in which the United States has engaged and certain "peacetime" veterans.

WIVES, WIDOWS AND MOTHERS

The wife of a disabled veteran is entitled to ten-point preference on all examinations, and all other veterans' advantages. She must show these facts to obtain preference: (1) that she is presently married to the veteran; (2) that her husband served on full-time active duty in the armed forces of the United States and received a discharge under honorable conditions; (3) that her husband is disqualified by his existing service-connected disability for Civil Service appointment along the general lines of his usual occupation. Only a Federal medical officer acting for the Office of Personnel Management may make the determination that the veteran on whose service the preference claim is based is disqualified by his service-connected disability for Civil Service appointment along the general lines of his usual occupation. This determination is required for wife preference and for certain claims for mother preference.

The widow of a veteran is entitled to ten-point preference if she meets the following requirements:

1. That she was married to the veteran and was not divorced from him.
2. That the veteran is actually and legally dead and the widow has not remarried since his death, or her remarriage has been annulled.
3. That the veteran had served on full-time active duty in any branch of the armed forces of the United States:
   a. During a war or a national crisis, or
   b. In a campaign or expedition for which a campaign badge (service medal) has been authorized.
4. That the veteran had been separated from such active duty under honorable conditions.

The mother of a veteran who lost his life while serving on active duty during periods listed under 3 in the preceding paragraph may qualify for mother preference if she meets these additional qualifications:

1. That she is, or was, married to the father of the ex-service child and is the natural mother of the ex-service child.
2. That if she is presently living with her husband:
   a. That the father of her ex-service child or the husband of her remarriage, as the case may be, is totally and permanently disabled.
   b. If she is widowed, divorced or separated:
      1. That she is widowed by the death of, or is divorced or separated from, the father of her ex-service child and has not remarried, or
      2. That if she has remarried she has been widowed by the death of, or is divorced or legally separated from, the husband of her remarriage.

The mother of a disabled ex-service son or daughter must meet the following conditions in addition to those listed under 1 and 2 of the preceding paragraph:

1. That the ex-service son or daughter was separated under honorable conditions from full-time active duty performed in any branch of the armed forces of the United States at any time.
2. That her son or daughter is living and has an existing service-connected disability which disqualifies for Civil Service appointment along the general lines of his or her usual occupation.

SOMETIMES PREFERENCE CAN BE LOST

Conditions arise under which a person entitled to veterans' preference can lose it. Examples:

DIVORCE FROM VETERAN: The wife of a veteran loses preference based on his service when she is divorced from him.

REMARRIAGE OF VETERAN'S WIDOW: The widow of a veteran loses preference when she remarries.

RECOVERY FROM DISABILITY: A veteran loses disability preference when he recovers from his disability, or ceases to receive compensation, pension, or disability retirement benefits. The wife of a veteran loses preference when her husband recovers from a service-connected disability. A mother loses her preference when she reunites with the father of her ex-service child, unless said father is permanently and totally disabled, or when she remarries, unless the husband of her remarriage is permanently and totally disabled. The mother of disabled ex-service sons or daughters loses preference when the child dies or recovers from disability to such an extent that he or she is no longer disqualified for Federal employment.

HOW TO SECURE A TEMPORARY JOB

We have learned that veterans get "first crack" at the many temporary positions available in government service. Probably the simplest way to learn about such temporary positions is to write directly to the agency for which you wish to work. Some persons even write to all Federal agencies, asking that they be put on the list for consideration for temporary work in their occupations.

HOW TO CLAIM VETERANS' PREFERENCE

In order to obtain preference the veteran must submit evidence that he or she is entitled to it. A candidate must answer questions about military service when filling out the application and later, when he or she is being considered for appointment, he or she will be required to submit the DD214.

NON-DISABLED VETERAN WHO SERVED IN TIME OF WAR: Claim for five-point preference based on war service is filed by answering the questions on the application form. Later you'll be asked to submit proof of honorable separation from the armed forces.

NON-DISABLED VETERAN WHO SERVED IN CAMPAIGN OR EXPEDITION FOR WHICH CAMPAIGN BADGE WAS AUTHORIZED: Preference goes also to persons who served in various campaigns, as distinguished from wars. If you're among the veterans who served in a campaign or expedition, you'll need to fill out Standard Form 15, which you can obtain at the same office which gives out application blanks. In addition you'll need to submit proof of honorable separation and official notice of the award of the campaign badge.

DISABLED VETERAN: If you are disabled, you file the following documents: Standard Form 15; proof of honorable separation from the armed forces; either an official statement from the Veterans' Administration, Army, Navy, Air Force, Coast Guard, or Public Health Service certifying the existence of a service-connected disability, or an official statement from the Veterans' Administration that you are receiving compensation or an official statement from the Veterans' Administration, Army, Navy, Air Force, Marine Corps, Coast Guard, or Public Health Service certifying that you are receiving disability-retirement benefits.

WIFE: The wife of a disabled veteran must submit the same documents required of the disabled veteran. If the veteran is retired from military service, the official statement should contain information concerning the nature and extent of her husband's disability. This statement will be issued by the service department at the veteran's request.

WIDOW: A widow files the following information: Preference Form 15; proof of her husband's honorable separation from the armed forces.

When the claim is based on service in a campaign or expedition for which a campaign badge has been authorized, she must file with the Office of Personnel Management the veteran's official notification of the award by the military organization in which the service was performed.

She is not required to furnish proof of death except under these special circumstances: If he died in line of duty, she must submit the official notification. If he has disappeared and his death cannot be established she must submit two or more affidavits certifying that he has not been seen or heard from for at least seven years.

MOTHER: The mother of a disabled veteran must submit the same documents required of a disabled veteran.

The mother of a deceased veteran files the following information: Standard Form 15; official notification of the veteran's death in line of duty.

CIVIL SERVICE REFORM ACT

Personnel Practices and Actions in the Federal Government Require:

- Recruitment from all segments of society, and selection and advancement on the basis of ability, knowledge, and skills, under fair and open competition.
- Fair and equitable treatment in all personnel management matters, without regard to politics, race, color, religion, national origin, sex, marital status, age, or handicapping condition, and with proper regard for individual privacy and constitutional rights.
- Equal pay for work of equal value, considering both national and local rates paid by private employers, with incentives and recognition for excellent performance.
- High standards of integrity, conduct, and concern for the public interest.
- Efficient and effective use of the Federal work force.
- Retention of employees who perform well, correcting the performance of those whose work is inadequate, and separation of those who cannot or will not meet required standards.
- Improved performance through effective education and training.
- Protection of employees from arbitrary action, personal favoritism, or political coercion.
- Protection of employees against reprisal for lawful disclosures of information.

Officials and Employees Who Are Authorized to Take Personnel Actions Are Prohibited From:

- Discriminating against any employee or applicant.

- Soliciting or considering any recommendation on a person who requests or is being considered for a personnel action unless the material is an evaluation of the person's work performance, ability, aptitude, or general qualifications, or character, loyalty, and suitability.
- Using official authority to coerce political actions, to require political contributions, or to retaliate for refusal to do these things.
- Willfully deceiving or obstructing an individual as to his or her right to compete for Federal employment.
- Influencing anyone to withdraw from competition, whether to improve or worsen the prospects of any applicant.
- Granting any special preferential treatment or advantage not authorized by law to a job applicant or employee.
- Appointing, employing, promoting, or advancing relatives in their agencies.
- Taking or failing to take a personnel action as a reprisal against employees who exercise their appeal rights; refuse to engage in political activity; or lawfully disclose violations of law, rule, or regulation, or mismanagement, gross waste of funds, abuse of authority, or a substantial and specific danger to public health or safety.
- Taking or failing to take any other personnel action violating a law, rule, or regulation directly related to merit system principles.

The New Organization for Personnel Management

As a result of Reorganization Plan No. 2, the U.S. Civil Service Commission is abolished January 1979, and its functions divided between two new agencies. An Office of Personnel Management (OPM) is to

28

provide leadership in managing the Federal work force. An independent Merit Systems Protection Board (MSPB) is to resolve employee complaints and appeals. A third new agency, the Federal Labor Relations Authority (FLRA), is to administer the Federal labor relations program and investigate unfair labor practices.

The functions of the agencies are described below:

Office of Personnel Management

The Office of Personnel Management helps the President carry out his responsibilities for management of the Federal work force. The Office is headed by a director and deputy director appointed by the President and confirmed by the Senate.

OPM takes over many of the responsibilities of the Civil Service Commission. These include central examining and employment operations, personnel investigations, personnel program evaluation, executive development, and training. OPM also administers the retirement and insurance programs for Federal employees and exercises management leadership in labor relations and affirmative action.

As the central personnel agency, OPM develops policies governing civilian employment in Executive branch agencies and in certain agencies of the Legislative and Judicial branches, and helps agencies carry out these policies. Subject to its standards and review, OPM also delegates certain personnel powers to agency heads.

Merit Systems Protection Board

The Merit Systems Protection Board is the independent agency to safeguard both the merit system and individual employees against abuses and unfair personnel actions. The MSPB is headed by three board members, appointed on a bipartisan basis to 7-year nonrenewable terms. The Board hears and decides employee appeals and orders corrective and disciplinary actions against an employee or agency when appropriate. It also oversees the merit system and reports annually to Congress on how the system is functioning.

Within the MSPB is an independent Special Counsel, appointed by the President for a 5-year term. The Special Counsel has the power to investigate charges of prohibited personnel practices, including reprisals against whistleblowers; to ask MSPB to stop personnel actions in cases involving prohibited personnel practices; and to bring disciplinary charges before the MSPB against those who violate merit system law.

Federal Labor Relations Authority

The Federal Labor Relations Authority oversees the creation of bargaining units, supervises elections, and deals with labor-management issues in Federal agencies. The FLRA is headed by a chairman and two members, who are appointed on a bipartisan basis to staggered 5-year terms.

Within the FLRA, a General Counsel, appointed to a 5-year term, investigates alleged unfair labor practices and prosecutes them before the FLRA. Also within the FLRA and acting as a separate body, the Federal Service Impasses Panel resolves negotiation impasses.

Performance Appraisal Systems

Each agency is to develop and phase-in its own appraisal system(s). Performance appraisals are to be a basis for decisions to train, reward, assign, promote, demote, retain, or remove employees (for reasons other than misconduct). Agencies are encouraged to have employees participate in establishing performance objectives for their jobs.

Specifically, the appraisal systems must make it possible for agencies to:
- advise employees on what the critical elements of their jobs are;
- establish performance standards that will permit accurate evaluation of job performance on the basis of objective, job-related criteria;
- assist employees to improve unacceptable performance; and
- reassign, demote, or remove those employees whose performance continues to be unacceptable, but only after they have been given an opportunity to show that they can perform acceptably and have failed to improve.

Agencies are required to inform employees of the critical elements and performance standards of their jobs.

If any agency proposes to remove or demote an employee because of poor performance, and if that employee's performance becomes acceptable and remains acceptable for one year, the record of the poor performance will be removed from agency files.

Procedures for Adverse Actions and Appeals

Adverse actions, such as removals, suspensions for over 14 days, and reductions in grade or pay, may be appealed to the Merit Systems Protection Board. Employees in organized bargaining units may be able under their negotiated agreements to ask their union to seek arbitration instead of appealing to MSPB.

If an agency proposes to demote or remove an employee because of unacceptable performance, that employee is entitled to:
- receive written notice from the agency 30 days before the proposed action;
- be represented by an attorney or other representative;
- answer orally and in writing within a reasonable time; and
- receive a written decision (agreed to by a higher level supervisor than the one who proposed the action) which states the reason for the action.

An agency's final decision will be provided in writing within 30 days after the end of the notice period.

If an agency decides to demote or remove an employee at the end of the notice period, the employee may appeal to the MSPB for a hearing, or, if within a bargaining unit, the employee may use the grievance arbitration procedure. The agency's decision will be upheld if it is shown by substantial evidence that the employee failed to meet performance standards for one or more critical elements of the job. For adverse actions based on grounds other than poor performance, an agency's decision to remove an employee must be supported by a preponderance of evidence.

An agency's decision will not be upheld if an employee shows that the decision:
- was based on harmful procedural errors on the part of the agency;
- was based on any prohibited personnel practice; or
- was unlawful.

The same standards will apply whether the adverse action is appealed to MSPB or resolved by an arbitrator.

Agencies whose decisions are reversed may be required in certain cases to pay employees for reasonable attorney fees. These payments might occur in cases where agencies engaged in prohibited personnel practices.

Decisions or orders of MPSB are appealable to the U.S. Court of Appeals, or, in matters of pay, the Court of Claims.

Complaints Involving Discrimination

Procedures to handle discrimination complaints in two situations are established.

The first situation includes agency actions which the employee claims were discriminatory and which are of a type that may be appealed to MSPB (e.g. removals and demotions). These are called "mixed cases." An agency has 120 days to try to resolve the discrimination issue by using counseling and investigation. If an employee is not satisfied with the final agency decision, or if time runs out, that employee may appeal to MSPB. Instead of going to MSPB with a "mixed case," the union may call for grievance arbitration.

An employee may not directly appeal a "mixed case" to the Equal Employment Opportunity Commission (EEOC). However, an employee may ask EEOC to review the MSPB decision. Other steps would be followed if EEOC and MSPB do not agree.

The second type of situation includes discrimination complaints about actions or failures to act which are not appealable to MSPB (e.g. promotions or working conditions). In this case, an employee may appeal the final agency action to EEOC, or a union may call for grievance arbitration procedures. Appeals to EEOC will follow the current procedures for processing discrimination complaints. MSPB plays no part in these decisions.

Regardless of whether the decision is made by MSPB,

EEOC, or an arbitrator, an employee will have the right to appeal that decision to a U.S. District Court.

EEOC is also responsible for approving agency goals and timetables in affirmative action plans.

Special Counsel Protections

The Special Counsel to the Merit Systems Protection Board is, in effect, an independent investigator and prosecutor. This individual is appointed by the President for a 5-year term.

Specifically, the Special Counsel investigates charges that agency officials:
- undertook prohibited personnel practices, including reprisals against whistleblowers;
- engaged in prohibited political activity;
- withheld information under the Freedom of Information Act without just reason;
- discriminated in violation of law; or
- carried out activities prohibited by any other civil service law, rule, or regulation.

After these investigations, the Special Counsel may bring disciplinary charges before the MSPB against officials if the evidence shows a probable violation. They may be reprimanded, removed, fined, or barred from Federal employment.

The Special Counsel has authority to protect *whistleblowers*. Whistleblowers are those employees or applicants who expose practices which they reasonably believe to be a violation of law, rule, or regulation, or which they believe constitute mismanagement, gross waste of funds, abuse of authority, or a danger to public health or safety. Employees or applicants who make disclosures specifically prohibited by law or Executive order will not be protected.

The Special Counsel investigates charges of reprisal without revealing the identity of the whistleblower, and may petition any member of the MSPB to stop any personnel action while the matter is under investigation. The results of the investigation will be reported to the whistleblower.

Agencies may be required to conduct investigations and prepare reports on the substance of complaints made by whistleblowers. In such cases, the Special Counsel will review the agency reports to determine whether they contain sufficient information and whether the findings appear reasonable. Copies of the agency reports will be sent to the President and to Congress, and to the persons who filed the complaints.

Grade and Pay Retention

Pay retention provisions will make it possible for employees to retain their grades for two years and to avoid taking considerable cuts in salary as the result of downgrading actions for which they were not responsible.

Employees to be placed in lower-graded positions as the result of reductions-in-force or reclassification actions may, (if they have held their current positions for one year), retain their current grades for two years from the date of demotion. Pay for these employees will not be reduced.

At the end of the two-year period, the grades of these employees will be lowered. Should their pay at that time exceed the maximum rate of their new grades, they will retain their current rate of pay but will receive only 50% of their annual comparability pay increases. If or when their pay is lower than or equal to the maximum rate of their new grades, they will then receive full comparability pay increases.

These special benefits will continue only as long as the employees remain in their same positions and will apply to all reductions-in-force or reclassification actions taken on or after January 1, 1977.

Veterans' Preference and Benefits

Veterans with service-connected disabilities of 30% or more are entitled to receive additional benefits, including:
- appointment without competitive examination, with a right to be converted to career appointments, and
- retention rights over other preference eligibles in reductions-in-force.

Veterans with disabilities of 30% or more also have the right to be notified in advance and respond to any decision in which:
- they are considered ineligible for a position due to physical requirements of the position;
- they would be passed over by an agency in the course of filling a position from a civil service

certificate; or
- they are deemed ineligible for retention in a position during a reduction-in-force due to the physical requirements of the position.

On October 1, 1980, veterans' preference is eliminated for non-disabled military retirees who retire from the service at or above the rank of major or its equivalent.

Changes in Federal Labor Relations

The Civil Service Reform Act contains a number of new provisions which clarifies the roles and responsibilities of labor organizations and which, to an extent, expands the rights of employees in collective bargaining units.

The Act affirms the basic rights of Federal employees to form, join, and assist labor organizations (or to refrain from doing so). It prohibits strikes and work slowdowns, as well as picketing that interferes with government operations.

For most matters, employees working in organized bargaining units must use the grievance arbitration procedures negotiated by the union. However, an exception is made for adverse actions and discrimination complaints. In such cases, employees may use either the negotiated procedures *or* the appeals procedure. The union is required to represent all employees in the bargaining unit who choose the negotiated procedures, whether or not they are members of the union.

The issues subject to collective bargaining are to generally continue. However, departments and agencies (such as OPM, OMB, and GSA) which issue government-wide regulations affecting Federal employees, are required to consult with labor organizations representing a substantial number of employees over any substantive changes. In addition, a union that represents, in one bargaining unit, a majority of affected employees is able to negotiate without regard to their own agency's regulations on matters otherwise within the scope of bargaining.

The Act makes all types of management actions subject to collective bargaining unless specific "management rights" exist. These reserve to agency officials the authority to make decisions and take actions which are not subject to the collective bargaining

process, and exclude bargaining on Federal pay and benefits or nonvoluntary payments to unions by employees. The changes in the management rights area will: (1) *prohibit* agencies from bargaining on mission, budget, organization, number of employees, or internal security; and (2) *permit,* but not require, them to negotiate over the methods, means, and technology of conducting agency operations. Management has the right to determine whether vacant positions may be filled only by persons within the agency *or* by persons within and outside the agency.

Other provisions in the Act include:
- A time limit of 45 days for agency heads to decide if a proposed action is negotiable. This decision will be appealable to the Federal Labor Relations Authority.
- Court enforcement of FLRA decisions and orders, including judicial review in unfair labor practice cases.
- Provisions for back pay and attorney fees for employees subject to unjustified or unwarranted personnel actions.
- Dues withholding—based on voluntary allotments by employees—at the exclusive union's request. (Allotments are irrevocable for one year, and the withholding service is at no charge to the employee or labor organization.)
- Official time during regular working hours for employees representing unions in negotiations.

Trial Period for New Managers and Supervisors

First-time supervisors and managers will be required to serve a trial period before their appointments become final. Those who do not satisfactorily complete the trial period will be returned to positions of no lower pay and grade than those they occupied before assuming their managerial or supervisory assignments.

Previously, ineffective first-time supervisors and managers could normally be removed only through the application of adverse action procedures. Those who do not perform well during the trial period are to be removed from managerial responsibilities forthwith.

Merit Pay for Managers and Supervisors

A merit pay system is implemented in which the pay increases of managers and supervisors in grades GS-

13 through GS-15 will be directly linked to their performance, rather than to their length of service. Employees covered will no longer receive automatic within-grade increases, but will be eligible each year for merit pay increases.

Managers covered under the merit pay system will receive a minimum of one-half of the annual comparability pay increases authorized for white collar employees, but this minimum can be increased by OPM. The funds for merit raises are to be derived from a combination of the remainder of the annual comparability increases and from funds formerly used for step increases and quality step increases for these employees.

The amounts agencies award in merit increases will vary to recognize distinctions in the performance of individual managers and supervisors and of the organizations they direct. Agencies must base their decisions on a formal appraisal system. Factors taken into account in awarding merit pay increases will include cost efficiency; timeliness of performance; and improvements in efficiency, productivity, and quality of work or service.

All managers and supervisors in grades GS-13 through GS-15 are to be brought into the merit pay system. No employee will suffer a salary loss in the conversion to the new system.

Senior Executive Service

The Senior Executive Service (SES) is to include managers at GS-16 through Executive Level IV or their equivalents in the Executive branch. The SES will make it easier for the Federal Government to attract and keep top managers, to use their abilities productively, and to pay them according to their performance.

The large majority of SES executives are to be career managers. There is a 10% government-wide ceiling on the number who may be noncareer. In addition, about 45% of SES positions will be career-reserved; that is, they can be filled only by career executives.

SES executives may be reassigned to other positions within their own agencies, but may not be involuntarily transferred to other agencies.

Entry Into SES

OPM will determine the number of SES positions in each agency. Individuals who presently occupy those positions which their agencies designate to become a part of the SES have 90 days in which to choose either to enter the Service or to remain under their present appointment authorities. Those who choose not to join the SES will keep their present pay and benefits, but will not be eligible for promotions. Those who enter the SES at a later date must have their managerial qualifications evaluated by qualification review boards within the Office of Personnel Management, and must serve a trial period of one year. Veterans' preference will not apply in the SES.

Compensation and Benefits

Base pay for SES executives will be set at one of five levels, with the minimum at the equivalent of GS-16, step 1, and the maximum at the salary for Executive Level IV. In addition, performance awards may be given to 50% of the career executives in amounts up to 20% of base salary. Each year, up to 5% of SES executives may receive the rank of "Meritorious Executive," with a special award of $10,000. Up to 1% may receive the rank of "Distinguished Executive," with a special award of $20,000. A ceiling will be set on total compensation for SES members equal to the pay of Executive Level I (now $66,000). Only career executives in the SES will be eligible for performance awards and ranks.

Retention and Removal

Retention in the SES will be based on good performance. Executives will be evaluated annually by their supervisors, who will measure their individual performance and that of the organizations they direct. Among the evaluation criteria are improvements in efficiency and productivity; work quality; timeliness of performance; and success in meeting affirmative action goals.

Ratings will range from "fully successful," a rating which makes one eligible for performance awards, to "marginal" or "unsatisfactory," ratings which indicate a need for corrective action and improvement. Failure to improve would cause removal from the SES.

Career executives who are removed from the SES for

poor performance cannot appeal but may state their case in a hearing before the Merit Systems Protection Board. They are entitled to placement in non-SES positions at GS-15 or above, at no loss in base pay. Executives with 25 years of government service or with 20 years of service at age 50 may choose retirement under such circumstances.

Agencies are to conduct minority recruitment programs to help eliminate underrepresentation of minority groups in the Federal work force. The Office of Personnel Management and the Equal Employment Opportunity Commission will provide guidelines and assistance.

Nonpaid work by students in connection with educational programs is permitted, provided they do not reduce opportunities for regular employees.

Employees who would otherwise be separated under reductions-in-force may be retrained for jobs in other agencies.

Employees who are age 50 with 20 years of service, or who, regardless of age, have 25 years of service, may choose early retirement in major reorganizations, transfers of function, or reductions-in-force.

OPM must notify the U.S. Employment Service about competitive examinations it administers. Agencies must provide both OPM and the U.S. Employment Service employment information about positions for which they are seeking candidates outside of the civil service system.

The mobility program authorized by the Intergovernmental Personnel Act has been extended to include additional types of organizations and individuals. Federal employees who accept these assignments must return to the Federal Government for a period equal to that of the assignments.

Subject to its standards and review, OPM may delegate authority for personnel management functions, including certain competitive examinations, to the heads of agencies employing persons in the competitive service.

The combined retirement pay and federal civilian salary received by future retirees of the uniformed services may not exceed the pay for Executive Level V.

Federal agencies are authorized to adopt OPM's merit system standards as a personnel requirement for grants to state and local governments.

YOU BECOME AN "ELIGIBLE"

People who are found to meet the requirements in the announcement are called "eligibles." Their names are put on a "list of eligibles." An eligible's chances of getting a job depend on how high he stands on this list and how fast agencies are filling jobs from the list.

Federal agencies can fill jobs in several ways—for instance, by promoting an employee already within the agency or by hiring an employee from another Federal agency who wants to change jobs. But when a job is to be filled from a list of eligibles, the agency asks the Civil Service examiners for the names of people on the list of eligibles for that job.

When the examiners receive this request, they send to the agency the names of the three people highest on the list. Or, if the job to be filled has specialized requirements, the examiners send the agency, from the general list, the names of the top three persons who meet those requirements. An applicant who has said he would not accept appointment in the place where the job is located is, of course, not considered.

The appointing officer makes a choice from among the three people whose names were sent to him. If that person accepts the appointment, the names of the other persons are put back on the list so that they may be considered for future openings.

That is the rule in hiring from all kinds of eligible lists, whether they are for typist, carpenter, chemist, or something else. For every vacancy, the appointing officer has his choice of any one of the top three eligibles on the list. This explains why the person whose name is on top of the list sometimes does not get an appointment when some of the persons lower on the list do. If the appointing officer chooses the No. 2 or No. 3 eligible, the No. 1 eligible doesn't get a job at once, but stays on the list until he is appointed or the list is terminated.

S118

VETERANS GET PREFERENCE

If you are a veteran, you may be eligible for additional benefits in getting a Government job and also in keeping it after you are hired. For example, "veteran preference" will add extra points to your passing score.

Disabled veterans or their wives, widows of certain veterans, and widowed or divorced mothers of some veterans who died in service or who were totally and permanently disabled get 10 extra points. Most other honorably discharged veterans get 5 points, depending upon length or dates of service.

KINDS OF APPOINTMENTS

If you are offered a job, the letter or telegram will show what kind of appointment is involved. Most appointments are either temporary, term, career-conditional, or career. You should know what these mean.

A *temporary* appointment does not ordinarily last more than 1 year. A temporary worker can't be promoted and can't transfer to another job. He is not under the retirement system. Persons over 70 can be given only temporary appointments, but they can be renewed.

A *term* appointment is made for work on a specific project that will last more than 1 year but less than 4 years. A term employee can be promoted or reassigned to other positions within the project for which he was hired. He is not under the retirement system.

If you accept a temporary or term appointment,

your name will stay on the list of eligibles from which you were appointed. This means that you will remain eligible for permanent jobs that are normally filled by career-conditional or career appointments.

A *career-conditional* appointment leads after 3 years' service to a career appointment. For the first year, the employee serves a probationary period. During this time, he must demonstrate that he can do a satisfactory job and may be dismissed if he fails to do so. A career-conditional employee has promotion and transfer privileges. After a career-conditional employee completes his probation, he cannot be removed except for cause. However, in reduction-in-force (layoff) actions, career-conditional employees are dismissed ahead of career employees.

A *career* employee also serves a probationary period, as described above, and has promotion and transfer privileges. After he completes his probation, however, he is in the last group to be affected in layoffs.

WHY YOU MAY BE BARRED

Applicants may be denied examinations and eligibles may be denied appointments for any of the following reasons:

1. Dismissal from employment for delinquency or misconduct.

2. Physical or mental unfitness for the position.

3. Criminal, infamous, dishonest, immoral, or notoriously disgraceful conduct.

4. Intentional false statements, deception, or fraud.

5. Refusal to furnish testimony which the Commission may require.

6. Drunkenness.

7. Any legal or other disqualification.

An old conviction for civil or criminal offense will not of itself bar an applicant from U. S. government employment. Ordinarily a person who has been convicted of a felony must wait two years after release before his application will be considered. Exceptions can be made by the Office of Personnel Management, which also decides whether or not to accept applications from persons who have been convicted of misdemeanors or who are under suspended sentence or on probation.

PART TWO

*Representative
Civil Service Jobs*

GENERAL INFORMATION FOR PART II

The following list of terms applies to most of the positions discussed in PART II. It is a good idea, therefore, to read through this list before you embark upon this highly informative section of FEDERAL CIVIL SERVICE JOBS, THE COMPLETE GUIDE. Exceptions to and/or qualifications of any of these terms will be indicated and described at length for relevant positions.

ACADEMIC YEAR: Consists of approximately 36 weeks of full-time study, 30 semester hours, 45 quarter hours, or the equivalent. One academic year equals approximately nine months of experience.

CREDITING EDUCATION or TRAINING: Study completed in an institution above the high school level is evaluated as evidence of ability in terms of its relatedness to the knowledges, skills, and abilities required to assume the position of interest successfully. Study completed in a business or secretarial school or other comparable institution above the high school level is creditable provided subjects related to the position of interest were studied. Study completed in a junior college, college, or university is creditable provided such study included a minimum of six semester hours, or the equivalent, per year in subjects which equipped the candidate with the knowledges, skills, and abilities required at the level of the position of interest.

FULL-TIME STUDY: In the case of business and commercial schools, it is the equivalent of at least 20 classroom hours of instruction per week, plus necessary outside study. Part-time study is prorated on this basis also but is creditable only in amounts equivalent to one-half academic year or multiples thereof.

INTERVIEWS: The purpose of interviews is to observe and evaluate personal characteristics and qualifications which are essential to the successful performance of the duties of the position.

PHYSICAL REQUIREMENTS: Applicants must be physically and mentally able to efficiently perform the essential functions of the position without hazard to themselves or others. Depending on the essential duties of a specific position, usable vision, color vision, hearing or speech may be required. However, in most cases, a specific physical condition or impairment of a specific function may be compensated for by the satisfactory use of a prosthesis or mechanical aid. Reasonable accommodation may also be considered in determining an applicant's ability to perform the duties of a position. Reasonable accommodation may include but is not limited to: the use of assistive devices, job modification or restructuring, provision of readers and interpreters, or adjusted work schedules. Also, all positions involving Federal motor vehicle operation carry the additional medical requirements.

QUALITY OF EXPERIENCE: For positions at any grade, the required amount of experience will not in itself be accepted as proof of qualifications. The candidate's record of experience and training must show that he/she has the ability to perform the duties of the position.

QUALITY RANKING FACTORS: A quality ranking factor is a knowledge, skill, or ability which could be expected to significantly enhance performance in a position, but could not reasonably be considered necessary for satisfactory performance. Quality ranking factors may be used to distinguish the better qualified candidates from among those who meet all other requirements, including selective factors.

SELECTIVE FACTORS: Selective factors must be job related, represent an extension of the basic knowledges and skills required of the position and be essential to successful performance of the position. Selective factors are knowledge and skills of a kind and level which reasonably could not be acquired on the job without undue interruption of the organization's production. Selective factors for positions at higher grades typically will be more narrowly defined and/or set at a higher level than is necessary at lower grades. What may be appropriate as a quality ranking factor at a lower grade may have to be a selective factor in a higher graded position.

* Alternative definition: a knowledge, skill, or ability that is essential for satisfactory performance in a position, and represents an addition to the basic minimum requirements in this standard.

CLERICAL POSITIONS

Clerk (various positions) GS−1/3

DESCRIPTION OF WORK

Clerical positions involve the orderly processing of the papers and performance of the routine work supporting an office or organization. Within a framework of procedures, regulations, precedents, and instructions, clerks process and maintain the records and written materials which represent the transactions or business of the office or organization served. Among the basic duties which may be performed are, for example: (1) maintaining records; (2) receiving, screening, reviewing, and verifying documents; (3) searching for and compiling information and data; (4) providing a central source of information on the activities of the organization orally or by correspondence; (5) preparing and/or verifying the validity of documents with which the organization is concerned; etc.

REQUIREMENTS

A. GENERAL BACKGROUND

In order to be considered for appointment the applicant's overall background, work history, personal characteristics, work habits, and general behavior and reputation in his/her community, school, and previous employment must be of such nature as to provide positive evidence that he/she can and will perform clerical or office type work in a successful and productive manner in an office type of environment.

B. EXPERIENCE

For grade GS−1, no written test, experience, training, or education is required.

GS−2.—Six months of general experience; or graduation from a full 4-year or senior high school or possession of a General Educational Development High School Equivalency Certificate (GED).

GS−3.—One year of general experience; or 1 academic year of business or secretarial school, junior college, or college which is in addition to graduation from high school.

WRITTEN TESTS

Applicants for positions at grades GS−2 and GS−3 are required to pass written tests.

For some positions, only applicants who receive suitably high scores on parts of the test specifically pertinent to the particular kind of work to be done will be considered.

BASIS OF RATING

For GS−1: An evaluation of the applicant's willingness to do simple and repetitive clerical work, dependability, and the ability to perform work safely.

For GS−2 and GS−3: The score on the written test *and* an evaluation of the extent and quality of experience, education, and training.

APPLICABLE STANDARDS FOR
CLERICAL POSITIONS ALSO
REQUIRING SKILL IN TYPING OR
STENOGRAPHY

Some positions requiring typing or stenographic skill as high as that required under the competitive standard for typing or stenographic work, are so constituted that other work skills or abilities, rather than typing or stenographic skills, form the main qualification requirements for the positions. An appropriate means should be used to assure that applicants possess sufficient skill in typing or stenography to perform the duties of all such positions (i.e., a performance test, certificate of proficiency, or some method of certification acceptable to the Office of Personnel Management).

REQUIREMENTS FOR CLERICAL POSITIONS INVOLVING PUBLIC CONTACTS

Some clerical positions (e.g., information receptionists) which involve substantial contact with others, require a clear speaking voice, tact, courtesy, and capacity for effective public contacts. In filling such positions competitively and noncompetitively, appointing officers will assure themselves by reference checks, personal interviews, or other appropriate means that applicants possess these qualities to the degree necessary for satisfactory performance of the duties of such positions.

Office Machine Operator (various positions) GS−1/3

DESCRIPTION OF WORK

Persons employed in these positions have as their primary responsibility the operation of the specific office machine described in the individual job title, although clerical work of varying degrees is also involved in many such positions.

EDUCATION AND EXPERIENCE REQUIREMENTS

GS−1.—No experience or education required; however, the appropriate tests must be passed.

GS−2.—Must pass the appropriate written test and—

Alternative 1. Pass appropriate performance test (if any);

or

Alternative 2. Have had six months of office clerical experience or office machine operation experience;

or

Alternative 3. Have completed a specialized course of instruction in the operation of the appropriate machine and either

a. had three months of general or specialized experience

or

b. have graduated from high school.

The specialized course of instruction on appropriate machines may have been completed as part of the high school curriculum. Evidence of successful completion of such courses will be required.

GS−3.—Must pass the written test *and* the appropriate performance test (if any) and have had either (a) one year of acceptable experience of which at least six months is specialized experience, or (b) one academic year of business or secretarial school or junior college. For occupations for which no performance test is available, education offered under (b) must have included training in the operation of appropriate office machines.

WRITTEN TESTS

All applicants are required to pass tests covering (a) verbal abilities and clerical abilities (alphabetizing and arithmetic) and (b) eye-hand coordination and perception of differences. All applicants for positions of operators of machines equipped with an alphabetic keyboard will be required to pass a performance test on a typewriter-style keyboard. Applicants for positions of EAM Operator must pass a test of abstract reasoning ability.

Higher scores may be required for the higher grades.

BASIS OF RATING

Applicants will be ranked on the basis of (a) their score on the verbal abilities test, and (b) the extent and quality of their experience and education. Other required tests must be passed but are not used to rank the eligibles.

GENERAL NOTE AS TO
APPLICABLE STANDARDS FOR
POSITIONS ALSO REQUIRING SKILL
IN TYPING OR STENOGRAPHY

Some office machine operator positions may require typing or stenographic skill at or above the level of proficiency required under the competitive standard for entry-level clerk-typist or clerk-stenographer positions, but may be so constituted that the machine operator skills, rather than the typing or stenographic skills, form the main qualification requirements for the positions. Positions so constituted are classified in the office machine operator series appropriate for the main requirement and are identified by the parenthical addition of the words "typing" or "stenography" to the titles otherwise prescribed for those series.

Secretary, All Grades
Secretary (Stenography), All Grades
Secretary (Typing), All Grades

DESCRIPTION OF WORK

This series includes all positions the duties of which are to assist one individual, and in some cases the subordinate staff of that individual, by performing general office work auxiliary to the work of the organization. To be included in this series, a position must be the principal clerical or administrative support position in the office, operating independently of any other such position in the office. The duties require a knowledge of clerical and administrative procedures and requirements; various office skills; and the ability to apply such skills in a way that increases the effectiveness of others. The duties do not require a technical or professional knowledge of a specialized subject-matter area.

EXPERIENCE REQUIREMENTS

The requirements at all levels discussed below are purposely stated in terms of knowledges, skills, and abilities, rather than specific duties. A candidate may demonstrate possession of the knowledges, skills, and abilities through various means. For example, a candidate with extensive writing experience could perhaps demonstrate the ability to compose nontechnical correspondence without ever having performed that specific duty. Volunteer work for organizations such as civic groups or church groups may be used to fulfill experience require-

ments to the degree that such work can be verified and evaluated when such work demonstrates possession of the knowledges, skills, and abilities applicable to secretarial work.

For positions at GS—3
A general background in the performance of routine clerical duties which demonstrates that a candidate has *all* of the following:
1.—basic knowledge of office routines and functions sufficient to refer visitors and telephone calls and to route correspondence by name or functional area.
2.—knowledge of clerical practices and filing procedures.
3.—knowledge of spelling, punctuation, and syntax.

Experience acquired through the performance of most kinds of clerical work in an office setting is normally considered qualifying.

For positions at GS—4
A background in the performance of a variety of clerical duties which demonstrates that a candidate has *all* of the following:
—working knowledge of many different office procedures such as those needed to request a variety of office equipment, supplies, publication material, and maintenance services, when each of these requires a different procedure;

AND

—ability to understand an organization and its

functions sufficient to establish file systems for classifying, retrieving, and disposing of materials; refer telephone calls and visitors; distribute and control mail; maintain leave records; and provide general and non-technical information.

For positions at GS–5 and above

Experience in administrative or clerical work which demonstrates possession of the knowledges, skills, and abilities required to serve as a principal office assistant at these levels, including *all* of the following:

1.—ability to organize effectively the flow of clerical processes in an office;
2.—ability to organize and design a filing system;
3.—ability to make arrangements for such things as travel, conferences, and meetings;
4.—ability to locate and assemble information for various reports, briefings, and conferences;
5.—ability to compose non-technical correspondence.

Length of experience will not necessarily in itself be considered qualifying. The candidate's record must show the ability to perform the duties of the position to be filled.

For positions at GS–3

A candidate must have had six months of qualifying experience at GS–2 in the General Schedule or equivalent experience outside the General Schedule.

For positions at GS–4 or GS–5

A candidate must have had one year of qualifying experience at the next lower grade in the General Schedule or equivalent experience outside the General Schedule.

For positions at GS–6

A candidate must have had six months of qualifying experience at GS–5 in the General Schedule or equivalent experience outside the General Schedule.

For positions at GS–7 through GS–11

A candidate must have had six months of qualifying experience at the next lower grade in the General Schedule or equivalent experience outside the General Schedule *OR* one year of qualifying experience at the second lower grade

in the General Schedule or equivalent experience outside the General Schedule.

For positions at GS–12 and above

A candidate must have had one year of qualifying experience at the next lower grade in the General Schedule or equivalent experience outside the General Schedule.

SUBSTITUTION OF EDUCATION FOR EXPERIENCE

Except for any requirement for passing performance tests to demonstrate skill in shorthand and/or typing (when required), the following will apply:

For positions at GS–3

All of the experience requirements for the GS–3 level may be met by completion of 1 academic year of full-time business school or 1 academic year of education above the high-school level.

For positions at GS–4

All of the experience requirements for the GS–4 level may be met by completion of 2 academic years of full-time business school or 2 academic years of education above the high-school level.

For positions at GS–5

All of the experience requirements for the GS–5 level may be met by completion of 4 academic years of education in an accredited college or university.

NOTE: Academic study alone is not creditable as qualifying experience for positions above the GS–5 level; i.e., no more than 4 years of academic study is creditable towards meeting experience requirements.

Combination of education and experience may be used to meet the minimum qualification requirements.

Courses that are not measurable in terms of credit hours (e.g., "certificate courses") should be treated as if they were work experience. However, no credit will be allowed for training which has been obtained only or primarily in the basic skills of shorthand or typing or refresher courses.

TYPING AND STENOGRAPHIC SKILLS

When secretary positions require skill in typing or stenography at or above the level of proficiency required under the competitive standards for these skills, the qualification standard for the skill should be used in conjunction with this standard to assure that candidates possess at least the minimum degree of skill required to perform the typing or stenographic duties of the position.

The level of stenographic proficiency required by positions classified as Secretary (Stenography) is based on the classification of the *stenography* duties and not necessarily on the grade level of the position. Therefore, before applying for positions of this type, first determine the skill level required by the stenographic duties.

WRITTEN TESTS

No written test will be required at any grade level to establish basic qualifications of candidates, or to rank candidates. Performance tests may be required to demonstrate possession of stenographic or typing skill.

BASIS FOR RATING AND RANKING CANDIDATES

Candidates who meet the minimum qualification requirements will be rated on a scale of 70 to 100 based on an evaluation of the quality and extent of their experience, education, training, or other achievements pertinent to the duties of the positions to be filled.

Some kinds of training and experience which enhance the candidate's qualifications may be treated as factors to award extra credit for rating and ranking purposes. These include, but are not limited to, the following:
—Possession of a certificate as a "Certified Professional Secretary";
—Successful completion of in-service courses which offered training in areas related to the secretarial function, general management or administration, or the program area with which the supervisor is concerned;
—Successful completion of work-related educational courses in excess of those used to meet minimum requirements;
—Recognition for exceptional work performance.

Personnel Clerk
Staffing Clerk
Classification Clerk
Employee Development Clerk
Employee Relations Clerk
GS—4/6

Personnel Assistant
Staffing Assistant
Classification Assistant
Employee Development Assistant
Employee Relations Assistant
GS—6/10

DESCRIPTION OF WORK

Personnel clerks perform a variety of clerical tasks in connection with processing paper work, compiling and presenting data for reports, and providing basic information on personnel matters. Individual assignments may involve such duties as processing personnel actions; maintaining registers and issuing certificates of eligibles; compiling data for and preparing periodic and special personnel reports; providing basic information about personnel regulations, procedures, programs, or benefits to employees, management officials, or the general public; or providing clerical support in a personnel office or specialized unit within a personnel office where the work requires substantial knowledge of civilian personnel rules, regulations, procedures, and program requirements.

Personnel assistants perform a variety of technical support work which is usually related to one of the recognized personnel management specialties. This work may take the form of assisting one or more fully qualified personnel specialists in a limited area of assignment. It also may involve independent performance of assignments in a prescribed segment of a personnel program where a fully qualified personnel specialist is not required.

EXPERIENCE AND EDUCATION

Except for the substitution of education or training provided for below, applicants must have had the kind and amount of experience shown in the following table, and as described in the statements immediately following:

Grade	Total (years)	General (years)	Specialized (years)
GS–4	2	1	1
GS–5	3	1	2
GS–6	4	1	3
GS–7 and above	5	1	4

NOTE: The work of *clerical* positions (as distinguished from *assistant* positions) at grades GS–5 and above requires the application of specialized knowledge gained through experience in civilian personnel operations. These positions are generally filled through noncompetitive action.

These requirements for directly related experience will ordinarily apply. However, the requirement may be waived under certain circumstances where a lateral reassignment is involved, as provided elsewhere in this stand-ard. In addition, the requirement for directly related experience may be waived for individuals under consideration for promotion in the relatively few instances where it can be clearly shown that the candidate's background gives positive evidence that he possesses to a superior degree the essential skills and abilities needed for the position.

Substitution of Education and Training for Experience.

For a maximum of three years of the required experience (one year of general plus two years of specialized experience) study successfully completed in a resident school or institution may be substituted as follows:

General experience only:

a. Study completed in a college, university, or junior college, above the high school level may be substituted on the basis of one-half an *academic year* of study for *six months* of experience.

b. Full-time study completed in a business or secretarial school or other comparable institution above the high school level may be substituted on the basis of one-half an *academic year* of study for *six months* of experience provided such subjects as business English, office machines, filing and indexing, office practices, business mathematics, bookkeeping or accounting were studied. No credit will be allowed for training which has been obtained only or primarily in the basic skills of shorthand or typing or refresher courses.

Specialized experience:

a. For the first year of specialized experience, study successfully completed in a resident school above the high school level may be substituted at the rate of one-half an *academic year* of study for *six months* of specialized experience provided the study included a minimum of six semester hours, or the equivalent, per year in subjects closely related to the personnel field. Such subjects include statistics; psychology; sociology or other social sciences; courses where primary emphasis is on writing skill; public administration; personnel administration, industrial relations, or similar courses dealing directly with subjects in the personnel field; organization and management; and management analysis.

b. For the second year of specialized experience, study of the type described in item a, above, may be substituted at the rate of one academic year of study for six months of specialized experience. Therefore, a full 4-year course of this type of study may be substituted for a maximum of three years of the required experience and is fully qualifying for grade GS—5.

COMPUTER POSITIONS

Computer Clerk, GS–2/4
Computer Assistant, GS–5/9

DESCRIPTION OF WORK

Computer Clerks and Computer Assistants perform a variety of work in support of specialists and computer operators engaged in the design and operation of computer systems. Employees in this occupation also support functional users of computer systems by accepting processing requirements, preparing them for execution, and in some cases performing or directing program execution through remote terminals, distributing the products and performing related control and processing support duties. These tasks are complementary to and support such specialized computer systems work as analysis, design, programming, installation, operations and system management.

Computer Clerks perform such tasks as: (1) labeling, maintaining and controlling tapes, disks and other storage media and documentation in tape libraries; (2) preparing processing schedules for jobs that are executed in simple sequence and have dependencies that are readily accommodated; (3) maintaining a variety of computer program files, records, manuals and related documents; or, (4) tracing sources of procedural errors in documents, data and control records.

Computer Assistants perform limited phases of computer specialist functions in addition to project control and scheduling work such as: (1) translating program routines and detailed logic steps designed by others into instructions, codes, or languages that machines can accept; (2) preparing charts showing the flow of documents and data in assigned subject areas; (3) preparing daily or longer schedules for program processing sequences where multiple systems, multiprocessing, dependencies, contentions and similar conditions affect the scheduling processes; (4) assembling, modifying controls, annotating instructions and staging the materials and docu-

mentation required for machine processing; and/or, (5) tracing and identifying the sources of processing failures, correcting those associated with system controls, introducing new or revised schedules of program processing and providing control stream modifications to take advantage of alternative operating system hardware configurations and processing techniques.

EXPERIENCE REQUIREMENTS

Applicants must have the kind, quality and amount of experience indicated in the following table and explanatory information.

Grade	General Experience (years)	Specialized Experience (years)	Total Experience (years)
1	0	0	0
2	½	0	½
3	1	0	1
4	2	0	2
5	2	1	3
6	2	2	4
7 and above	2	3	5

General Experience—any experience which includes work associated with following written directions, procedures, or systematic work methods such as in classifying and maintaining records, or comparable clerical support work which gives evidence of the ability to perform this kind of work.

Specialized Experience—any experience in computer clerical or other computer related support work requiring knowledge of computer terminology, processing methods, controls, media and data flow. OR: Experience requiring proficiency in translating actions into a computer programming language (COBOL, FORTRAN,

ALGOL, etc.); preparing and interpreting program and system charts and instructions; or other work requiring comparable knowledges of computer processing techniques.

Substitution of Education for Experience

Education may be substituted for work experience according to the following criteria:

GS–2 Graduation from a 4-year high school or GED equivalent.

GS–3 Successful completion of a 2-year course, including instruction and practice in data processing in high school which provides knowledge of electronic computer systems, programming, media (tape, disks, and/or drum), input and retrieval methods. Specific knowledge or ability as computer operators is not essential to this occupation and is not required when crediting high school ADP training. OR:
Successful completion of 1 year of education above the high school level that includes at least six semester hours, or equivalent, in data processing courses. OR:
Successful completion of a full time concentrated course of study of at least 6 months' duration which includes systems design and programming instruction and practice in a technical school above the high school level.

GS–4 Successful completion of two years of study above the high school level which includes at least 12 semester hours (or equivalent) in courses such as computer mathematics, basic and advanced programming, data processing, computer operations, or other ADP related courses of study and practice.

GS–5 Successful completion of four years of study above the high school level which includes at least 24 semester hours (or equivalent) in courses such as those described above for GS–4.

QUALITY OF EXPERIENCE

In evaluating combinations of experience, education and training, one academic year of study may be substituted for one year of general experience or six months of specialized experience. Academic study may be substituted for a maximum of one year of specialized experience.

The applicant's record of experience and training must show the ability to perform the duties of the positions. In addition:

For grade GS–5, except for those who qualify on the basis of education alone, the 1 year of required specialized experience must have been comparable in difficulty and responsibility to the GS–4 level in the same or closely related work.

For grade GS–6 and above, at least 1 year of the required specialized experience must have been comparable in difficulty and responsibility to the next lower grade in the Federal service or 2 years comparable to the second lower grade in the Federal service.

WRITTEN TEST

Applicants for competitive appointment to grades GS–2/4 must pass a written test. The written test is waived for applicants who qualify on the basis of specialized training or experience in the data processing field.

BASIS FOR RATING

GS–2/4 applicants will be rated on the basis of written test scores except for applicants for whom the written test is waived. For such applicants and for positions at grade GS–5 and above, applicants will be rated on an evaluation of the quality and extent of their experience, education or training.

For Supervisory and Nonsupervisory Positions
GS–2/13 in the Computer Operation Series

DESCRIPTION OF WORK

Computer Operators are primarily responsible for the operation of the control console of a computer and all elements of the system which are directly connected with it. This involves readying the equipment for operation, starting it, monitoring its operation, and taking prompt action in response to machine commands or unscheduled halts.

EXPERIENCE, EDUCATION, AND TRAINING REQUIREMENTS

Applicants must have the kinds, quality, and amounts of experience indicated in the following table and explanatory information.

Grade	General Experience (years)	Specialized Experience (years)	Total Experience (years)
2...................	½	0	½
3.................	1	0	1
4.................	2	0	2
5.................	2	1	3
6.................	2	2	4
7 & above	2	3	5

General Experience—experience in the operation of electric accounting machines; *or* clerical experience; *or* experience in the operation of office business machines and other machines such as card punch, verifier, and the like.

Specialized Experience—experience in the operation of a computer system or peripheral device used in support of computer operations.

Specialized experience also may be experience in other computer-related occupations such as those involving programming, systems analysis, production control, scheduling, or others that are directly related.

Substitution of Education for Experience

In crediting education above the high school level, one year of study is equal to 30 semester hours or the equivalent. Education may be substituted for work experience according to the following criteria.

GS–2—Graduation from a 4-year high school or GED equivalent.

GS–3—Successful completion of 1 year of study in a school above the high school level in any field of study,

OR

Successful completion of a full-time, or equivalent part-time, course of study in computer operations in an accredited vocational or technical school above the high school level.

GS–4—Successful completion of 2 years of study in a school above the high school level.

GS–5—Completion of 4 years of study above the high school level which includes at least 12 semester hours in any one or a combination of the following: mathematics, statistics, data processing, or other pertinent or related fields.

In evaluating combinations of experience, education and training, 1 academic year of study may be substituted for 1 year of general experience or 6 months of specialized experience. Academic study may be substituted for a maximum of 1 year of specialized experience.

QUALITY OF EXPERIENCE

For positions at any grade the amount of experience will not in itself be accepted as proof of qualification. The applicant's record of experience and training must show that he/she has the ability to perform the duties of the position. In addition:

For grade GS–5, except for those who qualify on the basis of education alone, at least 6 months of the required specialized experience must have been comparable in difficulty and responsibility to the GS−4 level in the same or related work.

For grade GS−6 and above, in addition to education, training, and/or experience credited at lower levels, at least 1 year of the required specialized experience must have been comparable in difficulty and responsibility to the next lower grade in the Federal service or 2 years comparable to the second lower grade in the Federal service.

WRITTEN TEST

Applicants for competitive appointment to grades GS−2/4 must pass a written test.

BASIS FOR RATING

For GS−2/4, applicants will be rated on the basis of written test scores. For positions at grade GS−5 and above, applicants will be rated on an evaluation of the quality and extent of their experience, education, or training.

RELATING QUALIFICATIONS OF CANDIDATES TO JOBS HAVING SPECIAL REQUIREMENTS

The numbers and kinds of computers, and the primary purposes they serve, differ among various work situations and may vary widely. Consequently, the particular demands of positions in these different work situations may vary widely. Referral of candidates for these positions may be limited to those whose records show evidence of the required capabilities.

Computer Systems Analyst GS−5/15
Computer Programer GS−5/15
Computer Programer Analyst GS−5/15
Computer Systems Programer GS−5/15
Computer Equipment Analyst GS−5/15
Computer Specialist GS−5/15

DESCRIPTION OF WORK

Positions in this series advise on, supervise, or perform work necessary to design or implement systems for solving problems or accomplishing work processes by the use of digital computers. Except for entry level positions, the primary requirement is knowledge of computer requirements and techniques.

Computer Systems Analysts are concerned with analysis of problems or processes and design of computerized systems for accomplishment of the work. Representative assignments include performance of feasibility studies for proposed computer applications in a subject matter area, development of an application's programing specifications, or analysis of existing applications systems to correct problems.

Computer Programers are concerned with translating system designs into the plans of instructions and logic by which computers can produce the desired actions or products. Knowledge of a particular programing language is an important consideration in recruitment for these positions.

Computer Programer Analysts perform work which is a combination of Computer Systems Analyst and Computer Programer duties.

Computer Systems Programers are concerned with systems software. This typically involves maintenance and modification of assemblers, compilers, debugging routines, and similar internal computer programs necessary for the processing of other programs.

Computer Equipment Analysts are concerned with the selection or utilization of computer equipment. These positions do not involve design or repair of equipment; concern is with the relative merits of equipment items (e.g., mainframe computers, disk memory devices, printers, terminals) and the arrangement of the items into equipment systems appropriate to an organization's needs.

Computer Specialists perform work of a kind or combination of duties that does not fall under one of the above specializations but does have as the main requirement knowledge of computer requirements and techniques.

Further information about the nature of the work performed by employees in the Computer Specialist Series may be obtained from the position classification standard.

KNOWLEDGES, SKILLS AND ABILITIES

KNOWLEDGES AND SKILLS

The requirements in this standard reflect the fact that proficiency in application of knowledges and skills at a given level indicates probability of success in similar work at the next higher level. The requirements are keyed to the progression of grade levels set forth in the classification standard. Successful accomplishment of assignments at the next lower grade in the normal line of promotion to the position being filled demonstrates capability to do work of the required level of difficulty and responsibility. Work in other fields which has provided the same kind and level of knowledges and skills similarly is qualifying. Education is substitutable for practical experience when the education has provided the knowledges and skills.

The GS-5 and GS-7 levels require basic analytic and communicative skills combined with broad general knowledges. The knowledges and skills required for GS-9 and above are more specialized. Persons typically gain and demonstrate the more specialized knowledges and skills through a) successful performance in lower grade level positions in this series, b) related work experience in other fields, or c) graduate study in

fields such as data processing or computer science.

SELECTIVE FACTORS

Selective factors are knowledges and skills of a kind and level which reasonably could not be acquired on the job without undue interruption of the organization's production. Selective factors must be job related, represent an extension of the basic knowledges and skills required of the position and be essential to successful performance of the position.

Owing to the diversity of work in the Computer Specialist Series, the use of selective factors normally will be required in filling positions above the developmental level. Some factors, such as knowledge of a certain level of mathematics, may be appropriate for positions at any level. At the GS-9 and higher grades, knowledges and skills typically will be needed which relate to both the specialty of the position and the particular duties and responsibilities involved. For example, patterns of selective factors for a sample of full performance positions might be:

—For a Computer Programer Analyst position, a) proficiency in the use of a particular higher level programing language (e.g., COBOL), b) skill in development and implementation of specifications for applications programs, and c) knowledge of techniques pertinent to the appropriate broad category of subject matter applications (i.e., scientific applications or business applications).

—For a Computer Systems Programer position, a) proficiency in the use of a particular assembly level programing language (e.g., ALC), b) knowledge of general techniques for analysis of system software requirements, and c) skill in development and implementation of specifications for system software programs.

—For a Computer Equipment Analyst position, a) knowledge of techniques for analysis of computer equipment requirements, b) knowledge of techniques for evaluation of computer equipment, c) skill in development of specifications for procurement of computer equipment, and d) knowledge of a broad category of equipment (e.g., telecommunications related computer equipment).

Positions at GS−12 and above commonly involve very demanding and responsible roles, often with little or no "back up" expertise available in the organizational unit. Therefore, selective factors for positions at these grades typically will be more narrowly defined. What may be appropriate as a quality ranking factor at a lower grade may have to be a selective factor in a higher graded position. For example, knowledge of statistical methods and accounting techniques normally would be a quality ranking factor in filling positions concerned with an automation project involving such methods and techniques. However, this knowledge normally would constitute a selective factor in filling the position of the project leader responsible for planning the overall approach and integrating segments of the system where these methods and techniques were of critical importance.

MINIMUM QUALIFICATION REQUIREMENTS

For the GS−5 Level
  A. A background which includes one year of work at no lower than GS−4 or equivalent and demonstrates:
    1. Skill in analyzing problems, to include identifying relevant factors, gathering pertinent information and recognizing solutions,
    2. Skill in doing thorough, accurate work that requires planning a logical sequence of steps, and
    3. Skill in communicating, both orally and in writing.

Such skills typically are gained in administrative, technical, or investigative lines of work. It is also possible to acquire these skills through a variety of other means, such as volunteer work, vocational training, or substantive clerical work.
OR
  B. Completion of a four year course in an accredited college leading to a bachelor's degree in any field.
AND
(In the case of A or B)
  C. Evidence of possession of any selective factors appropriate to the position to be filled.

For the GS−7 Level
  A. A background which includes one year of work at no lower than GS−5 or equivalent and demonstrates skills related to the computer field through performance of tasks such as:
    —translating detailed logical steps developed by others into language codes that computers accept where this requires understanding of procedures and limitations appropriate to use of a programing language.
    —interviewing subject matter personnel to get facts regarding work processes and synthesizing the resulting data into charts showing information flow.
    —operating computer consoles where this involves choice among various procedures in responding to machine commands or unscheduled halts.
    —scheduling the sequence of programs to be processed by computers where alternatives must be weighed with a view to production efficiency.
    —extracting and compiling information concerning an equipment feature where this involves selecting pertinent data from catalogs, manufacturer's literature, and previous studies.
    —preparing documentation on cost/benefit studies where this involves summarizing the materials and organizing them in logical fashion.

Such skills typically are gained as a trainee in the Computer Specialist Series, as a Computer Operator or Assistant, or through performance of work where the primary concern was the subject matter of the computer application (e.g., supply, personnel, chemical process control) and one or more of the above types of computer related efforts were required to facilitate the basic duties. Also, work in management analysis, program analysis, or a comparable field often provides such skills.
OR
  B. Superior Academic Achievement.
OR
  C. Completion of one full academic year of graduate study in any field.
AND
(In the case of A, B, or C)
  D. Evidence of possession of any selective

factors appropriate to the position to be filled.

For the GS−9 Level

A. A background which includes one year of work at no lower than GS−7 or equivalent and demonstrates knowledges of computer requirements and techniques in carrying out project assignments consisting of several related tasks. To be qualifying for the GS−9 level the assignments must have shown completion of the following, or the equivalent:

1. Analysis of the interrelationships of pertinent components of the system,
2. Planning the sequence of actions necessary to accomplish the assignment, and
3. Personal responsibility for at least a segment of the overall project.

Such knowledges and skills typically are gained in the Computer Specialist Series or through performance of work where the primary concern was the subject matter of the computer application, and the above types of computer related efforts were required to facilitate the basic duties. Also, work in management analysis, program analysis, or a comparable field often provides such knowledges and skills.

OR

B. Completion of two full academic years of graduate study, or all requirements for a master's or equivalent degree, in a computer related field such as computer science, data processing, or information processing science.

AND

(In the case of A or B)

C. Evidence of possession of any selective factors appropriate to the position to be filled.

For the GS−11 Level

A. A background which includes one year of work at no lower than GS−9 or equivalent and demonstrates accomplishment of computer project assignments that required a range of knowledges of computer requirements and techniques. For example, this level would be shown by assignments where, on the basis of general design criteria provided, the person developed modifications to parts of a system that re-

quired significant revisions in the logic or techniques used in the original development. In addition to the characteristics noted for the GS−9 level, qualifying accomplishments for the GS−11 level involve the following, or the equivalent:

1. Knowledge of the customary approaches, techniques, and requirements appropriate to an assigned computer applications area or computer specialty area in an organization,
2. Planning the sequence of actions necessary to accomplish the assignment where this has entailed a) coordination with others outside the organizational unit and b) development of project controls, and
3. Adaptation of guidelines or precedents to the needs of the assignment.

Such knowledge and skills typically are gained in the Computer Specialist Series or through performance of work where the primary concern was the subject matter of the computer application (e.g., supply, personnel, chemical process control) and the above types of computer related efforts were required to facilitate the basic duties. Also, work in management analysis, program analysis, or a comparable field occasionally provides such knowledge and skills.

OR

B. Completion of three full academic years of graduate study, or all requirements for a doctoral degree (Ph.D or equivalent), in a computer field such as computer science, data processing, or information processing science when 1) the position to be filled involves highly specialized work and 2) the graduate work is directly pertinent to the duties and responsibilities of the position.

AND

(In the case of A or B)

C. Evidence of possession of any selective factors appropriate to the position to be filled.

For GS−12 and above

A. A background which includes one year of work at no lower than the next lower grade or equivalent and demonstrates accomplishment of computer project assignments that required a wide range of knowledges of computer requirements and techniques pertinent to the position to be filled. This normally will have included knowledges of how the work is carried out in other organizations. In addition to the characteristics noted for the GS−9 and GS−11 levels, to be qualifying for the GS−12 and above the assignments will have involved performance of studies, such as feasibility studies, where alternatives were evaluated, reports prepared, and recommendations made.

Such knowledges and skills typically are gained in the Computer Specialist Series.

AND

B. Evidence of possession of any selective factors appropriate to the position to be filled.

RANKING QUALIFIED CANDIDATES

A suggested procedure is to analyze the requirements of the position and determine, in addition to selective factors essential to satisfactory performance, quality ranking factors which would distinguish the better qualified candidates among those who meet the minimum requirements. (Where appropriate, selective factors may also serve as quality ranking factors.)

Positions at GS−5 and GS−7

Evaluation of candidates for positions at GS−5 and GS−7 should be based on evidence indicating probable success at higher level assignments.

Other things being equal, candidates who can be expected to achieve full performance competence most quickly usually will be distinguished by:

1. The quality of achievements that indicate ability in analyzing problems,
2. The caliber, job relatedness, and extent of education or experience which provided familiarity with data processing concepts, terminology and techniques, and
3. For applications oriented positions (e.g., computer programer), the degree of subject matter knowledge of the work process to be automated.

Positions at GS−9 and above

Evaluation of candidates for positions at GS−9 and above should be based on:

1. Knowledges and skills specific to the position vacancy, and
2. Evidence of the capacity to accept change and keep pace with the rapidly evolving computer technology.

Examples of quality ranking factors specific to a position, when supported by the position description, could be the degree of: a. skill in planning, developing, and conducting training, b. knowledge of a specific application, c. familiarity with a specific model of computer, d. knowledge of techniques for development of ADP standards, e. knowledge of data base design, f. skill in simulation of new applications, and/or g. familiarity with specific operating modes.

Considerations in evaluating the capacity to accept change and keep pace with the technology could include the extent to which the candidate's background shows: a. success in a diversity of work in the computer field, b. development of systems or programs for which no precedents exist, c. accomplishments which involved the use of advanced design or programing techniques, and/or d. evidence of continuing self development, such as pertinent course work or publication of papers in ADP society journals.

ACCOUNTING, BUDGETING, AND FISCAL MANAGEMENT POSITIONS

Accounting Clerical, Supervisory, and Administrative Positions GS–7/15

EXPERIENCE, TRAINING, AND RELATED REQUIREMENTS

This standard is considered appropriate for filling such positions as Cash Accounting Assistant; Voucher Examiner; Time, Leave, and Payroll Supervisor; Benefit-Payment Roll Supervisor; etc.

A. LENGTH AND KIND OF TRAINING AND EXPERIENCE REQUIRED

Except for the substitutions provided for below, applicants must have had as a minimum the length of experience specified in the following table.

Grade of position	Total (years)	Length of experience required	
		General (years)	Specialized (years)
GS–7	4	2	2
GS–8	4½	2	2½
GS–9	5	2	3
GS–10	5½	2	3½
GS–11 and above ...	6	2	4

General experience is work in (1) accounting, auditing, or bookkeeping of a commercial type in such fields as cost accounting, financial accounting, etc., or (2) maintaining or examining fiscal records for the issuance, collection, safekeeping, or disbursing of money and securities by municipal, State, or Federal government agencies, or commercial, industrial, or eleemosynary concerns and institutions, or (3) supervising work described in (1) and (2) above with responsibility for the technical adequacy thereof, including supervision of machine accounting groups.

Specialized experience is experience in the kind of work which is to be done in the position for which the examination is held and for which application is made. (Specialized experience in excess of the required length may be accepted as general experience.)

B. PROVISION FOR SUBSTITUTION OF EDUCATION FOR EXPERIENCE

For a maximum of 2 years of the required general experience and 1 year of the specialized experience, applicants may substitute the following:

1. Study successfully completed in a resident school above high-school level with a major in the field of accounting or business administration on the basis of 1 academic year of study for 9 months of experience; *or*

2. Teaching of any of the fields named in (1) above in a resident school above high-school level on the basis of 1 academic year of teaching for 9 months of experience; *or*

3. Any time-equivalent combination of (1) and (2) above; *or*

4. The possession of a certificate as a Certified Public Accountant in a State, Territory, or the District of Columbia, provided the certificate number, date, and place of issuance are clearly stated in the application.

5. In addition, applicants who offer a bachelor's degree within 24 semester hours, or its equivalent, in any of the fields named in (1) above as a substitution for 2 years of the required general experience and 1 year of the specialized experience may substitute a master's degree in any of the fields named for 1 ad-

56

ditional year of specialized experience. Under this provision, an applicant with a master's degree in the named fields of study may qualify at the GS–7 level.

C. OTHER REQUIREMENTS

Quality of experience. Applicants must have had progressively responsible experience of a scope and quality sufficient to demonstrate conclusively the ability to handle the duties of the position. The degree of fiscal responsibility involved must have been proportionately greater for each successively higher grade for which the applicant is being considered. The prescribed lengths and levels of experience must be met, but

meeting them does not of itself entitle one to an eligible rating. The measure of total performance must be so full as to give promise of at least satisfactory performance at the grade or grades for which he is being considered.

For grades GS–12 and above, at least 1 year of the required specialized experience must have been at a level of difficulty comparable at least to that of the next lower grade in the Federal service. For grades GS–11 and below, at least 6 months of the required specialized experience must have been at a level of difficulty comparable to that of the next lower grade in the Federal service, or 1 year must have been at a level comparable at least to that of the second lower grade.

Budget and Accounting Officer GS–11/15

DESCRIPTION OF WORK

Budget and accounting officers are typically responsible for the day-to-day supervision over the budget and the accounting operations and may also be responsible for auxiliary areas such as credit and finance, internal audit, contractor accounts, etc. As specialists, budget and accounting officers serve as technical experts for the organization's management staff on budget and on accounting matters, provide specialized accounting and budget advice, interpret the results and needs of the budget and of the accounting programs, and coordinate these two separate functions (within the subordinate staff supervised) to the extent required for the effective conduct of each function.

To perform this work, the budget and accounting officer should have a high degree of knowledge of budget and/or accounting functions and operations, plus ability to manage and direct the accounting, budgeting, and auxiliary staffs so as to provide the organization's management staff with the necessary specialized accounting and budget information and advice which that staff needs.

EXPERIENCE

All applicants must have had a total of 6 years of progressively responsible administrative, technical, or specialist experience which provided a thorough knowledge of methods of supervision, administration, and management; a demonstrated ability to deal with others. Of the 6 years, at least 3 years must have been *specialized* experience as defined below. The applicant's experience must include significant supervisory or administrative responsibilities, and also responsible technical or specialist experience in either the budget or accounting field, but *preferably in both*. If actual experience has been obtained in only one of these fields, the applicant must demonstrate possession of basic knowledge of the other area.

For some positions the services of a professionally-qualified accountant are desirable. For such positions only those applicants will be considered who also meet the qualification requirements for the Accounting Series (including, where required, passing a written test). (Some types of experience may satisfy the requirements of both the Accounting Series and this standard and may be credited accordingly.)

Eligibility in any grade level will be based upon a clear showing that the applicant has had experience of a scope and quality sufficient to give him the ability to handle technical and/or supervisory problems commensurate with the duties of the grade for which he is being considered.

SPECIALIZED EXPERIENCE

Specialized experience is progressively responsible experience in the fields of budget administration and/or accounting, or in any of the major kinds of work which are to be supervised and/or managed in the position for which the applicant is being considered. Experience in closely related fields is also acceptable, provided that the experience demonstrated competence in and knowledge of budget or accounting functions and also demonstrated:

1. Ability to plan, direct, and coordinate a budget and accounting program, and to provide service thereon;
2. Ability to select, develop, and supervise a subordinate staff;
3. Ability to establish and maintain effective working relationships with all levels of key management officials and subordinate staff.

The degree of technical ability involved must be proportionately greater for each successively higher grade for which the applicant is considered. Among the kinds of work which may be accepted as specialized experience are the following:

a. The development, direction, evaluation, or revision of budgetary control systems;
b. Budget preparation and presentation, budget analysis and/or program analysis;
c. Supervision or maintenance of commercial type accounts in such fields as cost accounting, financial accounting, etc.;
d. Supervision of the maintenance or examination of records for the issuance, collection, safekeeping, or disbursing of money and securities by municipal, State, or Federal Government agencies or private industry (including such records as cost, time, payroll, expenses, revenues, expenditures, appropriations, revolving funds, working capital, trust funds, or other fiscal records);
e. Planning, directing, or supervising a program for collecting, classifying, compiling or evaluating accounting data;
f. Planning, developing, or installing new accounting systems, or revising existing accounting systems;
g. Preparing financial or cost statements and reports used to evaluate performance or to determine status of activities or programs;
h. Auditing or examining accounting systems, records, or financial statements;
i. Examining or appraising organizational procedures, operations, or internal controls which involve financial systems or are accomplished primarily for budget or accounting purposes;
j. Preparing or reviewing reports of financial audits;
k. Experience as an office manager, owner, etc., which has involved direct supervision of accountants, auditors, or budget analysts provided that budget and accounting responsibilities comprised a major part of the position.

QUALITY OF EXPERIENCE

For grade GS–11, at least 6 months of the required specialized experience must have been at a level of difficulty comparable to that of the next lower grade in the Federal service, or 1 year must have been at a level comparable at least to that of the second lower grade. For grades GS–12 and above, at least 1 year of the required specialized experience must have been at a level of difficulty comparable at least to that of the next lower grade in the Federal service.

EDUCATIONAL AND OTHER SUBSTITUTIONS

1. Successfully completed study in a residence school above high school level in any field may be substituted for a maximum of 3 years of general experience at the rate of 1 academic year of study for 9 months of experience.
2. Full-time graduate education may be sub-

stituted for experience on the following basis. The education must have equipped the candidate with the knowledge and ability to perform fully the work of the position for which he is being considered.

a. *For 1 year of specialized experience.*—One full academic year of graduate education in business administration, public administration, economics, industrial engineering or industrial management, government, political science, or in other directly related fields.

b. *For 2 years of specialized experience.*—

Completion of all requirements for a master's or an equivalent degree, or 2 full academic years of graduate education, which is in the fields described in paragraph "a" above.

3. The possession of a certificate as a Certified Public Accountant obtained through written examination in a State, Territory, or the District of Columbia, provided the certificate number, date, and place of issuance are clearly stated in the application, may be substituted for 3 years of general experience.

Accounting Series, GS–5/15
Auditing Series, GS–5/11–5/15

DESCRIPTION OF WORK

Accountants and auditors perform professional work in any of several capacities depending upon the accounting system involved, the organizations and operating programs served, the financial data sought, and the needs of management. Accountants classify and evaluate financial data; record transactions in financial records; develop and install new accounting systems, revise existing accounting systems; and prepare and analyze financial statements, records and reports. Auditors examine accounts for the purpose of certifying or attesting that as of a certain date or for a stated period various financial statements fairly present the financial position of the activity audited in terms of assets, liabilities, net worth, and income and expenses. Auditors evaluate such matters as (a) the degree of compliance with laws, regulations and principles of sound financial management; (b) the effectiveness, economy, and efficiency of resource utilization and management systems; and (c) the extent to which desired results or benefits are being achieved. Audit emphasis includes evaluating internal controls to determine the reliability of reported results; and assuring that generally accepted accounting principles have been consistently applied by the activity audited.

BASIC REQUIREMENTS FOR ALL GRADES

Candidates for all grades must meet the requirements of paragraph A, B, or C below:

A. A full 4-year course of study in an accredited college or university which meets all of that institution's requirements for a bachelor's degree with an accounting major.

B. A full 4-year course of study in an accredited college or university that meets all requirements for a bachelor's degree and that included or was supplemented by at least 24 semester hours in accounting.[1]

C. At least 4 years of experience in accounting, or an equivalent combination of accounting experience, college-level education, and training that provided professional accounting knowledge equivalent in type, scope, and thoroughness to that acquired through successful completion of a 4-year college curriculum in accounting as in A above. → The background of candidates who meet the requirements of this paragraph must also include one of the following: ←

---

[1]Generally, for editorial convenience, the term "accounting" is used in lieu of "accounting and/or auditing." Similarly "accountant" should be interpreted, generally, as "accountants and/or auditors."

1. Twenty-four semester hours in accounting or auditing courses of appropriate type and quality. Note: Resident or home-study academic courses conducted by a Federal agency or a nonaccredited institution that are determined to be fully equivalent to accounting and auditing courses in an accredited college may be accepted.

2. A certificate as Certified Public Accountant or a Certified Internal Auditor, obtained through written examination.

3. Recognized, well-established professional stature in accounting or auditing based on a combination of (a) successful experience in a variety of highly responsible accounting functions in positions equivalent to GS–12 or higher, and (b) significant documented contributions to the accounting or auditing profession through publications, leadership in professional organizations, development of new methods and techniques, or comparable achievements.

4. Completion of the requirements for a bachelor's or higher degree with major study in accounting, auditing or a related field which includes substantial course work in accounting or auditing, e.g., 15 semester hours, but which does not fully satisfy the 24 semester hour requirement of paragraph B provided that (a) the candidate has successfully demonstrated the ability to perform work of the GS–12 or higher grade level in accounting, auditing or a related field, e.g., valuation engineering or financial institution examining; (b) a panel of at least two higher level professional accountants or auditors have determined that the candidate has demonstrated a good knowledge of accounting and of related and underlying fields that equals in breadth, depth, currency, and level of advancement that normally obtained with successful completion of the 4-year course of study in paragraph A; and (c) except for literal nonconformance to the requirement of 24 semester hours in accounting, the candidate's education,

training, and experience fully meet the specified requirements.

GS–5.—The basic requirements are fully qualifying for grade GS–5.

ADDITIONAL EXPERIENCE AND TRAINING REQUIREMENTS

Candidates for grades GS–7 and above must have had either professional experience or graduate education, or an equivalent combination of both, in addition to meeting the basic requirements. This professional experience or graduate education must have been in or directly related to accounting or auditing or in a field closely related to the position to be filled.

1. EXPERIENCE

In addition to the basic requirements, the following amounts of professional experience are required for grades GS–7 and above:

Grade:	Years
GS–7	1
GS–9	2
GS–11 and above	3

For grades GS–11 and below at least 6 months of the required experience must have been at a level of difficulty comparable to that of the next lower grade or 1 year comparable to the second lower grade in the Federal service. For grades GS–12 and above at least 1 year of the required experience must have been at a level of difficulty comparable to that of the next lower grade in the Federal service.

2. EDUCATION

In addition to the basic requirements, the following amounts and levels of education are qualifying for grades GS–7 and above. This education must have been either in accounting and auditing or in directly related fields.

GS–7 .... One full academic year of graduate education.

GS–9 .... Completion of all requirements for a master's or equivalent degree; or two full academic years of graduate education.

Equivalent combinations of professional experience and graduate education of the type described above are acceptable at each grade.

3. ALTERNATE REQUIREMENTS

a. Superior academic achievement at the baccalaureate level or 1 year of student trainee experience in accounting or auditing is qualifying at grade GS–7. A combination of superior academic achievement at the baccalaureate level and 1 year of appropriate professional experience is qualifying at grade GS–9.

b. Technician experience: For positions at GS–7 only, candidates who have completed the required 24 semester hours in accounting and who have experience—in addition to that needed to satisfy the basic requirement for all positions—as an accounting technician equivalent to grade GS–5 or higher may have that experience credited for GS–7 on a month-for-month basis up to a maximum of 12 months.

SELECTIVE AND QUALITY RANKING FACTORS

In general, candidates who meet the "Basic Requirements For All Grades" are qualified for positions at the entrance and lower levels in any specialized branch of accounting such as cost, systems, staff, and auditing. Specific knowledges, skills, and/or abilities will be used as quality ranking factors under justification that shows: (a) how the quality ranking factor is directly related to the duties and responsibilities of the position; and (b) why possession of the desired knowledge, skill and/or ability would predict superior performance.

For other specialized positions, only candidates who possess specific job-related knowledges, skills, and/or abilities may be qualified. Justification for selective placement factors must show: (a) how the selective factor is directly related to the duties and responsibilities of the position; and (b) why possession of the knowledges, skills, and/or abilities identified as selective factors are necessary for successful performance in the position.

The Office of Personnel Management Position-Classification Standard for the Accounting Series and the Auditing Series includes a great deal of valuable information on the various specialized branches of accounting.

BASIS OF RATING

No written test is required. Candidates will be rated on a scale of 100 on the extent and quality of their experience and training. Ratings will be based upon candidates' statements in their applications and upon any additional information that may be secured by the Office of Personnel Management.

Professional knowledge of accounting is defined as (a) a thorough knowledge of the concepts, theories, principles and practices of general and cost accounting; public industrial and/or governmental accounting; auditing, taxation, budgeting and analysis of financial statements; and trends and current developments in the accounting profession in government, industry and public accounting firms; (b) an understanding of the legal principles that govern financial transactions and relationships in government or industry; and (c) a basic foundation in related fields such as banking, mathematical analysis, statistics, automatic data processing systems and techniques, business organization, and the principles and processes of management.

Professional ability to apply accounting knowledge is defined as the ability to (a) apply fundamental and diversified professional accounting concepts, theories, and practices to achieve financial management objectives with versatility, judgment, and perception; (b) adapt and apply methods and techniques of related disciplines such as economics and statistical analysis; and (c) organize, analyze, interpret, and evaluate financial data in the solution of management and accounting problems.

Positive and continuing development of professional knowledge and ability is defined as an action program involving activities such as the following as appropriate to the circumstances:

(a) Developing new approaches, methods or techniques for the solution of problems in accounting or auditing;

(b) Formal or informal training and guidance on the job by specialists or more mature professionals;

(c) College-level academic study;

(d) Participations in seminars, conferences, and technical committees of professional societies and other organizations;

(e) Review and study of the professional literature of accounting and related fields;

(f) Publication of professional papers.

Professional work in accounting, like that of other professions, is marked by continuing personal effort to keep abreast of the advancing and changing discipline. Continuing education in accounting and related fields is an important element of full professional competence as an accountant which should be considered in evaluating the qualifications of candidates for professional accountant positions. Accounting technicians who desire to make the upward mobility transition to professional accountant must not only satisfy the essential requirement of 24 semester hours in accounting, but should plan on continued academic course work.

EDUCATION IN ACCOUNTING

UNDERGRADUATE EDUCATION

Most accounting majors consist of 24 semester hours of accounting courses that have easily recognizable titles such as elementary accounting, intermediate accounting, advanced accounting, auditing, Federal tax accounting, cost accounting, CPA problems, accounting systems, internal auditing, government accounting, accounting theory, accounting seminar, and the like. However, not all professional accounting courses have the words accounting or auditing in their titles. Courses entitled, for example, analysis of financial statements, business budgeting, cost analysis and control, investment analysis, and statement and report presentation and analysis are considered professional accounting courses when they: (a) have as a prerequisite one or more clearly identifiable professional accounting courses such as principles of accounting; and (b) are primarily concerned with the development, analysis, and presentation of financial data and/or the interpretation and evaluation of financial information and its application to management problems.

GRADUATE EDUCATION

Graduate education may have been either in accounting or in directly related fields such as business administration, finance, comptrollership, and management. Normally such study includes one or more courses in accounting.

ACCEPTANCE OF TECHNICIAN EXPERIENCE

At grade GS–7, for competitive appointment and for inservice placement accounting technician experience at the grade GS–5 level and above may be accepted toward meeting the professional experience requirements as described on page 60, provided the candidate meets the basic requirements for all grades on page 59.

Accounting Technician GS–4/9

DESCRIPTION OF DUTIES

Accounting technicians perform nonprofessional work necessary to insure the effective operation of established accounting systems. They apply a basic understanding of accounting concepts and procedures in performing such functions as classifying accounting transactions; maintaining, balancing and reconciling accounting records; examining accounting records to verify accuracy; determining appropriate adjustments and special entries; preparing and verifying accounting statements and reports; and performing prescribed analyses of accounting data and reports. These functions may involve a narrow range of accounts or may encompass the entire accounting system of the activity, depending on the nature and level of assignments.

EXPERIENCE REQUIREMENTS

Except for the substitutions provided for below, candidates must have had the kind and amount of experience shown in the table and described in the statements immediately following.

Grade	General experience (years)	Specialized experience (years)	Total experience (years)
GS–4	2	0	2
GS–5	2	1	3
GS–6	2	2	4
GS–7	2	3	5
GS–8 and above	2	4	6

1. *General experience* is clerical work which has demonstrated arithmetic aptitude and ability, accuracy and attention to detail, and the ability to apply established procedures for recording and compiling data. Such work may have involved—

(a) maintaining various types of records requiring accuracy in selecting, posting, and consolidating pertinent data;

(b) coding, compiling, or verifying statistical data;

(c) making arithmetic computations, applying formulas or conversion tables, etc.;

(d) screening various types of documents to verify the accuracy of codes, amounts, or similar data in numeric form against related documents or guides;

(e) operating various calculating or posting machines provided this work included responsibility for verifying accuracy; or

(f) similar work which demonstrated the relevant abilities.

2. *Specialized experience* is work which required the candidate to acquire and apply a knowledge of established accounting procedures and techniques in the performance of such functions as—

(a) analyzing and classifying or recording transactions;

(b) balancing, reconciling, adjusting, or examining accounts;

(c) developing or verifying accounting data for reports, statements, and schedules; or

(d) performing prescribed analyses of accounting data.

Directly related specialized experience is defined as experience gained in the same specialized area of accounting technician work as the position for which application is made.

3. *Quality of experience.*—Candidates for any grade must have at least 1 year of experience at a level of difficulty comparable to the next lower grade or 2 years of experience at the level of difficulty comparable to the second lower grade in the Federal service.

SUBSTITUTIONS ALLOWED

1. Study successfully completed in a resident college, university, or junior college may be substituted for *general* experience on the basis of *one-half academic year* of study for *6 months* of experience provided it included at least 3 semester hours per year in the fields of bookkeeping or accounting.

2. Study successfully completed in a resident business or commercial school or other comparable institution above the high school level may be substituted for *general* experience on the basis of *one-half academic year* of study for *6 months* of experience provided such study included accounting or bookkeeping as well as other subjects such as business English, office machines, filing and indexing, office practices or business mathematics. No credit will be allowed for training which has been obtained only or primarily in the basic skills of shorthand or typing or refresher courses.

3. Study of the nature described in 1 and 2 above may be substituted for the *first year* of specialized experience on the basis of *1 academic year* of study for *6 months* of specialized experience.

Under these provisions a 2-year course of study of the above nature meets the experience requirements for grade GS–4 and a full 4-year course of study meets the experience requirements for grade GS–5.

WRITTEN TEST

A written test of abilities necessary to learn and perform the duties of these positions is required for positions at grade GS–4.

BASIS OF RATING

Competitors for all positions will be rated on a scale of 100. Rankings are made:

1. For competitive appointments at GS–4: on the basis of the written test.
2. For competitive appointments above GS–4 and for in-service placement actions at all grades: on the basis of the extent and quality of experience and training relevant to the duties of the position.

IN-SERVICE PLACEMENT PROVISIONS

1. SUBSTITUTION FOR SPECIALIZED EXPERIENCE

Responsible work in closely related occupations which has demonstrated potential for advancement and aptitude for accounting technician work may be substituted for a *maximum of 1 year* of specialized experience. Experience in related work may be credited provided it involved—

(a) demonstrated analytical ability in interpreting and applying a body of regulations and procedures under varying conditions;
(b) substantial responsibilities for verifying the accuracy and completeness of data in source and supporting documents or reports and for tracing and correcting discrepancies; *and*
(c) reconciling records maintained with related accounting data *or* performing prescribed analyses of the records maintained.

Work in related areas which does not fully meet the above conditions is creditable as *general* experience only.

2. WAIVER OF DIRECTLY RELATED EXPERIENCE REQUIREMENT

The requirement for directly related experience may be waived under the following conditions:

(a) For lateral reassignments when:
  (1) The candidate has had experience that provided a general familiarity with the work of the position for which he is being considered; *and*
  (2) A review of the candidate's experience and performance discloses possession of the necessary skills and abilities, and evidences potential for successful performance of the work.
(b) For promotion actions, where it is clearly shown that:
  (1) Despite the lack of directly related experience, the candidate's background gives positive evidence that he possessed to a superior degree the essential skills and abilities needed for the position; *and*
  (2) The candidate has had experience that has provided a general familiarity with the work of the position for which he is being considered; *and*
  (3) The overall evaluation of the candidate's background provides strong evidence that he can successfully perform the higher grade work without prolonged training.

3. SUGGESTIONS FOR EVALUATING EMPLOYEES FOR IN-SERVICE PLACEMENT

In evaluating candidates for in-service placement to accounting technician jobs, it is suggested that inquiries be made of former supervisors of the candidate to elicit detailed information concerning demonstrated abilities, type of work experience and past responsibilities.

Inquiries should develop information on:

(a) The kind and extent of knowledges of double entry accounting processes or of closely related recordkeeping techniques. (NOTE: The accounting and finance unit is not the only place where such pertinent experience can be gained);
(b) The degree of responsibility for interpreting guidelines and procedures, and the relative degree of supervision; and
(c) Such personal characteristics and interests as—
  • interest and aptitude in working with figures;
  • ability to maintain a high level of accuracy in work requiring close attention to detail;

- interest in the purpose and effect of prescribed procedures; or
- initiative in questioning unusual actions or in obtaining information to support or verify questionable actions.

In ranking individuals, other things being equal, the greatest credit should be given to those with the greatest amount of directly related experience, and to those who have had the greatest responsibility and freedom from supervision. Extra credit may be given for a broader range of experience (in addition to any required directly related experience) when the broader experience will be of benefit in the position and if it gives evidence of greater potential for development. Extra credit may also be given for completion of correspondence courses or part-time study, not credited under educational substitution provisions, in accounting or bookkeeping.

Budget Analyst, GS–5/15
Budget Officer, GS–11/15
Budget Examiner, GS–5/15 (OMB only)

DESCRIPTION OF WORK

Positions in this series perform, advise on, or supervise work in the phases or systems of budget administration currently in use in the Federal service. Such work primarily requires knowledge and skill in the application of related laws, regulations, policies, precedents, methods and techniques of budgeting.

Budget Analysts perform a segment, but less than the full range of the budget administration work done in the employing component or installation. The work requires a knowledge of the particular phase(s) of budgeting, analytical methods, processes, and procedures used in budgeting for assigned organizations, programs or activities. Budget analysts analyze the relative costs and benefits of alternate courses of budget and program action, check the propriety of obligations and expenditures, establish standard rates and charges to customers of industrially-funded activities, or develop budgetary policy and regulatory guidance.

Budget Officers are responsible for the full complement of budgetary operations which support the programs and personnel of the employing organizational component and level. At a minimum a budget officer's responsibilities include formulation and execution of the annual operating budget for the employing component. However, most budget officers also provide expert staff advice and assistance to managers by developing budget plans and estimates, interpreting budget laws, policies, and regulations, analyzing the cost effectiveness of program operations, and recommending alternate sources of program funding.

Budget Examiners are budgetary experts in the Office of Management and Budget (OMB) actively engaged in the review, analysis, and control of the budgetary operations of Federal agencies and departments. Budget examiners approve, disapprove, or adjust agency requests for funds in proposed and approved annual budgets and provide budgetary guidance to Federal agencies. These positions are established only in OMB.

For a more complete description of the work performed by budget analysts, budget officers, and budget examiners, refer to the position classification standard for the Budget Analysis Series.

EXPERIENCE REQUIREMENTS

Applicants must show that they have met the general and specialized experience requirements summarized in the following chart:

Grade	Specialized (years)	General (years)	Total (years)
GS–5	0	3	3
GS–7	1	3	4
GS–9	2	3	5
GS–11 and above	3	3	6

General experience is experience from which the applicant gained a general knowledge of financial and management principles and practices applicable to organizations. Experience in specialized fields which are closely related to budget analysis or excess specialized experience is acceptable as general experience.

Specialized experience is experience which provided specific knowledge and skill in the application of budgetary principles, practices, methods and procedures directly related to the work of the position to be filled. Such experience must have included substantially full-time work or its part-time equivalent in one or more of the following budgetary functions.

—budget preparation, justification, and presentation;

—budget execution (i.e., monitoring and control of obligations and expenditures);

—development of budgetary policies, procedures, and guides;

—development, evaluation, or revision of budgetary control systems; or

—planning and budgeting for the operations of a working capital fund.

QUALITY OF EXPERIENCE

Applicants must demonstrate progressively responsible experience of a scope, quality, and degree such as to have equipped them with the capability to perform duties at the grade level of the position for which application is made. Typically, this is demonstrated by accomplishment of assignments of the difficulty and responsibility described in the position classification standard used to evaluate positions at the next lower grade in the normal line of promotion to the position being filled.

Specialized experience which involved less than the majority of the candidate's time is to be prorated and credited on a month-for-month basis. In crediting experience gained in the Federal service, the grade of specialized experience may or may not be equivalent to the grade level of the position in which it was gained. Whenever possible, determination of the grade level of specialized experience should be based upon the classification evaluation of the budget work performed.

SUBSTITUTION OF EDUCATION

Education may be substituted for the required experience as follows:

1. Undergraduate Education
   a. Successful completion of a four year course of study in an accredited college or university leading to a bachelor's degree or the equivalent is acceptable as meeting all requirements for the GS–5 level.
   b. Part-time undergraduate education of the type described above may be substituted at the rate of 1 year of education for 9 months of general experience.
2. Graduate Education
   a. Successful completion of one full academic year of relevant graduate education in business administration, economics, accounting, governmental budgeting, public administration, industrial engineering, political science, or an equally relevant field with comparable course work meets all requirements for grade GS–7.
   b. Successful completion of all requirements for a master's or equivalent degree, or 2 full years of graduate education which is in one of the fields described in paragraph (a) above meets all requirements for grade GS–9.
   c. For some positions, notably those which also require intensive knowledge of the Congressional budget process, economics, or statistics, completion of all requirements for a doctoral degree in a field directly related to the work of the position to be filled is accepted as qualifying for grade GS–11.
   d. Part-time graduate education of the type described above may be substituted at the rate of 30 semester hours for 1 year of specialized experience, or 15 semester hours for ½ year of specialized experience.
3. Education may not be substituted for the required experience above the GS–11 level.

SPECIAL PROVISIONS FOR INSERVICE PLACEMENT

Positions covered by this standard may be filled at the GS–5 and GS–7 levels without regard to experience or educational requirements of Part I of this standard by inservice lateral reassignment of employees from positions in the Budget Clerical and Assistance Series, the Accounting Technician Series, the General Accounting Clerical and Administrative Series, or other series which provided comparable financial skills. Unless otherwise qualified under experience and educational requirements described in other parts of this standard, employees reassigned under this provision must serve at least 1 year in the position at the grade level at which reassigned before promotion within this series.

This provision is not to be used to promote an employee from a clerical, assistant, or technician occupation directly into a position in this series.

BASIS OF RATING

Candidates for competitive appointment to all positions will be rated on the basis of their experience and/or education as it relates to the work or the position to be filled.

GUIDE FOR EVALUATING CANDIDATES

Positions at all grade levels in this series require:
1. Ability to effectively express ideas and recommendations orally and in writing;
2. Ability to reason in quantitative terms (e.g., in numerical concepts);
3. Analytical ability which includes the ability to conceptualize, generalize, and draw meaningful inferences and conclusions from financial and narrative data;
4. Ability to work effectively under pressure of tight time frames and rigid deadlines;
5. In addition, some positions in this series require skill in presenting and gaining the acceptance of budgetary requests, recommendations, and decisions during formal negotiations with fund granting and reviewing authorities.

For positions at the entry level (GS–5 and GS–7) credit should be given for experience and education which has demonstrated the candidate's ability to communicate effectively, both orally and in writing.

Analytical ability of the type required in this series is often demonstrated through completion of college-level courses in logic, philosophy, economics, mathematics (e.g., probability and statistics), computer science, chemistry and physics. In ranking candidates, courses which included analytical methods and techniques commonly used in budget analysis may also be considered. While courses in business mathematics, financial management, statistics, economics, and accounting are highly desirable, they have not been specified as minimum educational requirements because to do so could possibly exclude some candidates who would otherwise be well-qualified to do the work.

SELECTIVE PLACEMENT FACTORS

In filling positions at grades above the entry levels, selective factors may be appropriate for screening candidates. If selective factors are used, the requirements must be job related, and need for them must be reflected in the official position description or other official communication. These will vary considerably, depending upon the nature of the position to be filled.

QUALITY RANKING FACTORS

Candidates who meet or exceed the basic requirements, including any selective factors, may be ranked according to their degree of proficiency on quality ranking factors which have been identified for use. Examples of quality ranking factors could include:
1. Knowledge of the programs and work processes of organizations for which budgetary services are provided.
2. Skill in developing and presenting briefings on budgetary matters.

Volunteer service (e.g., in charitable, religious, or service organizations) is to be counted toward meeting experience requirements of this standard.

Savings and Loan Examiner GS–5/15
Farm Credit Examiner GS–5/15
Investment Company Examiner GS–5/15
Savings and Loan Examining Officer GS–12/15
Farm Credit Examining Officer GS–12/15
Investment Company Examining Officer GS–12/15

DESCRIPTION OF WORK

Examiners in positions of these kinds make examinations and audits of savings and loan associations, farm credit associations, cooperative banks, investment institutions, national banks, or other financial institutions to determine financial condition, soundness of operations, compliance with regulatory laws and provisions, integrity of accounts, and other pertinent matters.

Examining Officers in positions of these kinds plan, manage, and direct the work of examiners of financial institutions.

EXPERIENCE REQUIREMENTS

Except for the substitutions provided for below, applicants must have had experience of the kinds and amounts specified below:

Grade	Total (years)	General (years)	Specialized (years)
GS–5	3	3	. . . .
GS–7	4	3	1
GS–9	5	3	2
GS–11 and above	6	3	3

GENERAL EXPERIENCE

(1) Experience in positions requiring a thorough knowledge and the application of commercial accounting or auditing principles and practices (but less than full professional accounting knowledges), i.e., experience which has provided an understanding of debits and credits, the principles of journalizing, balance sheets, and operating statements; or

(2) Experience with a savings and loan association, savings or commercial bank, or other financial institution, requiring knowledge of accounting or auditing principles as applied to such institutions; or

(3) Any time-equivalent combination of (1) and (2) above.

SPECIALIZED EXPERIENCE—TYPE A (USUAL REQUIREMENT)

(4) Progressively responsible experience requiring a thorough knowledge and the application of accounting or auditing principles and practices (but less than full professional accounting knowledge) with a financial institution engaged in mortgage lending operations, with the mortgage loan department of an insurance company, or with a Federal agency making, insuring, guaranteeing, or supervising mortgage lending; *or*

(5) Progressively responsible experience in the examining or auditing of such financial institutions as savings and loan associations, savings or commercial banking institutions or trust companies, Federal Reserve Banks, farm credit associations, or Federal or State credit unions; *or*

(6) For up to a *maximum of 2 years* of experience, professional accounting or auditing work which provided a broad knowledge of the application of accounting or auditing principles and practices; *or*

(7) Any time-equivalent combination of (4), (5), and (6) above.

SPECIALIZED EXPERIENCE—TYPE B (OPTIONAL REQUIREMENT)

(8) Experience which has provided a thorough knowledge of Federal and State laws ap-

plicable to the type of financial institution involved and of the operations and practices of such institutions.

Specialized experience, Type B may be required for some positions but when required, this will not increase the total length of required experience. The specialized experience, Type B may be required, therefore, in lieu of part of the above stated requirement for either general experience or specialized experience, or both. For grade GS–7, specialized experience, Type B may be the sole specialized experience which is required.

Specialized experience, Type A in excess of that required may be substituted for general experience.

SUBSTITUTION OF EDUCATION FOR EXPERIENCE

1. Study successfully completed in a resident institution above the high school level may be substituted for general experience at the rate of 1 academic year of study for 9 months of experience provided that such study included an average of 6 semester hours (or the equivalent) in either one or two of the following, or directly related fields: accounting, banking, business administration, commercial or banking law, economics, or finance. For some positions 12 semester hours of this study must have been in accounting. A total of 4 academic years of study as described in this paragraph is qualifying for grade GS–5.

2. Full-time graduate education may be substituted for experience on the following basis.

a. *For 1 year of specialized experience.*—One full academic year of graduate education in one of the following: accounting, banking, business administration, economics, finance, or other directly related fields. (This amount and kind of education meets all the requirements for grade GS–7.)

b. *For 2 years of specialized experience.*— Completion of all requirements for a master's or an equivalent degree, or 2 full academic years of graduate education, which is in the fields described in paragraph "a" above. (This amount and kind of education meets all the requirements for grade GS–9.)

3. Applicants may substitute the possession of a certificate as a Certified Public Accountant in a State, Territory, or the District of Columbia for all of the 3 years of general experience, provided the certificate number and date of issuance are clearly shown.

QUALITY OF EXPERIENCE

The prescribed lengths and levels of experience must be met, but meeting them does not of itself entitle one to an eligible rating unless the quality of the applicant's total background gives promise of satisfactory performance at the grade level for which the applicant is being considered.

For grades GS–11 and below, at least 6 months of the required specialized experience must have been at a level of difficulty comparable to that of the next lower grade in the Federal service, or 1 year must have been at a level of difficulty comparable at least to that of the second lower grade. For grades GS–12 and above, at least 1 year of the required specialized experience must have been at a level of difficulty comparable to that of the next lower grade in the Federal service.

ADDITIONAL REQUIREMENTS

All applicants must demonstrate ability to meet and deal successfully and effectively with the public.

WRITTEN TEST

Applicants for grade GS–5 and GS–7 positions must pass an appropriate written test.

Applicants for all positions at grades GS–9 and above will not be required to take a written test.

BASIS OF RATING

Applicants for GS–5 and GS–7 positions will be rated on the basis of their test scores and an evaluation of their education and experience.

Applicants for all positions at GS–9 and above will be rated on the basis of the quality, diversity, and extent of their experience and its relevance to the duties of the position to be filled. Such ratings will be based on the competitors' statements in their applications and on any additional evidence which is obtained.

LAW ENFORCEMENT POSITIONS

Investigator
Supervisory Investigator
Criminal Investigator
Supervisory Criminal Investigator
GS–5/15

COVERAGE

These standards are intended to be used primarily in filling investigator and criminal investigator positions which involve the performance of factfinding and reporting duties and related responsibilities described below, and other positions in these series for which actual investigative experience is essential. All parts of these standards apply to positions in both the General Investigating Series and the Criminal Investigating Series; where variations exist involving differences in investigating duties, specialized experience, physical standards, and minimum age requirements, these are so indicated.

DESCRIPTION OF WORK

INVESTIGATORS

Investigators plan and conduct investigations relating to the administration of, or compliance with, Federal laws and regulations. The duties performed typically include: Collecting facts and obtaining information by observing conditions, examining records, and interviewing individuals; writing and securing affidavits; administering oaths; preparing investigative reports to be used as a basis for court or administrative action; testifying before administrative bodies, courts, or grand juries, or serving as a witness for the Government. The work occasionally may involve criminal investigations.

Performance of these duties may require work at irregular hours and considerable travel. In-

vestigators may also be required to operate motor vehicles.

CRIMINAL INVESTIGATORS

Criminal investigators plan and conduct investigations relating to alleged or suspected violations of Federal laws. The duties typically performed include: obtaining physical and documentary evidence; interviewing witnesses; applying for and serving warrants for arrests, searches, and seizures; seizing contraband, equipment and vehicles; examining files and records; maintaining surveillance; performing undercover assignments; preparing investigative reports; testifying in hearings and trials; and assisting U.S. Attorneys in the prosecution of court cases. Most criminal investigators are required to carry firearms and to be proficient in their use. The work may occasionally involve noncriminal investigations.

Performance of these duties frequently requires irregular unscheduled hours, personal risks, exposure to all kinds of weather, considerable travel, and arduous exertion, under adverse environmental conditions. Criminal investigators may also be required to operate motor vehicles.

TYPES OF POSITIONS

The kind of investigative work performed varies in respect to the investigative jurisdiction and functions of the employing agencies. The grade levels of the positions vary with the scope, com-

71

plexity, and importance of investigations and the degree of individual responsibility required. At the higher grade levels, investigators may also serve as team leaders, group supervisors, case reviewers, unit coordinators, or in similar capacities, with responsibility for supervising the work of other investigators; or they may be responsible for the management or direction of an investigative program or program segment.

The duties of some positions require experience or equivalent educational backgrounds (*a*) which have been obtained in or are closely related to particular industries, business operations, commercial enterprises, professions, or other occupational areas; or (*b*) which have been obtained in both the investigative and the criminal investigative areas.

EXPERIENCE REQUIREMENTS

Except for the substitutions provided for below, applicants must have had experience of the length shown in the table and of the nature described in the paragraphs following:

Grade	General experience (years)	Specialized experience (years)	Total experience (years)
GS–5	3	0	3
GS–7	3	1	4
GS–9	3	2	5
GS–11 and above ...	3	3	6

GENERAL EXPERIENCE

This must have been progressively responsible experience which has required (1) ability to work or deal effectively with individuals or groups of persons, (2) skill in collecting and assembling pertinent facts, (3) ability to prepare clear and concise reports, and (4) ability and willingness to accept responsibility. Acceptable general experience may have been gained in types of work such as the following:

(1) Adjustment or investigation of claims arising under law, contract, or governmental order;

(2) Analysis of reports or data or the preparation of surveys, studies, or reports, requiring the development, organization, evaluation and interpretation of substan-

tive program, technical, or similar information;

(3) Examining, administrative, or professional experience with Government regulatory bodies requiring review of regulatory material or reports on compliance with regulations;

(4) Experience requiring ability to determine applicability of laws, rules, and regulations, and to explain legal requirements;

(5) Responsible auditing and accounting work which included analyzing books and records, and preparation of statements and reports in accordance with recognized accounting standards, procedures, and principles;

(6) Adjudication or examination of claims which required the collection and analysis of pertinent data and the preparation of written reports and recommendations on such claims;

(7) Performance of preliminary record inspection, verification and procurement of documents required to establish prima facie cases from courts and law enforcement agencies and securing of related information from records of such courts and agencies;

(8) Experience as a teacher of accounting or law in a resident college or university;

(9) Experience described below under "Specialized Experience" for either Investigator or Criminal Investigator;

(10) Any time-equivalent combination of any of the above or comparable types of experience.

SPECIALIZED EXPERIENCE

This must have been progressively responsible investigative experience which demonstrated (1) initiative, ingenuity, resourcefulness, and judgment required to collect, assemble, and develop facts and other pertinent data; (2) ability to think logically and objectively, to analyze and evaluate facts, evidence, and related information, and arrive at sound conclusions; (3) skill in written and oral reports and presentation of investigative findings in a clear and concise manner; and (4) tact, discretion, and capacity for obtaining the cooperation and confidence of others.

For Investigator positions, this may be either investigative or criminal investigative experience, or comparable experience. For Criminal Investigator positions, this must have been criminal investigative experience, or comparable experience.

INVESTIGATOR POSITIONS

Acceptable investigative experience may have been obtained in types of work such as the following:

(1) Investigations of difficult casualty or insurance claims;
(2) Investigations conducted for a private detective agency which involved responsible factfinding and reporting on substantial issues;
(3) Newspaper reporting where the major responsibility involved personal investigations of facts pertaining to violations of law;
(4) Investigations in connection with the prosecution or defense of civil or criminal cases;
(5) Investigations for a Federal, State, county, or municipal agency;
(6) Investigations of important cases for practicing attorneys; or practice of law involving a substantial amount of investigative work or analysis of issues of fact and law;
(7) Legal experience involving such activities as personal participation in court cases and interviewing of suspects or witnesses;
(8) Investigations concerning compliance with, or violations of, governmental law, rules, and regulations;
(9) Investigations of individuals for character, conduct, suitability, and fitness for employment;
(10) Any of the types of specialized experience described for Criminal Investigators, below;
(11) Any time-equivalent combination of the above types or similar types of experience.

CRIMINAL INVESTIGATOR POSITIONS

Acceptable criminal investigative experience may have been gained in types of work such as the following:

(1) Investigative experience as a member of a military intelligence or criminal investigative component in any of the branches of the Armed Forces or in any of the various intelligence or investigative branches of the public service, in which the principal duties consisted of the supervision of or the independent conduct of investigations of security, intelligence, or criminal cases, the preparation of comprehensive documented reports, and responsibility for testifying in court;
(2) Investigation of complex casualty or insurance claims which included a substantial number of cases involving suspected crimes or alleged fraud;
(3) Investigation of criminal cases for practicing attorneys requiring the use of recognized investigative methods and techniques;
(4) Experience in the general practice of criminal law which required appearing in court and interviewing suspects and witnesses, or which required a substantial amount of complex criminal investigative work;
(5) Experience as a uniformed law officer where the principal duties (at least 50% of the time) were criminal investigations requiring the use of a variety of investigative methods and techniques such as surveillance, assuming an undercover role, etc. (Investigative experience of this nature which has been acquired on less than a full-time basis will be pro-rated for credit.);
(6) Any time-equivalent combination of the above types or similar types of experience.

NONQUALIFYING EXPERIENCE

There are some types of experience which are related to investigative work but which are not acceptable as either general or specialized experience for either the Investigator positions or the Criminal Investigator positions. Applicants who offer only these kinds of experience will be disqualified. Experience is not acceptable if (*a*) it has not afforded training in, or required the application of the knowledges, abilities and skills described above, or (*b*) it has been acquired in essentially clerical tasks or assignments. Examples of the kinds of experience which are not qualifying are:

(1) Experience in performing the normal duties of policeman, guard, watchman, or private detective assigned principally to the protection of life or property, or similar experience in other kinds of positions;

(2) Experience as a probation or parole officer which did not require pre-sentence investigations, investigations of parolees, objective development of facts, preparation of reports, or appearance in court to defend investigative findings;

(3) The investigation of minor insurance damage claims or of the financial standing of individuals or firms for credit associations or for collection agencies;

(4) Clerical work performed incidental to the adjudication of claims;

(5) Experience generally acquired in such positions as payroll clerk or reviewer, or voucher clerk or reviewer; cash accounting clerk; cashier; teller; time and leave clerk; disbursing clerk; fiscal clerk; administrative clerk; and similar positions;

(6) Experience as an inspector whose principal duties were to examine materials, plant facilities, or equipment to determine whether they conformed to prescribed specifications or standards.

QUALITY OF EXPERIENCE

Length of experience is of less importance than demonstrated success in positions of a responsible nature, and of less importance than the breadth and scope of the pertinent knowledges, skills, and abilities possessed by the applicant and applied by him in the performance of the duties of such positions. Although no additional amount of experience beyond that required for grade GS–11 is required for grades GS–12 through GS–15, applicants for these higher grade

levels must have had a progressively higher quality of experience.

For all grades through GS–11, at least 6 months of the required specialized experience must have been of a level of difficulty and responsibility comparable to that of the next lower grade, or at least 1 year of the specialized experience must have been at a level of difficulty and responsibility comparable to that of the second lower grade in the Federal service. For the GS–12 level and above, at least 1 year of the specialized experience must have been at a level of difficulty and responsibility comparable to that of the next lower grade in the Federal service.

EDUCATIONAL AND OTHER SUBSTITUTIONS

1. *For a maximum of 3 years of general experience* (for both Investigator positions and Criminal Investigator positions):

   a. Study successfully completed in an accredited college or university may be substituted at the rate of 1 year of study for 9 months of experience. (Four years of study in a college or university or completion of all requirements for a bachelor's degree qualifies for positions at grade GS–5.)

   b. Possession of a certificate as a Certified Public Accountant in a State, Territory, or the District of Columbia.

2. Full-time graduate education may be substituted for experience on the following basis:

   a. *For 1 year of specialized experience.—For Investigator and Criminal Investigator positions:* One full academic year of graduate education. (This amount and kind of education meets all the requirements for both types of positions at grade GS–7.)

   b. *For 2 years of specialized experience.—For Investigator positions:* Completion of all requirements for a master's or an equivalent degree, or 2 full academic years of graduate education in public administration, industrial relations, political science, government, business administration, law enforcement, police administration, criminology, or directly related fields. (This amount and kind of education meets all the requirements for these positions at grade GS–9.)

For Criminal Investigator positions: Completion of all requirements for a master's or an equivalent degree, or 2 full academic years of graduate education in law enforcement, police administration, criminology, or directly related fields. (This amount and kind of education meets all the requirements for these positions at grade GS–9.)

3. Completion of a total of at least 6 years of legal and pre-legal education which meets all the requirements for an LL.B. or J.D. degree will provide eligibility in full at grade GS–9 for both Investigator positions and Criminal Investigator positions.

PERSONAL QUALITIES

In addition to meeting all other requirements, applicants for these positions must possess certain personal qualities essential for investigative work. Among these qualities are ability in oral expression; poise and self-confidence; good personal appearance; tact; initiative and drive; capacity for effective public relations; and practical intelligence.

WRITTEN TEST

Competitors for positions at the GS–5 and GS–7 levels must pass an appropriate written test.

No written test is required for positions at GS–9 and above.

BASIS OF RATING

Competitors for GS–5 and GS–7 will be rated on the basis of the written test and an evaluation of their experience and education.

Competitors for GS–9 and above will be rated on the basis of an evaluation of their experience, education, and investigative skills.

INTERVIEW

Competitors who pass the written test, as required, and who meet the experience and training requirements may be requested to appear for an interview at the time of consideration for appointment.

SPECIAL PHYSICAL REQUIREMENTS

INVESTIGATOR POSITIONS

Applicants must be physically able to perform efficiently the duties of the position for which application is made. Good distant vision in one eye and ability to read without strain printed material the size of typewritten characters are required, glasses permitted. Ability to hear the conversational voice, with or without a hearing aid, is required. In most instances, an amputation of arm, hand, leg, or foot will not disqualify an applicant for appointment, although it may be necessary that this condition be compensated by use of satisfactory prosthesis. Applicants must possess emotional and mental stability. Any physical condition which would cause the applicant to be a hazard to himself or to others will disqualify him for appointment.

CRIMINAL INVESTIGATOR POSITIONS

The duties of the positions require moderate to arduous physical exertion involving walking and standing, use of firearms, and exposure to inclement weather. Manual dexterity with comparatively free motion of finger, wrist, elbow, shoulder, hip, and knee joints is required. Arms, hands, legs, and feet must be sufficiently intact and functioning in order that applicants may perform the duties satisfactorily. Applicants must possess sufficiently good vision, with or without glasses, each eye, in order that they may perform the duties satisfactorily. Near vision, glasses permitted, must be acute for the reading of printed material the size of typewritten characters. The ability of applicants to hear the conversational voice and whispered speech without the use of a hearing aid is required. Since the duties of the position are exacting and responsible, and involve activities under trying conditions, applicants must possess emotional and mental stability. Any physical condition which would cause the applicant to be a hazard to himself or to others will disqualify for appointment.

MOTOR VEHICLE LICENSE

For some positions, applicants (*a*) must possess a valid automobile license at the time of appointment, and (*b*) must also qualify after appointment for authorization to operate motor vehicles in accordance with applicable Civil Service regulations and with related requirements of the employing agency.

AGE

INVESTIGATOR POSITIONS

Minimum of 18.

CRIMINAL INVESTIGATOR POSITIONS

Minimum of 21; not waived for any applicants including those persons entitled to veterans' preference. Maximum entry age under 37; waived only for those already in a Federal civilian law enforcement position.

EVALUATION OF EXPERIENCE AND EDUCATION FOR COMPETITIVE AND IN-SERVICE PLACEMENT PURPOSES

(1) Education which has been acquired in fields directly or closely related to the positions to be filled should be rated at a higher level than that which has been acquired in less closely or unrelated fields.

(2) Quality levels for rating investigator and criminal investigator experience should be established in accordance with the following guides:

(a) experience which has concerned matters involving substantial ramifications or elements of investigative complexity should be rated at a higher quality level than experience which did not involve such ramifications or elements (ordinarily investigative complexity can be gauged by such indicators as the size, diversity, and interrelationships of operations and activities investigated; the numbers of investigative matters growing out of the original case assignment; the numbers, size, and complexity of structure and subsidiary activities of the organizations involved; the geographic dispersion of the operations investigated; the degree of involvement of other principals; the degree of controversy surrounding the case; the potential deterrent value in successfully bringing the case to a conclusion; the delicacy of the legal issues involved; the absence of precedents; etc.);

(b) experience which has required individual responsibility on the part of the investigator for complete investigations should be rated at a higher quality level than experience which has involved responsibility for a segment or phase of an investigation, or which has involved limited responsibility for a complete investigation;

(c) experience which has required the exercise of sound independent decisionmaking and judgment while working under general technical and administrative supervision and direction should be rated at a higher quality level than experience which has been acquired while working under closer supervision;

(d) experience which has required the exercise of a high degree of ingenuity, resourcefulness, and creative thinking should be rated at a higher quality level than experience which called for these qualities to a lesser degree.

RATING PROCEDURE

Evaluation of the scope and level of the applicants' knowledges, skills, and abilities is of greater importance than evaluation of length of experience in individual types of positions.

Police Officer GS-2/5
Detective GS-6/7
Supervisory Police Officer GS-5/9
Supervisory Detective GS-7/8

DESCRIPTION OF WORK

Police perform or supervise performance of law enforcement work involved in the protection of life, property, and the rights of individual citizens. They enforce Federal, State, county, and municipal statutes, laws, and ordinances, and agency rules and regulations. They preserve the peace; prevent, detect, and investigate accidents and crimes; arrest violators; and aid citizens in emergency situations.

EXPERIENCE, TRAINING, AND RELATED REQUIREMENTS

All candidates for positions in grade GS-2 must take a written test to demonstrate their abilities to understand the written word, and to follow oral directions.

Candidates for positions at GS-3 and above are required to show experience of the length and nature described below:

MINIMUM EXPERIENCE AND TRAINING

Grade	Total experience required (years)
GS-2	None
GS-3	1
GS-4	2
GS-5	3
GS-6	4
GS-7 and above	5

ACCEPTABLE EXPERIENCE

For positions at GS-3, acceptable experience is that which clearly demonstrates that the candidate possesses a knowledge of general law enforcement methods and techniques that could be applied in performing police functions. This experience must have included protecting property, equipment, or materials; and person-to-person relationships in enforcing various rules and regulations.

For positions at GS-4 and above, acceptable experience is that which has given the candidate a broad knowledge of police operations, practices, and techniques. The experience must have included making arrests, protecting life and property, maintaining law and order, investigating accidents, preventing crime, and preserving the peace. Experience of this type normally may be acquired through regular, active service as a member of a Federal, state, county, municipal, or local police force or similar organization; or through service as a military police officer in the Armed Forces or Coast Guard.

QUALITY AND LEVEL OF EXPERIENCE

For nonsupervisory positions, at least 6 months of the required experience must have been at a level of difficulty and responsibility comparable to that of the next lower grade, or at least 1 year of required experience must have been at a level of difficulty and responsibility comparable to that of the second lower grade in the Federal service.

NONQUALIFYING EXPERIENCE

Experience as a prison or jail guard, night watchman, or other position which did not provide knowledges and skills in general law enforcement methods and techniques that could be applied in the performance of police functions, will not be considered as acceptable experience.

SUBSTITUTIONS

(1) Successful completion of police recruit training in a large civilian police force, a police academy, or police school, may be substituted for the experience requirements at GS–3.

(2) Successful completion of a Reserve-Police training course which included a minimum of 36 hours of actual lecture or training in police department procedures and methods, and local laws and regulations; and which led to the award of a certificate of proficiency or issuance of a badge, may be substituted for a maximum of 6 months of the experience →required for GS–3←.

(3) Successful completion of 1 year of study in a resident school above high school level may be substituted in full for the GS–3 requirements, provided each semester of study included 3 semester hours, or the equivalent, in one or more of the following subjects: police administration, police law and evidence, police investigation, criminology, law enforcement, general law, or similar subjects pertinent to police work.

(4) Successful completion of 2 years of study in a resident school above high school level may be substituted in full for the GS–4 requirements, provided each semester of study included 3 semester hours, or the equivalent, in one or more of the following subjects: police administration, police law and evidence, police investigation, criminology, law enforcement, general law, or similar subjects pertinent to police work.

(5) Successful completion of a full 4-year course of study required for a B.S. degree in Police Science from a resident school above high school level may be substituted in full for the GS–5 requirements.

MOTOR VEHICLE OPERATOR QUALIFICATIONS

For positions requiring the operation of a Government-owned motor vehicle, candidates must:

—Pass a practical road test, driving the appropriate type vehicle supplied by the agency to which the candidate is provisionally certified;

—Possess a valid State or territory motor vehicle operator's license or obtain one within 30 days after entry on duty;

—Have a satisfactory safe driving record.

BASIS OF RATING

Competitors for all positions will be rated on a scale of 100. The basis of rating will be:

For GS–2: Competitors will be rated only on the basis of the written test. They will be rated on a scale of 100. A rating of at least 70 must be obtained on the test as a whole.

For GS–3 and above: An evaluation of experience and training. Candidates must present evidence of ability to discharge the duties of the position.

PERSONAL QUALITIES

Candidates, in addition to other qualifications, must demonstrate that they possess traits and characteristics which are important to success in police work. Among these are: alertness, ability to work in stress situations, ability in oral expression, tact, integrity, capacity for effective public relations, practical intelligence, and good judgment.

AGE LIMITS

Persons appointed to police positions must be at least 21 years of age. This requirement may be waived only for veterans. Persons between the ages of 20 and 21 may file applications for examinations. Such persons will be examined but only veterans may enter on duty before attaining the age of 21 years.

PHYSICAL REQUIREMENTS

Applicants must be physically able to perform efficiently the duties of the position, which are described elsewhere in this standard. →For most positions, applicants must have binocular vision correctible to 20/20 (Snellen). Uncorrected vision must test at least 20/70 (Snellen) in each eye. Near vision corrected or uncorrected must be sufficient to read Yaeger Type 2 at 14 inches. However, there may be some positions suitable for persons with good vision in one eye only.← Ability to distinguish basic colors is essential. Ability to hear the conversational voice, without the use of a hearing aid, is required. Persons with an amputation of arm, hand, leg, or foot should not apply. Applicants must possess emotional and mental stability. Any physical condition which would cause the applicant to be a hazard to himself or to others will disqualify for appointment.

Correctional Officer GS-6/13

DESCRIPTION OF WORK

Correctional Officers supervise and perform work concerned with the correctional treatment, supervision, and custody of criminal offenders in correctional institutions or community-based treatment or rehabilitation centers. They have primary responsibility for guiding inmate conduct, supervising work details, carrying out plans for the correctional treatment and modification of attitudes of inmates, instructing and counseling inmates on institutional and personal problems, and generally ensuring the custody, safety, and well-being of inmates. On occasion, Correctional Officers are required to carry firearms.

Supervisory Correctional Officers have either (*a*) responsibility for planning, directing, coordinating and implementing programs to accomplish the work described above, and for supervising a force of Correctional Officers on all shifts, or (*b*) responsibility for the immediate supervision of correctional officers assigned to a shift or to a physical area or activity of an institution.

EXPERIENCE AND TRAINING

Except for the substitution of education provided below, applicants must have had the following kinds and length of experience:

Grade	General experience (years)	Specialized experience (years)	Total experience (years)
GS-6	3½	None	3½
GS-7	3½	1	4½
GS-8	3½	2	5½
GS-9/13	3½	3	6½

NOTE: When positions are to be filled at grades below the normal GS-6 level, the qualification requirements should be determined by a downward extension of the criteria in this standard, e.g., 3 years of general experience is qualifying for grade GS-5.

GENERAL EXPERIENCE

Experience, paid or voluntary, full or part time, that demonstrates the applicant's aptitude for acquiring the skills and knowledges needed for correctional work, and in addition, demonstrates the possession of personal attributes important to the effectiveness of correctional officers, such as:
—ability to meet and deal with people of differing backgrounds and behavioral patterns;
—ability to be persuasive in selling or influencing ideas;
—ability to lead, supervise, and instruct;
—sympathetic attitude towards the welfare of others;
—capacity to adapt to new ideas and changing conditions;

—ability to reason soundly and to think out practical solutions to problems;

—ability to pay attention to detail;

—ability to make decisions and act quickly, particularly under stress;

—poise and self-confidence, and ability to remain calm during emergency situations.

The following types of experience are illustrative of acceptable general experience, providing they meet the above criteria (this list is not intended to be all inclusive).

(1) Social case work in a welfare agency;

(2) Classroom teaching or instructing;

(3) Responsible rehabilitation work, e.g., in an alcoholic rehabilitation program;

(4) Supervision of planned recreational activities;

(5) Active participation in community action programs;

(6) Employment with a counseling service in interviewing and counseling people;

(7) Management of, or supervising work in, a business or other organization that included personnel management responsibilities in addition to directing work performance;

(8) Sales work (other than taking and filling orders as in over-the-counter sales);

(9) Active participation, as an officer or member, in extracurricular activities in college, such as student government, service organizations, college magazines or newspapers, fraternal organizations, etc.

SPECIALIZED EXPERIENCE

This is experience in the correctional custody and supervision, in accordance with modern penological concepts, of inmates of a penal or correctional institution or community based correctional treatment facility. This experience must satisfy all of the following requirements:

(a) must have included satisfactory completion of a federally operated inservice training course for correctional officers, or completion of a comparable training course covering modern correctional concepts and techniques;

(b) must have demonstrated the ability to supervise and control inmates in groups of 20 or more, and to make sound decisions in critical circumstances;

(c) must have shown the capacity to relate successfully to inmates with respect to matters such as close and continuous counseling, singly and in groups; and

(d) must have shown the ability to work independently and to assume responsibility for the correctional custody and supervision of inmate activities; to direct, observe, and correct inmate behavior; and to take precautionary measures to ensure control in situations relatively critical to the security of the institution.

In addition:

For grade GS–8, the applicant must have demonstrated the ability and knowledge necessary to perform difficult post assignments that require the judgment, maturity, and knowledge of inmate behavior developed through experience gained in performing a variety of correctional assignments; to use, and to make reports and recommendations based on the use of techniques such as informal counseling, guidance, interview, and observation, and to deal adequately with special problems of correctional custody made difficult by unusual conditions of supervision and control.

For grade GS–9 nonsupervisory positions, the applicant must have demonstrated the knowledge of, and ability to apply technical treatment and/or counseling skills and techniques acquired through formal classroom and supervised practical training. These skills may have been utilized in a variety of assignments, typically as part of structured treatment or rehabilitation programs under the guidance of professionals in the behavioral sciences or social work.

QUALITY OF EXPERIENCE

The applicant's record of experience and training must show that he has the ability to perform the duties of the position.

In addition:

For grade GS–6, applicant must have had at least 6 months of general experience comparable in difficulty and responsibility to that of the next lower grade, or 1 year comparable to the second lower grade in the Federal service.

For grades GS-7 through GS-11, at least 1 year of the specialized experience must have been comparable in difficulty and responsibility to the next lower grade, or 2 years comparable to the second lower grade in the Federal service.

For grades GS-12 and above, at least 1 year of the specialized experience must have been comparable in difficulty and responsibility to the next lower grade in the Federal service.

SUBSTITUTION OF EDUCATION AND TRAINING FOR EXPERIENCE

To be acceptable as substitution for general or specialized experience, the level and quality of the education and/or training (or of the combined experience and education and/or training) must have equipped the candidate to perform correctional duties at the grade level of the position to be filled.

GENERAL EXPERIENCE

(1) Two years of study successfully completed in a resident school above high school level may be substituted for two years of general experience.

(2) Successful completion of a full 4-year course of college study may be substituted for three years of general experience.

(3) One full semester of graduate study successfully completed in an accredited college or university, except as noted below, may be substituted for six months of general experience, and is fully qualifying for grade GS-6.

At any grade, post-high school education may be partially substituted for required experience at the rates of substitution indicated above.

SPECIALIZED EXPERIENCE

One full semester of graduate study in correctional administration, criminology, penology, sociology, or social work successfully completed in an accredited college or university may be substituted for six months of specialized experience, up to a total of 18 months.

Credit for appropriate education and training

other than that outlined above (such as manpower development programs, "New Careers" programs, rehabilitated offender programs, or inservice training programs) will be granted depending on the nature, extent, and applicability of the training in relation to the position to be filled.

SELECTIVE PLACEMENT

Additional knowledges and abilities may be required for some positions because of the concentration of inmates in distinct age, ethnic, cultural, or other specific groups in certain institutions. It is desirable for these institutions to have sufficient numbers of correctional officers who can successfully relate to the members of these groups. Selective placement consideration may be given to applicants having a thorough knowledge and understanding of the customs, language patterns, and problems of specific groups of inmates.

BASIS OF RATING

Applicants for all grades will be rated on the basis of an evaluation and appraisal of experience, education, and training.

EMPLOYMENT INTERVIEW

The personal qualities and characteristics of the applicant are the most critical of all the requirements for positions of Correctional Officer. He must be willing to perform arduous and prolonged duties on any of the three shifts. He must possess certain personal qualities in order to effectively relate to inmates in a correctional setting. These qualities include: empathy, objectivity, perceptiveness, resourcefulness, adaptability and flexibility, stability and maturity.

Before appointment, candidates may be required to appear before a panel of specialists in correctional administration for an employment interview. The interview will also serve to acquaint the applicant with further details of, and the environment surrounding, the position. A determination by the panel that a person who is otherwise qualified does not possess such personal characteristics to the required degree may result in removal of his application from further consideration. Notice will be given in advance of the date and place of the interview.

AGE

At time of appointment, applicants must not have reached their 37th birthday unless they have previously served in a Federal civilian law enforcement position.

PHYSICAL REQUIREMENTS

The duties of these positions involve unusual mental and nervous pressure and require arduous physical exertion involving prolonged walking and standing, restraining of prisoners in emergencies, and participating in escape hunts. Applicants must be physically capable of performing efficiently the duties of the position, be free from such defects or disease as may constitute employment hazards to themselves or others, and have no deformities, disfigurements, or abnormalities which tend to be conspicuous. Persons having remediable defects or curable diseases, and who are otherwise qualified, will he admitted to the examination but must submit proof, during the time the list of eligible competitors exists, that the defects or diseases have been remedied or cured before they may be considered for appointment.

No height or weight limits are specified but weight must be in proportion to height. Male applicants under 66 inches and female applicants under 63 inches in height will be especially evaluated for stamina and vigor.

Vision: Uncorrected vision must be no less than 20/100 (Snellen) in each eye, capable of full correction to 20/30 (Snellen) in each eye, provided that defective vision is not due to active or progressive organic disease.

Hearing: Hearing in each ear must be normal, that is, 15/15 in each ear by the whispered voice test. Hearing aids are not acceptable.

General: Hernia (with or without truss); organic heart disease (whether or not compensated); severe varicose veins; serious deformities or disabilities of extremities (including weak feet); chronic constitutional disease: marked abnormality of speech; facial disfigurement; or other serious physical defect or disease will disqualify for appointment. Disease of the nervous system or history or presence of mental disease or emotional instability may disqualify an applicant for appointment. Before entrance on duty, appointees will be given, without expense to themselves, a physical examination by a Federal medical officer, and will be rejected if they do not meet the standards specified above. Persons who are offered appointment must pay their own expenses in reporting for duty. Any person reporting for duty at the place of assignment and found ineligible because of physical defects cannot be appointed, and no part of his expense for reporting and returning home can be borne by the Government.

PROFESSIONAL POSITIONS

Paralegal Specialist, GS–5 and above

DESCRIPTION OF WORK

Paralegal specialist positions involve such activities as (a) legal research, analyzing legal decisions, opinions, rulings, memoranda, and other legal material, selecting principles of law, and preparing digests of the points of law involved; (b) selecting, assembling, summarizing, and compiling substantive information on statutes, treaties, contracts, other legal instruments, and specific legal subjects; (c) case preparation for civil litigation, criminal law proceedings or agency hearings, including the collection, analysis, and evaluation of evidence, e.g., as to fraud and fraudulent and other irregular activities or violations of laws; (d) analyzing facts and legal questions presented by personnel administering specific Federal laws, answering the questions where they have been settled by interpretations of applicable legal provisions, regulations, precedents, and agency policy, and in some instances preparing informative and instructional material for general use; (e) adjudicating applications or cases on the basis of pertinent laws, regulations, policies and precedent decisions; or (f) performing other paralegal duties requiring discretion and independent judgment in the application of specialized knowledge of particular laws, regulations, precedents, or agency practices based thereon. These duties may or may not be performed under the direction of a lawyer.

EXPERIENCE AND TRAINING REQUIREMENTS

Except for the substitution of education provided for below, candidates must have had both general and specialized experience as follows:

Grade	Experience		
	General (years)	Specialized (years)	Total (years)
GS–5	3	0	3
GS–7	3	1	4
GS–9	3	2	5
GS–11 and above	3	3	6

GENERAL EXPERIENCE

This is progressively responsible experience which demonstrated the ability to explain, apply or interpret rules, regulations, procedures, policies, precedents, or other kinds of criteria. Such experience may have been gained in administrative, professional, investigative, technical, high level clerical, or other responsible work.

SPECIALIZED EXPERIENCE

This is legal, quasi-legal, paralegal, legal technician, or related work that demonstrated:
— Ability to evaluate pertinent facts and evidence;
— Ability to interpret and apply laws, rules, regulations, and precedents;
— Skill and judgment in the analysis of cases;
— Ability to communicate effectively orally and in writing;
— As required, ability to deal effectively with individuals and groups;
— As required, knowledge of the pertinent subject area.

Qualifying specialized experience may have been acquired in positions which involved, for example:

(1) Preparation, development, examination, review, or authorization of action on claims in accordance with applicable laws, rules, regulations, precedents, policies, office practices and established procedures; or

(2) Examination and/or preparation of contracts, legal instruments, or other documents to assure completeness of information and conformance to pertinent laws, rules, regulations, precedents, and office requirements which has required the application of a specialized knowledge of particular laws, or of regulations, precedents or practices based thereon; or

(3) Analysis of legal decisions, opinions, rulings, memoranda, and other legal material and preparation of digests of the points of law involved for the internal use of the agency; or

(4) Interpretation and application of laws and related regulations in determining individual or agency responsibility; or

(5) Selection, compilation, and summarization of substantive information on statutes, treaties, and specific legal subjects for the use of others; or

(6) Conduct of hearings or adjudication of appeals arising under statute or regulations of a Government agency; or

(7) Investigation and analysis of evidence of alleged or suspected violations of laws or regulations.

QUALITY OF EXPERIENCE

The candidate's record of experience and training must show the ability to perform the duties of the position. For positions at grades GS–11 and below, at least six months of the required specialized experience must have been at a level of difficulty and responsibility equivalent to that of the next lower grade, or one year of such experience at a level equivalent to the second lower grade in the Federal service. For positions at grades GS–12 and above, at least one year of the required specialized experience must have been at a level equivalent to the next lower grade in the Federal service.

SUBSTITUTION OF EDUCATION FOR EXPERIENCE

(1) Successful completion of a full 4-year course in an accredited college or university leading to a bachelor's degree may be substituted for three years of general experience. Such education successfully completed in a residence school above high school level may be substituted at the rate of one academic year of study for nine months of experience up to a maximum of four years of study for three years of general experience.

(2) Completion of all requirements for an LL.B., J.D., or higher degree from a recognized law school, including at least six full years of resident college work, will meet the requirements for grade GS–9.

(3) Successful completion of one full academic year of study in a paralegal or legal curriculum may be substituted for one year of specialized experience required for grades GS–7 and above; less than one full year of study will be credited on a pro rata basis.

WRITTEN TEST

Candidates for competitive appointment to grades GS–5 and GS–7 must pass an appropriate written test. In addition, the test may *not* be used in evaluating or ranking eligible employees unless the test is approved for this purpose by the Office of Personnel Management.

BASIS OF RATING

Competitors for all positions are rated on a scale of 100. Rankings are made:

1. *For competitive appointment at grades 5 and 7*—On the basis of the written test.
2. *For competitive appointments above GS–7*—On the basis of the extent and quality of experience and training relevant to the duties of the position.

SPECIAL PHYSICAL REQUIREMENTS

Ability to read without strain printed material the size of typewritten characters is required, corrective lenses permitted. Ability to speak without impediment may be required for some positions. Ability to hear the conversational voice, with or without a hearing aid, is required for most positions; however, some positions may be suitable for the deaf.

Statistician GS–5
Statistician (appropriate subject-matter specialization) GS–7/15
Survey Statistician GS–7/15

DESCRIPTION OF WORK

Statisticians do professional work or provide professional consultation requiring the application of statistical theory and technique in the collection, compilation, analysis and interpretation of quantitative information in a variety of subject-matter fields, including the biological, social and physical sciences, engineering, agriculture, and administration.

Statisticians (appropriate subject-matter specialization) are primarily concerned with the use of statistical theory, techniques and methods to determine meaningful relationships or to measure the significance of quantified information in a particular subject-matter field, e.g., biology, demography, engineering, economics, etc.

Survey Statisticians are concerned with the application of statistical theory and technique to the planning, organization, and operation of programs for collecting, verifying, adjusting, processing, summarizing, and presenting information expressed numerically.

BASIC REQUIREMENTS FOR ALL GRADES

1. Applicants for all grades must have successfully completed one of the following, A *or* B:

A. A full 4-year course leading to a bachelor's degree in an accredited college or university which has included 15 semester hours in statistics, (or in mathematics and statistics provided at least 6 semester hours are in statistics) and 9 additional hours in one of the following: the physical or biological sciences; medicine; education or engineering; or in the social sciences, including demography, history, economics, social welfare, geography, international relations, social or cultural anthropology, health sociology, political science, public administration, psychology, etc. Credit toward meeting statistical course requirements should be given for courses in which 50 percent of the course content appears to be statistical method.

B. Courses are given in A above, plus additional appropriate experience or education which when combined with these courses will total 4 years of education and experience and give the applicant a technical knowledge comparable to that which would have been acquired through successful completion of a full 4-year course.

2. The experience offered in combination with specified educational courses to meet the requirements specified in paragraph B above should include evidence of professional statistical work such as (a) sampling; (b) collecting, computing and analyzing statistical data; (c) applying known statistical techniques to data such as measurement of central tendency, dispersion, skewness, sampling error, simple and multiple correlation, analysis of variance and tests of significance.

Without other indication of professional statistical experience, work in the processing of numerical or quantified information by other than statistical methods is not considered appropriate qualifying experience.

3. For positions involving highly technical research, development or similar complex scientific functions, selection may be restricted to eligibles who show the successful completion of a full college course in the appropriate field as designated above.

GS–5.—The basic requirements which apply to all grades are fully qualifying for grade GS–5.

ADDITIONAL EXPERIENCE AND TRAINING REQUIREMENTS

Candidates for grades GS–7 and above must have had either professional experience or graduate education (or an equivalent combination of both) in addition to meeting the basic requirements. Such professional experience or graduate education must have been in, or directly related to, statistics or an appropriate subject-matter field. For statistician positions at GS−9 and above in one of the specializations listed below, the experience or education must have provided specialized knowledge of the subject-matter field:

Subject-Matter fields:
1. Agriculture
2. Biology
3. Health
4. Medicine
5. Engineering
6. Social Science
7. Operations and Administration including logistics
8. Economics
9. Demography
10. Education
11. Physical Science

1. EXPERIENCE

In addition to the basic requirements, the following amounts of professional experience are required for grades GS−7 and above:

	Minimum amount of professional experience in appropriate subject-matter fields
Grade:	(years)
GS−7	1
GS−9	2
GS−11 and above	3

For grades GS−11 and below, at least 6 months of the required experience must have been at the level of difficulty comparable to that of the next lower grade, or 1 year comparable to the second lower grade, in the Federal service. For grades GS−12 and above, at least 1 year of the required experience must have been at a level of difficulty comparable to that of the next lower grade in the Federal service.

2. EDUCATION

In addition to the basic requirements, the following amounts and levels of education are qualifying for grades GS−7 and above, as shown:

Grade:	*Minimum amount or level of education in appropriate subject-matter fields*
GS−7—	One full academic year of graduate education.
GS−9—	Completion of all requirements for a master's or equivalent degree; *or*
	Two full academic years of graduate education.
GS−11—	Completion of all requirements for a doctoral degree (Ph.D. or equivalent); *or*
	Three full academic years of graduate education.
GS−11 (Analytical positions)—	Completion of all requirements for a master's or an equivalent degree for which at least 2 years of graduate study is required when—
	a. The position involves primarily analytical work of a creative or advanced scientific nature.
	b. The knowledge required for the work is *typically and preferably* acquired through graduate study.
	c. The work is of such character that the academic preparation will equip the candidate to perform fully the professional work at the GS−11 level after a short orientation period.

To be acceptable, the graduate education must have included a course in statistical or related theory for which knowledge of calculus is required.

3. COMBINATIONS OF PROFESSIONAL EXPERIENCE AND GRADUATE EDUCATION

Equivalent combinations of professional experience and graduate education of the types described above are acceptable at each grade.

4. ALTERNATE REQUIREMENTS

Superior academic achievement at the baccalaureate level or 1 year of student trainee experience is qualifying at grade GS−7. A combination of superior academic achievement at the baccalaureate level and 1 year of appropriate professional experience is qualifying at grade GS−9.

BASIS OF RATING

No written test is required. Applicants' qualifications will be rated on a scale of 100, and will be evaluated on the basis of their education, training, and experience as shown in the application, and on corroborative evidence obtained by the Office of Personnel Management.

Librarian
Administrative Librarian
Supervisory Librarian
Library Director
(with specializations as appropriate)
Grades GS–7/15
Librarian Trainee
(Special provision at GS–5)

DESCRIPTION OF WORK

Positions involve work that primarily requires a full professional knowledge of the theories, principles, and techniques of librarianship. An inherent requirement of these positions is a knowledge of literature resources. Such work is concerned with the collection, organization, preservation, and retrieval of recorded knowledge in printed, written, audio-visual, film, wax, near-print methods, magnetic tape, or other media. Typical library functions include one or more of the following: selection, acquisition, cataloging and classification of materials, bibliographic and readers' advisory services, reference and literature searching services, library management and systems planning, or the development and strengthening of library service. Some positions may involve work in connection with the development of information retrieval systems.

SPECIALIZATIONS

Since many libraries are highly specialized, the work often lies chiefly in one subject-matter field, or closely related subject areas. To serve subject specialists who are the principal users of these libraries, some librarians require a knowledge of a specialized subject or field of endeavor. Such subject-matter knowledge typically covers a broad field, rather than a deep subject knowledge and competence related to a specific discipline or a full knowledge of the state of the art. Because materials in libraries are often in foreign languages, some librarians also must have a proficient knowledge of one or more foreign languages.

To provide qualified personnel for librarian positions requiring knowledge of a subject-matter field and/or proficient knowledge of several foreign languages, the following specializations are authorized:

Subject-matter specializations

Biological Sciences	Education
Medical Sciences	Fine Arts
Physical Sciences	Humanities
Social Sciences	Law
Business and Industry	Music
Engineering	

Foreign language specializations

Germanic	Slavic
Oriental	Arabic
Romance	

EXPERIENCE AND EDUCATION REQUIREMENTS

All Librarians must meet the requirements for professional education in library science or possess equivalent experience as shown in IA, IB, IC or IIA, below. The usual way of entering the profession is to qualify at grade GS–9 on the basis of a master's degree in library science. However, it is possible to qualify for entrance at the GS–7 level on other bases as indicated.

For Librarian (appropriate specialization) positions all candidates must also meet requirements which are directly related to the subject matter or language of the specialization. These requirements are in addition to the basic professional library science requirements which apply to all positions. However, these requirements may be included within, or may be supplemental to, those specified for all positions at GS–7 and GS–9.

I. REQUIREMENTS FOR LIBRARIAN POSITIONS, GS–7

To qualify for all Librarian GS–7 positions, the applicant must meet the requirements specified in paragraphs A, B, or C below. (*Note:* Applicants who qualify under provisions of paragraphs A or B will not be required to take a subject-matter test in library science.)

A. Completion of 1 full academic year of graduate study in library science in an accredited college or university, in addition to completion of all work required for a bachelor's degree; *or*

B. Completion of all requirements for a "5th-year" bachelor's degree in library science. *In addition*, the applicant must have had at least 1 year of library experience which included the performance of duties in one or more functional areas of librarianship at the GS–5 or higher grade level; *or*

C. A total, in some combination, of not less than 5 years of college-level education, training, and/or experience. To qualify on this basis, the applicant must establish conclusively that the education, training, and/or experience has provided a knowledge and understanding of the theories, principles, and techniques of professional librarianship; a knowledge of literature re-

sources; and the knowledges and abilities essential for providing effective library services. Under this provision:

(1) Applicants must pass a subject-matter test in library science.

(2) If the applicant qualifies on the basis of a college level education, he must have had at least 1 year of library experience comparable in difficulty and responsibility to that of a GS–5 or higher level) library technician, technical information specialist, or subject-matter specialist performing library services.

(3) If the applicant qualifies on the basis of experience alone, with no college level education or training, he must have had at least 2 years of library experience comparable in difficulty and responsibility to that of a GS–5 (or higher level) library technician.

(4) The applicant may qualify under any time and quality equivalent combinations of the requirements shown in paragraphs (2) and (3).

(5) Specialized training, e.g., training at a school for library technicians or through "in-house" courses, will be allowed appropriate credit depending upon its applicability and extent.

To qualify for Librarian (appropriate specialization) positions GS–7, the applicant must also possess specialized knowledges of a subject-matter field and/or proficiency in one or more foreign languages which are directly related to the positions being filled. When such knowledges *are required by the position,* the applicant's education or experience must have included or been supplemented by the requirements specified in one of the paragraphs below:

(a) A full 4-year course of study in an accredited college or university which meets all academic requirements for a bachelor's degree, and also (1) has included at least 24 semester hour credits in the specialized field for which the applicant is being considered, *or* (2) has included any combination of subjects with at least 15 semester hour credits in a major subject which is especially applicable to the position for which the applicant is being considered; *or*

(b) Completion of at least 24 semester hours

of legal study in an accredited law school for positions primarily concerned with providing library services in law or legislative reference; *or*

(c) Four years of successful and pertinent experience of such nature and level to provide a knowledge of the basic principles, theories, practices, techniques, terminology and expressions of the appropriate discipline or subject-matter field; an understanding of the standard methods, procedures, and techniques of research and analysis in the subject-matter field; ability to acquire additional information about the field and related fields; and some knowledge of literature resources in the field.

(d) Any time equivalent combination of experience as described in item "(c)" with education as described in item "(a)" or "(b)" above.

(e) Demonstrated ability as shown by education or experience to read or translate information from one or more foreign languages into English.

II. REQUIREMENTS FOR LIBRARIAN POSITIONS, GS–9

A. Completion of all requirements for a master's degree or 2 full academic years of graduate study in library science, in an accredited college or university, meets all requirements for Librarian positions, GS–9.

B. In addition to meeting one of the requirements for GS–7 (A, B, or C above) must have had professional *or* advanced experience *or* graduate study as follows:

(1) One year of professional experience in librarianship which included the performance, supervision, or administration of one or more major functional areas of librarianship.

   Some positions are highly specialized in one functional area, and may require that the advanced experience be in the appropriate function to qualify at these higher grade levels.

(2) One year of professional or advanced experience in the subject matter or language which has provided the applicant with the professional, technical, language, or other specialized knowledges and abilities required by the par-

ticular position for which he is being considered.

   Graduate education in a subject-matter field which is especially applicable to the position, and provides the knowledges required to perform the duties of the position, as follows:

(a) Completion of all requirements for a master's degree; *or*

(b) Two full academic years of graduate education.

III. REQUIREMENTS FOR LIBRARIAN POSITIONS, GS–11 AND ABOVE

A. In addition to meeting the requirements for GS–9 (either A or B) candidates must have had either:

(1) One year of professional experience in librarianship; *or*

(2) One year of professional or advanced experience in a subject-matter or language area appropriate to the position.

B. Completion of all the requirements for a doctoral degree (or equivalent) or 3 full academic years of graduate education in library science.

C. In addition to possessing professional education in library science (or equivalent experience) as required for entrance at grades GS–7 or GS–9, candidates must have completed graduate study in a subject matter or language area appropriate to the position as follows:

(1) All requirements for a doctoral degree (Ph.D. or equivalent); *or*

(2) Three full academic years of graduate education.

IV. COMBINATIONS OF PROFESSIONAL EXPERIENCE AND GRADUATE EDUCATION

Equivalent combinations of professional experience and graduate education of the types described above are acceptable at each grade.

QUALITY OF EXPERIENCE

For grades GS–11 and below, at least 6 months of the required experience must have been at the level of difficulty comparable to that of the next lower grade, or 1 year comparable to the second lower grade, in the Federal service. For grades GS–12 and above, at least 1 year of the required experience must have been at a level of difficulty comparable to that of the next lower grade in the Federal service.

SUPERVISORY AND ADMINISTRATIVE POSITIONS

For positions concerned with administration, management, or direction of library programs, candidates must meet all other requirements for the particular grade and also show that they possess the required administrative and/or managerial ability to perform successfully the duties of such positions. Education, training, or experience of the candidate should demonstrate, e.g., ability to manage or direct a library, group of libraries, or library system; ability to plan, organize, and direct the development and execution of library programs, policies, and procedures; ability to plan or conduct management studies, public relations and educational activities; ability to plan, develop and carry out administrative activities of the library or library system concerned with budget and finance, personnel, plant and equipment, etc.

BASIS OF RATING

All competitors who meet the education and experience requirements for GS–7 and above, who pass the written test in library science when required, will be rated based upon an evaluation of their experience and training in library work. The library science written test, when required, will be used for qualification purposes only.

EVALUATING EXPERIENCE AND TRAINING

In evaluating experience and training, consideration will be given to the type, level, and scope of experience relating directly to the particular position or positions under consideration, as indicated in the application, and to any additional pertinent information obtained from references, employees, associates and colleagues.

NONQUALIFYING EXPERIENCE AND TRAINING

No credit will be given toward meeting the experience requirements for positions in this series for work in the following situations:

1. Work with collections of fiction, recreational or other reading material where no formal cataloging or classification of material is performed.

2. Experience in wholesale or retail bookstores, circulating fiction and club libraries, or hospital record departments.

3. Experience as a library page, as a library attendant or as a clerical worker, even though the duties included such work as charging and discharging books or typing catalog cards or orders for books and materials.

4. Nonprofessional work in a library on a part-time basis or on a volunteer basis.

5. No credit will be given for training in the particular use of libraries and library facilities such as is given in orientation courses to college freshmen.

WRITTEN TESTS

Applicants for all grades who (1) have a master's degree or the required education in library science, or (2) have a 5th-year bachelor's degree in library science, will *not* be required to take a written test.

Applicants for *all grades* who qualify on the basis of experience alone or a combination of experience and education *must pass a subject-matter test* in library science. This written test is designed to measure the candidate's knowledge of the fundamentals underlying professional library science and his understanding of its methods and techniques and their applications to effective library science. Questions will be asked on facts, principles, applications, tools, practices, and theory of professional librarianship as found in a variety of libraries.

SPECIAL PROVISIONS

A. *For all librarian positions*

At GS–9 and above, Librarian positions concerned with acquisition, cataloging, or reference work are sometimes highly specialized. In filling such positions, consideration may be limited to those eligibles who have had experience in the appropriate specialization at a qualifying level of difficulty.

SPECIAL PROVISION FOR FILLING POSITIONS OF LIBRARIAN (TRAINEE), GS–5

This is a special provision which may be used when there is a shortage of candidates who are fully qualified for GS–7 level Librarian or Librarian (appropriate specialization) positions. This provision is included because of the reported dearth of fully-qualified librarians. It is intended for use in those situations where the

Librarian (Trainee) can be expected to complete his/her education or training in library science within a reasonable period of time, and thus meet requirements for librarian positions at the GS–7 level.

Under this provision, applicants for positions of Librarian (Trainee), GS–5 must meet the following requirements: completion of a full 4-year course of study in an accredited college or university which meets all academic requirements for a bachelor's degree, or equivalent experience.

—Qualification of candidates under this provision is demonstrated by eligibility on a civil service register, or an appropriate subject-matter register. Appointing officers may request certification of eligible candidates with major study in a subject-matter field which is considered appropriate for the position being filled.

Individuals hired as Librarian (Trainee), GS–5, *may not* be employed or promoted to a position of Librarian GS–7 until they fully meet the requirement specified for GS–7 Librarian positions.

Social Worker GS– 7/15
Social Work Program Specialist GS–9/15

DESCRIPTION OF WORK

Social Workers perform professional social work involved in carrying out agency programs of service to people with whom they are concerned, such as patients in agency-operated hospitals and clinics, wards of child welfare agencies and their families, inmates of correctional institutions, etc.

Most positions involve direct professional services to individuals. Some positions also include working with clients in groups when appropriate, and/or working with and advising members of the community in the development of local resources to prevent or alleviate social problems. There are positions which are primarily concerned with supervision of social work staff and/or students, with directing programs of social work, or with research to improve social work practice.

Social Work Program Specialists advise on, develop, evaluate, and promote social welfare programs and services administered by State agencies and other public and nonprofit organizations and institutions. More specifically, they develop and issue material on new knowledge, set minimum standards for administration and operation of programs; evaluate the soundness and effectiveness of program administration and operation; and work with State, community, and professional leaders who are interested in strengthening service programs, etc.

MINIMUM EDUCATION REQUIREMENT

Applicants must have successfully completed a course of study in an accredited school of social work which has fulfilled all of the requirements for the master's degree in social work. The recognized accrediting association in the field is the Council on Social Work Education.

ADDITIONAL TRAINING AND EXPERIENCE REQUIREMENTS

For GS–7:   No additional training or experience needed.

For GS–9:   In addition to meeting the requirements for grade GS–7, applicants must have successfully completed one of the following:

A. Related practice training in professional social work during field placement as part of the graduate study.

B. At least 1 year of professional social work experience under professional supervision.

For GS–11:   In addition to meeting the requirements for grade GS–9, applicants must have had a minimum of → 1 year ← of professional social work experience under professional supervision. Experience must have demonstrated the ability to perform advanced assignments independently.

For GS–12/15:   In addition to meeting the requirements for GS–11, applicants must have had a minimum of 1 additional year of professional social work experience which has demonstrated broad knowledge of the field of social work and superior skill and judgment in professional practice.

For program specialist positions, the experience must have included one or, in some cases, a combination of two or more functions, such as program planning, program development, program evaluation, consultation, and cooperative community relationships in an agency providing social work service to families, children, or adults; *or*

Supervisory, administrative, or consultative work in a public or voluntary welfare or health agency with an organized social work program. For positions with staff development responsibilities, the required experience must have included experience in planning or conducting a social work education or staff development program in a health or welfare agency, or teaching in an accredited school of social work.

QUALITY OF EXPERIENCE AND TRAINING

The number of years of experience required for any grade level represents the minimum amount of time necessary to qualify for the appropriate position, but length of time is not of itself qualifying. The applicant's work experience must also have been of a quality and scope sufficient to enable him to perform satisfactorily assignments typical of the grade level for which he is being considered. The evaluation of the applicant's performance and potentialities will be based upon information acquired through confidential inquiry of his supervisors and others familiar with the nature and quality of his work.

For positions at grade GS–9, at least 1 year of experience must have been at a level comparable in scope and difficulty to that of grade GS–7 in the Federal service; for grade GS–11, at least → 1 year ← of the required experience must have been comparable in scope and difficulty to that of GS–9; and for GS–12 and above, at least 1 year must have been comparable in scope and difficulty to that of the next lower grade.

NONQUALIFYING EXPERIENCE

Except for the substitution of supervised field training completed as part of an educational curriculum (see above), experience acquired prior to completion of all requirements for the master's degree is not considered as qualifying.

An applicant who has been out of social work practice for 10 or more years may be asked to provide additional evidence that his qualifications fully meet the requirements of competence to practice in terms of current professional knowledge and standards of practice.

QUALIFICATION INQUIRIES

For all grades of these positions, confidential inquiries, including contacts with the applicant's supervisors and associates, or with other persons familiar with his qualifications, may be made to obtain further information about qualifications, character, and suitability for these positions.

SELECTIVE PLACEMENT

Some positions will require the background and approach of a particular method of practice. For such positions, consideration may be restricted to eligibles who possess the pertinent experience and knowledge required to perform the duties of the positions covered in this occupation. At grade GS–11 and above there are some positions that require experience specifically related to such fields of practice as programs of service to medical and psychiatric patients in hospitals and clinics, programs of rehabilitation for inmates of correctional institutions, or programs for the protection of children.

For some program specialist positions, some of the qualifying experience must have provided a knowledge of specific aspects of an agency program such as foster care, work with the ag-ing, services to unmarried mothers, community planning, volunteer services, etc.

Other positions may require experience which has provided a knowledge of one or more specific areas of child welfare, such as adoptions, foster family care, group care, day care, services to children in their own homes, homemaker service, services for mentally retarded and emotionally disturbed children, etc.

Some positions in *Medical Programs* require experience which has provided a knowledge of health and medical care social services for mothers and children.

Agencies requesting selective referrals must show the connection between the kind of training or experience on which they wish to base selective consideration and the duties of the position to be filled.

DRIVER'S LICENSE

For certain positions, applicants may be required to have a driver's license.

WRITTEN TEST

No written test is required. Applicants will be rated on a scale of 100 on the basis of education, experience, training, and personal qualifications in relation to the requirements of the specific position for which they are being considered. Ratings will be based upon competitors' statements in their applications and upon any additional evidence which may be secured through qualification inquiries or similar means.

SPECIAL PHYSICAL REQUIREMENTS

There may be a few positions in larger offices where the casework load would permit the employment of a blind person in a restricted area of activity.

HEALTH CARE POSITIONS

Physician's Assistant GS-7/11

DESCRIPTION OF WORK

Physician's Assistants help physicians by providing diagnostic and therapeutic medical care and services under the physician's supervision. The work requires knowledge of specific observation and examination procedures, and ability to perform designated diagnostic and therapeutic tasks. The work does not include the full scope of interpretation of medical findings requiring the professional background of the licensed physician.

In clinics or during hospital rounds, physician's assistants assist in the observation and evaluation of patients by performing such duties as taking case histories, conducting physical examinations, and ordering laboratory studies. As directed by a physician, physician's assistants carry out special procedures such as applying and removing casts, performing lumbar punctures, or suturing minor lacerations.

EXPERIENCE, TRAINING, AND RELATED REQUIREMENTS

REQUIREMENTS FOR GS-7

Candidates for positions at GS-7 must meet requirements (1) and (2) below:
(1) A broad background of knowledge of the medical environment, practices, and procedures such as would be acquired by a bachelor's degree in a health care occupation such as nursing, medical technology, or physical therapy or by 3 years of responsible and progressive health care experience such as medical corpsman, nursing assistant, or medical technician, *and*
(2) Successful completion of a course of study of at least 12 months, including clinical training or preceptorship, specifically designed for professional-caliber physician's assistants.

The course of study or training must be approved by a nationally-recognized professional medical body such as the American Medical Association or the Association of American Medical Colleges, or by a panel of physicians established by a Federal agency for this purpose.

REQUIREMENTS FOR GS-9 AND GS-11

In addition to the requirements for GS-7, the following amounts of pertinent professional-caliber experience comparable to the work of a physician's assistant are required for grades GS-9 and GS-11:

Grade	*Minimum amount of experience (years)*
GS-9	1
GS-11	2

The required education, training, and experience must have demonstrated the ability to perform professional-caliber medical work as a physician's assistant with minimal supervision, including the exercise of a degree of judgment in integrating and interpreting diagnostic findings and in determining the need for referral to a physician.

For all grades, at least 6 months of the required experience must have been at the level of difficulty comparable to that of the next lower grade, or 1 year comparable to the second lower grade, in the Federal service.

ACCEPTANCE OF PROFESSIONAL MEDICAL EDUCATION

Candidates who have completed 3 full years of a curriculum in an accredited medical school

94

leading to the doctor of medicine or doctor of osteopathy degree may be rated eligible at GS–9.

Candidates who have completed the requirements for the degree of doctor of medicine or osteopathy but who lack licensure to practice medicine in the United States, may be rated eligible at GS–11.

SELECTIVE PLACEMENT

Some positions demand specific competence in a particular specialty. For such positions, consideration may be limited to those candidates whose records show evidence of the required knowledges, abilities, skills, and personal characteristics.

BASIS OF RATING

Ratings will be based upon candidates' statements in their applications and all available evidence concerning the quality and scope of their knowledge and ability including the candidate's education, experience, training, avocations, and personal characteristics.

REQUIRED KNOWLEDGES AND ABILITIES

Candidates will be rated on the degree to which they possess the knowledges and abilities of the kinds listed below, as appropriate to the grade level:

1. Ability to identify a medical problem and determine appropriate action to meet the problem, including referral to a physician.
2. Knowledge and understanding of the environment, principles, ethics, and special human relationships in the field of medicine.
3. Knowledge of the medical, biological, and physical sciences related to the applicable area of medicine.
4. Knowledge of and ability to perform specified diagnostic and therapeutic practices and procedures.
5. Ability to work responsibly with physicians and other members of the medical team, and to deal effectively with patients.
6. Ability to communicate effectively, both orally and in writing.

Nonsupervisory Nonprofessional Nursing Care Positions GS–1/6
Nursing Aid
Nursing Assistant
Operating Room Nursing Assistant
Psychiatric Nursing Assistant

DESCRIPTION OF WORK

Nursing Aids, under close supervision, perform simple and repetitive personal and nursing care procedures. Nursing aid positions are normally established for training purposes.

Nursing Assistants receive on-the-job training in nursing care which requires some knowledge of human body functions and behavior for the purpose of providing personal nursing care, support duties for diagnostic procedures, technical treatment procedures, patient charting, and patient teaching.

Operating Room Nursing Assistants assist registered nurses and surgeons in a variety of operating room and delivery room activities. They position and drape patients, ensure proper lighting, pass instruments and materials, maintain sterile conditions, assist in sponge and needle counts, and dispose of contaminated materials.

Psychiatric Nursing Assistants give general nursing care, observe and report changes in behavior, and provide reassurance and technical support to mentally ill patients.

EXPERIENCE, TRAINING, AND RELATED REQUIREMENTS

Except for the substitutions provided for below, candidates must have had qualifying experience in the amounts shown in the following table:

Minimum Amounts of Experience

Grade	General experience (years)	Specialized experience (years)	Total experience (years)
GS–1	none	none	*none
GS–2	½	none	½
GS–3	1	none	1
GS–4	1½	½	2
GS–5	2	1	3
GS–6	2	2	4

*It should be noted that for grade GS–1, no experience, training or education is required. No written test is required. Candidates must be willing to do personal and nursing care work and show evidence of likelihood of success in assignments.

GENERAL EXPERIENCE

This is experience which has demonstrated the ability:
(1) to learn and perform nursing care duties;
(2) to deal successfully with people; and
(3) to be adaptable to the work situation.

SPECIALIZED EXPERIENCE

This is experience in nonprofessional nursing care work in a hospital, outpatient clinic, nursing home, or other supervised medical, nursing, or patient care facility. Illustrative examples of nursing care work follow:
(1) Caring for mentally ill patients, including observing, recording, and reporting changes in their behavior;
(2) Providing reassurance and encouragement to mentally ill patients;
(3) Assisting surgeons and registered nurses in operating room activities, including passing instruments, maintaining sterile conditions, and draping and positioning patients;
(4) Providing pre- and post-operative care; and
(5) Setting up and operating special medical equipment and apparatus.

Candidates are not required to be proficient in all tasks listed above. However, their experience, education, and training must clearly show that they possess the skills and knowledges required to perform the work of the job at the grade level for which application is made. As a minimum, the candidate must show:
(*1*) A practical knowledge of:
   (a) human body structure,
   (b) sterile techniques and procedures, and
   (c) how to meet, deal, and work with medical, surgical, and psychiatric patients; and
(*2*) Knowledge of, and skill in, the performance of personal and nursing care procedures and techniques pertinent to the specialized area and grade for which application is made.

QUALITY AND LEVEL OF EXPERIENCE

Applicants must demonstrate progressively responsible experience of a scope, quality, and degree such as to have equipped them with the ability to perform duties at the grade level of the position for which application is made. Typically, this is demonstrated by accomplishment of assignments of the difficulty and responsibility described in the position classification standard used to evaluate positions at the next lower grade in the normal line of promotion to the position being filled.

SUBSTITUTION OF EDUCATION AND TRAINING FOR EXPERIENCE

Successfully completed education and training of acceptable type and quality may be substituted for experience requirements as specified below:

(*1*) Graduation from a high school or its equivalent may be substituted in full for the experience requirements at the GS–2 level. (High school education or its equivalent may not be substituted for any part of the experience requirements for GS–3 and above.)

(*2*) Successful completion of a 2-year associate degree program in an accredited community college, junior college, or college or university in a field of study appropriate to the specialization of the position being filled, psychiatric technician, or operating room technician may be substituted for the 2 years of experience required for GS–4.

(*3*) Partial completion of professional or practical nurse training in a school approved by the State-approving body may be substituted on a month-for-month basis up to 1 year of specialized experience when the following provisions are met. The candidate must have been in good standing when the training was interrupted. In order to substitute the training for specialized experience, the applicant must have satisfactorily completed courses which involved clinical practice in medical and surgical nursing and infant and child care. Candidates lacking clinical practice in infant and child care may substitute clinical practice in psychiatric or another specialized field of nursing. Any excess specialized training may be credited as general experience.

(*4*) Education and training other than that outlined above will be allowed appropriate credit for either general or specialized experience, depending upon its applicability and extent.

The maximum amount of experience for which education or training of any kind may be substituted is 3 years (2 years of general and 1 year of specialized experience).

WRITTEN TEST

Candidates for positions at GS–2 and GS–3 must pass a written test of abilities necessary to learn and perform the duties of these positions. The written test should be waived for candidates who qualify on the basis of successful completion of specialized education or training that is substitutable for specialized experience.

BASIS OF RATING

Applicants who meet the minimum qualification requirements, including a passing score on the written test, when required, will be rated on a scale of 70 to 100 based on:

For positions at grade GS–1—an evaluation of the applicant's willingness to do simple and repetitive work of the occupation, dependability, and ability to work safely;

For positions at grades GS–2/3—the applicant's score on the written test or for those competitors not required to pass the written test (see Written Test section above), an evaluation of education, training, and/or experience; and

For positions at grade GS–4 and above—an evaluation of the quality and extent of the applicant's experience, education, training, or other achievements pertinent to the duties of the position to be filled.

For Positions in the Public Health Nurse Occupation, Grades GS–5/15

Public Health Nurse
Consulting Public Health Nurse
Public Health Nurse (Training)
Research Public Health Nurse

DESCRIPTION OF WORK

Public health nurses supervise or give public health nursing care, health teaching, and guidance to individuals and families in homes and schools. Such positions typically are found in public health nursing services which emphasize comprehensive care for mothers and children, and services to patients having communicable diseases and chronic illnesses.

A few public health nurse positions primarily involve advice and consultation on public health nursing programs, teaching or training in public health nursing programs, teaching or training in public health nursing, or research in public health nursing.

EDUCATION, EXPERIENCE, AND OTHER REQUIREMENTS

I. BASIC EDUCATIONAL REQUIREMENTS

Candidates for all positions must meet one of the following requirements:

A. Graduation from a baccalaureate or higher degree program in nursing approved by the legally-designated State approving body. To be acceptable the program must have been accredited by the nationally recognized accrediting agency (or else must have included course content and field practice in public health nursing equivalent to that of programs that are accredited).

B. Graduation from either a diploma or associate degree program in professional nursing approved by the legally-designated State approving body and at least 1 academic year in a university public health nursing program accredited by the nationally recognized accrediting agency.

C. Graduation from a foreign school of professional nursing, provided that the nursing education and the nursing knowledge acquired therefrom are substantially comparable and equivalent to that of graduates of nursing schools as described in paragraph A above. Such equivalence must have been evaluated by a school of nursing accredited by the nationally recognized accrediting agency as equivalent to that of its program.

Candidates for positions which involve highly technical research or development or comparable highly technical and scientific functional areas of nursing work must meet the requirements described in paragraph A above.

II. REGISTRATION REQUIREMENTS

Applicants for all positions must have active, current registration as a professional nurse in a State, District of Columbia, the Commonwealth of Puerto Rico, or a Territory of the United States.

An applicant who has, within the past 12 months, graduated from a baccalaureate or higher degree program in nursing approved by the legally-designated State approving body, with qualifying preparation in public health nursing, may be appointed at the entrance grade level for which qualified pending attaining State registration as a professional nurse within 6 months after appointment. No person appointed pending registration may be retained beyond 6 months or promoted if registration has not been attained.

GS–5.—The basic requirements which apply to all grades are fully qualifying for grade GS–5.

ADDITIONAL EXPERIENCE AND TRAINING REQUIREMENTS

Candidates for grades GS–7 and above must have had either professional experience or graduate education (or an equivalent combination of both) in addition to meeting the basic educational requirements. Such professional experience must have been in public health nursing, general nursing, or another specialty area of nursing that is directly applicable to the position to be filled. For GS–9 at least 1 year, and for GS–11 and above at least 2 years of the required professional nursing experience must have been in the public health nursing field.

Such graduate education must have been in nursing in a field that is directly applicable to the position to be filled. An exception to this requirement is that 1 year of the graduate education may have been in directly related fields. Graduate education in the "directly related fields" is qualifying for grade GS–7 only.

1. EXPERIENCE

In addition to the basic educational requirements, the following amounts of professional experience are required for grades GS–7 and above:

Grade:	Minimum amount of professional experience in appropriate subject-matter fields (years)
GS–7	1
GS–9	2
GS–11 and above	3

For grades GS–11 and below, at least 6 months of the required experience must have been at the level of difficulty comparable to that of the next lower grade, or 1 year comparable to the second lower grade, in the Federal service. For grades GS–12 and above, at least 1 year of the required experience must have been at a level of difficulty comparable to that of the next lower grade in the Federal service.

2. EDUCATION

In addition to the basic educational requirements, the following amounts and levels of education are qualifying for grades GS–7 and above, as shown:

Grade	Minimum amount or level of education in appropriate subject-matter fields
GS–7	One full academic year of graduate education.
GS–9	Completion of all requirements for a master's or equivalent degree; *or* Two full academic years of graduate education.
GS–11	Completion of all requirements for a doctoral degree (Ph.D. or equivalent); *or* Three full academic years of graduate education.

3. COMBINATIONS OF PROFESSIONAL EXPERIENCE AND GRADUATE EDUCATION

Equivalent combinations of professional experience and graduate education of the types described above are acceptable at each grade.

4. ALTERNATE REQUIREMENTS

Superior academic achievement at the baccalaureate level or 1 year of student trainee experience is qualifying at grade GS–7. A combination of superior academic achievement at the baccalaureate level and 1 year of appropriate professional experience is qualifying at grade GS–9.

SELECTIVE PLACEMENT

Some public health nurse positions demand specific competence in a particular specialty and/or in special functional areas such as giving advice and consultation, teaching, research. For such positions, consideration may be limited to those candidates whose records show evidence of the required knowledges, abilities, skills, and personal characteristics.

PERSONAL CHARACTERISTICS REQUIRED

Public health nurse positions require the ability (a) to work harmoniously and effectively with others in the organization and (b) to establish and maintain satisfactory working relationships with others in hospitals, clinics, the school, social agencies, etc. Public health nurses must have the ability to inspire confidence and motivate patients and the patient's family to follow the treatment program and to use the available health facilities.

Many public health nurses perform their work in homes and schools in which direction and supervision may not be immediately available. In these situations the work requires an extra measure of personal traits such as maturity, objectivity, resourcefulness, and sound judgment.

Some public health nurses require the knowledges, abilities, and skills to give advice and leadership to States and/or localities on the nursing aspects of health services in a specialty area such as maternal and child health, psychiatry, tuberculosis, etc.

These factors should be considered in evaluating candidates in relationship to the requirements of the specific position to be filled.

INTERVIEW

Applicants who meet the education, experience, and other requirements may be requested to appear for an employment interview.

QUALIFICATION INQUIRIES

Reference inquiries, including contacts with candidate's teachers, supervisors, or other persons familiar with the candidate's qualifications, may be made to obtain further information about the candidate's professional and personal qualifications for these positions.

BASIS OF RATING

No written test is required. Applicants will be rated on the extent and quality of their education and experience.

Nurse GS–4/15

Occupational Coverage: Nurse, Clinical Nurse, Community Health Nurse, Occupational Health Nurse, Operating Room Nurse, Psychiatric Nurse, Nurse Anesthetist, Nurse Consultant, Nurse Educator, Nurse Midwife, Nurse Practitioner, Nurse Specialist, Research Nurse.

DESCRIPTION OF WORK

Nurses apply a professional knowledge of nursing to advise on, administer, supervise, or perform direct or indirect care of patients in hospitals, clinics, health units, homes, schools, and communities; they administer anesthetic agents and supportive treatments to patients undergoing surgery or other medical procedures; promote better health practices; teach;

perform research; act as nurse midwives or consult with and advise nurses who provide direct care to patients.

Professional nursing includes a wide variety of categories of work, many of which are highly specialized. For example:

Clinical Nurses provide direct nursing service in the assessment, planning, implementation and evaluation of patient care in hospitals, clinics or other patient care facilities. They frequently work in a specialized clinical area, e.g., surgical ward, ambulatory care, emergency room.

Community Health Nurses provide therapeutic services and coordinate patient and family health information and services to, between, or in homes, hospitals, clinics, schools and communities. They function as client advocates and promote the health maintenance activities of early detection and prevention.

Occupational Health Nurses provide nursing and health services to employees in relation to their occupations and working environments. This entails both the nursing care and treatment of injuries and illnesses of employees, and participation in preventive health programs, health education, and counseling aimed at prevention of disease and health maintenance, and environmental surveys.

Operating Room Nurses provide specialized nursing care to meet the needs of patients undergoing surgical procedures, providing for patient counseling and continuity of care. This involves responsibility for and supervision of the preparation of the operating room and necessary equipment, and for the scheduling of facilities and personnel.

Psychiatric Nurses provide direct nursing service to patients in psychiatric hospitals, psychiatric units in general medical and surgical hospitals, or mental health clinics. This work requires advanced knowledges, skills, and experience in counseling and guidance, and communicative skills which contribute to the redirection of behavior of patients or their families.

Nurse Anesthetists administer anesthetic agents and provide supportive treatment to patients undergoing surgery or other medical procedures.

Nurse Consultants provide consultative and advisory service with respect to one or more facets of the nursing field. They work independently, and the services cover a broad range of activities involving assessing, planning, implementing, coordinating and evaluating nursing programs both within and outside the employing agency.

Nurse Educators develop, provide and administer educational programs and activities for nurses. They teach courses, develop technical phases of educational programs, plan curriculum content and methods of teaching, and advise on the application of approved educational methods for individual schools and communities.

Nurse Midwives provide care for mothers and babies throughout an essentially normal maternity cycle within the framework of a medically directed health service, and are responsible for management, counseling and teaching.

Nurse Practitioners, through advanced competence in primary health care, provide direct, comprehensive nursing, preventive and therapeutic health services to individuals, families or groups. This includes assessing the health status of individuals, managing the care of selected patients, and providing treatment, health teaching, counseling, guidance, and instructions to individuals/families so that they participate in a plan of care.

Nurse Specialists have an advanced level of competence in the special field for which applying, with experience in clinical practice that demonstrates ability to develop innovative techniques, practices and approaches for patient care.

Research Nurses perform, participate in and/or direct research activities toward development of new or expanded knowledge of the field of nursing or health systems which improve patient care and enhance the clinical practice of nursing.

BASIC REGISTRATION REQUIREMENTS FOR ALL NURSE POSITIONS

Applicants for nurse positions must have active, current registration as a professional nurse in a State, District of Columbia, the Commonwealth of Puerto Rico, or a Territory of the United States.

An applicant who has within the past 12 months, graduated from a school of professional nursing approved by a legally designated State approving agency at the time of graduation, may be appointed at the entrance grade level for which qualified pending attaining State registration as a professional nurse within 6 months after appointment. No person appointed pending registration may be retained beyond 6 months or promoted if registration has not been attained.

BASIC EDUCATIONAL REQUIREMENTS FOR ALL NURSE POSITIONS

Candidates for positions at all grades must meet one of the following requirements:

A. Graduation with a bachelor's or higher degree in nursing from a school of professional nursing, approved by the legally designated State accrediting agency at the time the program was completed by the candidate.

B. Graduation from a 3-year (at least 30 months) diploma program of professional nursing approved by the legally designated State accrediting agency at the time the program was completed by the candidate.

C. Graduation from an associate degree program or other program of at least 2 years, in a school of professional nursing approved by the legally designated State accrediting agency at the time the program was completed by the candidate.

D. Graduation from a school of professional nursing (including foreign schools), of at least 2 years in length other than one covered by A, B, or C above, provided that the professional nurse training and the nursing knowledge acquired therefrom are substantially comparable and equivalent to that of graduates of an approved school as described above. Comparability should be evaluated by a State Board of Nursing. Registration as defined above meets this requirement.

NOTE.—Successfully completed college level course work in nursing, the behavioral, physical or biological sciences related to nursing; nutrition; public health; and maternal and child health in excess of the minimum basic education requirement may be substituted for professional nursing experience at the rate of 1 academic year of appropriate education for 9 months of professional nursing experience in establishing eligibility for the GS–5 level. Tutorial or remedial work cannot be substituted.

BASIC EDUCATIONAL REQUIREMENTS FOR CERTAIN SPECIALIZED POSITIONS

In addition to meeting the basic requirements for all nurse positions:

Community Health Nurse.—Candidates for these positions at GS–5 and above must have graduated from a baccalaureate or higher degree program in nursing approved by the legally designated State approving body.

Nurse Anesthetist.—Candidates for nurse anesthetist positions at GS–9 and above must have graduated from at least an 18 month course in a school of anesthesia for nurses accredited by the American Association of Nurse Anesthetists for the year of the applicant's graduation.

Nurse Midwife.—Candidates for nurse midwife positions must have completed an organized program of study and clinical experience recognized by the American College of Nurse Midwives.

ENTRY LEVEL CREDIT FOR MILITARY EXPERIENCE

Nurse experience gained while in the military as a military corpsman will be accepted for initial appointment at grade GS–4 to the extent that it is accepted by a State licensing body.

EDUCATION AND EXPERIENCE ABOVE THE ENTRY LEVELS

Candidates for grades GS–7 and above must have had either professional experience or graduate education (or an equivalent combination of both) in addition to meeting the basic educational requirements for all nurse positions. Such professional experience must have been in nursing. Such graduate education must have been in nursing with a concentration in a field of nursing or closely related non-nursing fields directly applicable to the requirements for the position to be filled.

1. EXPERIENCE

The required amounts of professional experience are:

	Associate degree program or diploma program of less than 30 months (years)	Diploma program of 30 months or more (years)	Baccalaureate degree program (years)
GS–4	0	0	0
GS–5	1	0	0
GS–7	2	1	1
GS–9	3	2	2
GS–11 and above	4	3	3

For positions at GS–5: graduates of an associate degree or diploma nursing program of less than 30 months' duration may have experience as a practical nurse or nursing assistant (either voluntary or paid) credited for grade GS–5 on a month-for-month basis to a maximum of 12 months. The practical nurse or nursing experience must have been:

(a) gained under the supervision of a professional nurse;

(b) equivalent to GS–4 or higher; and

(c) relevant to the position to be filled.

For grades GS–7 through 11 at least 6 months of the professional nursing experience must have been at the level of difficulty comparable to that of the next lower grade in the Federal service, or 1 year comparable to the second lower grade.

For specialized positions at GS–9 and above, 1 year of professional nursing experience must be sufficiently related to the specialty in both subject-matter and grade-level, to demonstrate the candidate's ability to perform the major duties of the position being filled.

Candidates for positions at GS–12 and above must have at least 1 year of experience at the next lower grade, and must demonstrate a record of accomplishment, professional competence, leadership, and recognition in the profession as in the planning, organizing, directing, and coordinating of nursing projects, or in well-established service as an expert and consultant.

2. EDUCATION

In addition to the basic requirements, the following amounts and levels of education are qualifying for grades GS–7 and above, as shown:

Grade:	Minimum amount or level of education in appropriate subject-matter fields
GS–7	One full academic year of graduate education.
GS–9	Completion of all requirements for a master's or equivalent degree *or* Two full academic years of graduate education.
GS–11	Completion of all requirements for a doctoral degree (Ph. D. or equivalent) *or* Three full academic years of graduate education.

Currency of Knowledges and Skills

At all grade levels, greater credit may be given to applicants who have knowledges of and skills in current nursing practices.

Alternate Requirements

Superior academic achievement at the baccalaureate level is qualifying at grade GS–7. A combination of superior academic achievement at the baccalaureate level and 1 year of appropriate professional experience is qualifying at grade GS–9.

3. COMBINATIONS OF PROFESSIONAL EXPERIENCE AND GRADUATE EDUCATION

Equivalent combinations of professional experience and graduate education of the types described above are acceptable at each grade. Specialized areas of nursing (see Description of Work) may require particular specialized education and experience.

POSSIBLE SELECTIVE FACTORS

Many nursing positions GS–9 and above demand competence in a particular area, gained through specialized experience and/or training. Selective factors for these positions should be reflected in the knowledges, skills and abilities described in the position description.

INTERVIEW

Applicants who meet the education, experience, and other requirements may be required to appear for an employment interview.

QUALIFICATION INQUIRIES

Reference inquiries, including contacts with candidate's teachers, supervisors, or other persons familiar with the candidate's qualifications may be made to obtain further information about the candidate's professional and personal qualifications for these positions.

BASIS FOR RATING

No written test is required. Applicants will be rated on the extent and quality of their education and experience. Such ratings will be based upon the applicant's statements in the application and upon any additional information that may be secured, including that secured by inquiries made to supervisors, schools and other references.

Dietitian GS–5/15
Nutritionist GS–5/15
Public Health Nutritionist GS–9/15

DESCRIPTION OF WORK

Dietitians and nutritionists advise on, administer, supervise, or perform work which requires the application of a professional knowledge of the science of nutrition. Dietitians and nutritionists are both concerned with human nutrition needs and are responsible for the development of diet plans or programs for individuals or groups, for instructing others in nutrition matters, and for applying a knowledge of socioeconomic conditions which affect the eating habits of individuals and groups. Dietitians usually perform work which is associated with institutional health care, such as hospitals, domiciliaries, or privately operated group care facilities in the community, and involves responsibility for individual diet plans and for the management of the food service system. Public Health Nutritionists perform work associated with public health services and programs designed to meet the health needs of target groups within the population, such as maternal and child health, geriatrics, and American Indians. Nutritionists perform in nontreatment food assistance programs designed to help target groups within the population, or in research. Major specialties and subspecialties are summarized as follows:

Dietitians are responsible for nutritional care in managing individual or group feeding, in imparting knowledge concerning food and nutrition, and in applying knowledge to developing and implementing plans for health maintenance and/or improvement.

Administrative Dietitians are members of the management team, responsible for planning and evaluating the food service system, directing and managing food service personnel, planning budgets and managing resources, establishing standards of safety and sanitation, developing specifications for the procurement of equipment and supplies, and developing menu patterns and evaluating client acceptance.

Clinical Dietitians are members of the health care team concerned with continuously providing for the nutritional needs of individuals and groups in acute, intermediate, long-term care and hospital based community care facilities generally involving a specialized program. They are primarily concerned with assessing nutritional needs, developing therapeutic diets, recording progress in the medical records, providing nutritional education to the patient and family, and recommending changes to the physician. A dietitian may be responsible for one or more wards in a hospital involving patients with general or specialized problems, or for a nutrition or an outpatient clinic which provides similar care for ambulatory or outpatients.

Community Dietitians serve as members of the community health team, responsible for assessing the nutritional needs of individuals and groups located in nursing homes, private homes, or other group care facilities, and for evaluating and advising on the nutritional services provided by the institution to the individual.

Research Dietitians assist physicians or research scientists by planning the diet for the proposed study, by developing precise and complete data on patient nutrient intake and output, and by stimulating participation by patients or volunteer subjects.

Consultant Dietitians provide advice or services in nutritional care which affect the management of resources, such as the evaluating of food service systems, developing budgets and records systems, developing educational materials, recommending layout designs and equipment needs, or counseling clients and consulting with health care teams.

Teaching Dietitians plan, schedule or conduct educational programs for professional staff development, inservice training of nonprofessional staff, and may include training for medical interns, nurses, volunteers, patients, or dietetic interns or students.

Nutritionists are specialists in human nutrition concerned with nutritional or food assistance services provided by social, agricultural, or educational agencies to target populations. They perform such duties as assessing nutritional needs of groups, evaluating the nutrition component of programs, interpreting nutrition research or legislation, provide consultation and training, or participating in research.

Public Health Nutritionists serve as members of the health team, and are responsible for planning and administering the community nutrition program for a geographical area or specialty area. This involves such duties as assessing the nutritive quality of food eaten by people in the community; providing consultation and training to administrators, health professionals, and food service personnel in a variety of programs with a food service, nutrition education, and/or health component; conducting dietary studies and providing patient education to groups or individuals in normal and therapeutic nutrition; and consult-

ing on the development and improvement of standards or services provided.

Nutritionists in specialized areas. Current major specializations include maternal and child health, school nutrition and health, group feeding, gerontology, chronic disease, rehabilitation, clinical dietetics, group food service, research, education, and training. The nutritionist plans, develops, implements, evaluates, and promotes the nutrition component of the specialty area to serve the needs of the target population.

Community Nutritionists function as members of the community health team assessing nutrition needs of individuals and groups in the community and providing education and information through individual and group counseling, and through displays, newspapers, radios, and other informational devices.

Nutritionists in Administration plan policy and action related to changing health, service or program needs as influenced by nutrition practices and socioeconomic forces, determine program priorities through the projection of anticipated benefits and expected costs, and evaluate the effectiveness of program services provided.

EXPERIENCE AND TRAINING REQUIREMENTS

1. BASIC REQUIREMENTS FOR ALL GRADES

Successful completion of a full 4-year course of study in an accredited college or university creditable toward a baccalaureate or higher degree in dietetics, food, nutrition, food service management, institution management, or closely related science.

Dietitian: For positions of dietitian the curriculum must have been in accordance with the qualifying requirements established by The American Dietetic Association (ADA) in effect at the time of graduation. (Professional registration as a registered dietitian (R.D.) is evidence of meeting ADA requirements.)

GS–5—For dietitians and nutritionists, completion of the basic requirement is qualifying for GS–5.

Public Health Nutritionist: Successful completion of a master's degree in public health nutrition, community nutrition, or in nutrition supplemented by public health courses from an accredited college or university.

GS-9—For public health nutritionists, completion of the basic requirement is qualifying for GS-9.

2. ADDITIONAL EXPERIENCE AND TRAINING REQUIREMENTS

Candidates for grades GS-7 and above must have had either professional experience or graduate education, or an equivalent combination of both, in addition to meeting the basic requirements. This professional experience or graduate education must have been in or directly related to dietetics or nutrition, or in a field closely related to the position to be filled.

a. Experience
In addition to the basic requirements, the following amounts of professional experience are required for grades GS-7 and above:

Grade:	Years
GS-7	1
GS-9	2
GS-11 and above	3

Completion of a coordinated undergraduate program, internship, or other clinical component approved by The American Dietetic Association, which was conducted as part of the undergraduate program, or after completion of the basic requirements for a baccalaureate degree, is qualifying at grade GS-7 for dietitians or nutritionists.

Candidates possessing professional registration as a Registered Dietitian meet the full requirements for eligibility at GS-7.

For grades GS-11 and below at least 6 months of the required experience must have been at a level of difficulty comparable to that of the next lower grade or 1 year comparable to the second lower grade in the Federal service. For grades GS-12 and above at least 1 year of the required experience must have been at a level of difficulty comparable to that of the next lower grade in the Federal service.

For any grade, the required amount of experience will not, in itself, be accepted as proof of qualification for a position. The quality of experience, rather than its length, will be given primary consideration. The applicant's total education and experience must give positive evidence of ability to perform all of the duties of the position.

b. Substitution of Education for Experience
In addition to the basic requirements, the following amounts and levels of education are qualifying for grades GS-7 and above. This education must have been either in dietetics or nutrition, or in directly related fields such as public health nutrition.

GS-7.... One full academic year of graduate education.

GS-9.... Completion of all requirements for a master's or equivalent degree; or two full academic years of graduate education.

GS-11... Completion of all requirements for a doctoral degree (Ph.D. or equivalent); or,
Three full academic years of graduate education.

c. Combinations of professional experience and graduate education.
Equivalent combinations of professional experience and graduate education of the type described above are acceptable at each grade.

Professional experience is defined as nonroutine work that required and was characterized by (1) a knowledge of the principles, theories, and methods of dietetics or nutrition; (2) ability to apply such knowledge in the work situation; and (3) positive and continuing development of knowledge and ability, to keep abreast of the advancing and changing discipline.

d. Superior academic achievement
Superior academic achievement cannot be substituted for experience requirements of positions in this series.

EMPLOYMENT INTERVIEW

Applicants who meet the education, experience, and other requirements may be requested to appear for an employment interview.

BASIS OF RATING

No written test is required. Candidates will be rated on the extent, quality and recency of their experience and training, since a professional must keep abreast of constant changes in technology and trends. Ratings will be based upon candidates' statements in their applications and upon any additional information that may be secured, including that secured by inquiries made to supervisors, schools, and other references.

SELECTIVE FACTORS

For some specialized positions, only candidates who possess specific job-related knowledges, skills, and/or abilities may be qualified. For example, if a position requires highly developed skill in research techniques or in maternal and child care, that skill or knowledge may be used as an "in-or-out" selective placement factor. Justification for selective placement factors must show: (a) how the selective factor is directly related to the duties and responsibilities of the position; and (b) why possession of the knowledges, skills, and/or abilities identified as selective factors are necessary for successful performance in the position.

Specialized requirements, for example, are most commonly found in the following areas:

—Research positions, some of which require advanced preparation in dietetics or nutrition as well as in research techniques, to plan, investigate, interpret, evaluate, apply, and expand knowledge in one or more phases of dietetics or nutrition, and to communicate findings through reports and publications.

—Teaching positions, some of which require advanced preparation in dietetics, nutrition, and/or education, to plan, conduct, and evaluate educational programs in one or more dietetic or nutrition subject matter areas.

—Professional registration, (or other acceptable evidence of demonstrated ability to perform at the required level), is required for many positions of director of a dietetic or public health nutrition program in a hospital or other health care facility.

GUIDE FOR EVALUATION OF CANDIDATES

CANDIDATES FOR POSITIONS AT GS–5/7

Evaluation of candidates for these grades is based largely on their academic career, with consideration also being given to any experience they may have had.

1. Education: When evaluating a candidate's academic record, consideration should be given to the extent to which the courses successfully completed contribute to the basic knowledge required in the particular position to be filled.

2. Internship: In evaluating experience gained through an internship, the experience should be related to the duties to be performed.

3. Registration: A Registered Dietitian is a person who meets the qualifications established by the Commission on Dietetic Registration of The American Dietetic Association. Among the requirements for registration are successful completion of the examination for professional registration and the maintaining of continuing education requirements. Since the purpose of the examination and the continuing education requirements is to assure that the dietitian possesses and maintains the common core of knowledge of the profession, registration may be considered in the evaluation of the candidates.

CANDIDATES FOR POSITIONS AT GS–9 AND ABOVE

For positions at these levels, evaluation of undergraduate college training is less important than the consideration of graduate education and professional work experience. The same factors that are used to evaluate the undergraduate academic record may also be used to evaluate the graduate record.

1. The evaluation of a candidate's work experience should consider its nature and significance, its relationship to the requirements of the position, and whether it has involved the performance of professional work of increasing difficulty and complexity, and the assumption of more responsibility.

2. Candidates qualifying on the basis of a master's degree or Ph.D. may be evaluated for completion of a clinical component.

3. Registration by the Commission on Dietetic Registration of The American Dietetic Association may be considered in the evaluation of candidates for positions of dietitian or public health nutritionist.

4. Candidates may also be evaluated for active membership in and presentations before professional organizations, technical publications, participation in seminars and study groups, patents, awards, etc. Technical publications should be evaluated for their contribution to advancing knowledge in dietetics and nutrition, rather than on their quantity alone.

5. Recency of education and experience, and evidence of continuing education in dietetics and nutrition and in related fields, are important elements of full professional competence and may be considered in the evaluation of candidates.

6. Candidates for positions at GS–9 and above should also be evaluated for such skills and abilities as:
—Ability to plan work and evaluate results;
—Skill in analyzing, adapting, or developing materials, such as criteria, specifications, menus, and patient's needs and progress;
—Skill in interpersonal relationships, such as leadership, flexibility, and persuasiveness;
—Skill in oral communications for explaining nutrition to individuals or groups having a wide range of backgrounds, and for teaching students, other professionals, and communicating with groups;
—Skill in written communications for developing technical reports, informational materials, specifications, procedures, and similar tools;
—Ability to stay abreast of changes and new developments within the discipline and closely related areas;
—Ability to work independently, including originating workable solutions.

SPECIAL PHYSICAL REQUIREMENTS

Most positions involve moderate physical exertion, including moving substantial distances, within hospitals or similar facilities, standing, bending, and lifting of light objects, such as medical or procurement records. Ability to read printed material and handwriting, is required in most positions, as well as the ability to communicate effectively and efficiently with patients and others. Many positions involve some amount of exposure to contagious diseases, noise and hazards of kitchen equipment. Protective clothing is required in some situations. A few positions require travel to remote parts of the country.

Dental Aid, GS–1
Dental Assistant, GS–2/5
Dental Assistant (Expanded Function), GS–5/6

DESCRIPTION OF WORK

Dental Assistants provide assistance to the dentist by receiving and preparing patients for dental treatment, preparing materials and equipment for use by the dentist, assisting the dentist at chairside or bedside in the treatment of patients, taking dental radiographs, and maintaining records related to appointments, examinations, treatment and supplies. Dental Assistants may work in general dentistry or in a specialized field of dentistry such as prosthodontics or oral surgery.

Dental Assistants (Expanded Function) are primarily concerned with the performance of reversible intra-oral procedures, such as placing and finishing restorations in teeth prepared by a dentist. Dental Assistants (Expanded Function) also perform chairside assistance and other services typically provided by dental assistants.

MINIMUM QUALIFYING EXPERIENCE

For positions at GS–1, no written test, experience, training, or education is required. Candidates must be willing to perform simple dental aid work and show ability to follow specific instructions. Evidence of this ability may be obtained from personal references, interviews, etc.

For positions at GS–2, six months of experience is required which has provided a knowledge of simple clinic maintenance procedures such as clearing work areas of used materials; replacing soiled linens; storing medical and dental supplies; and filing records in alphabetic or numeric order.

For positions at GS–3, one year of experience is required which has provided all of the following knowledges:

—knowledge of clinical routines and procedures such as receiving, routing, and scheduling patients, ordering supplies, requesting medical or dental laboratory work;
—knowledge of the use, care and storage of dental, medical, or laboratory instruments, materials and equipment;
—knowledge of sterilization techniques sufficient to sterilize dental instruments and materials; and
—knowledge of dental or medical terminology to maintain records related to patients, supplies and recurring medical or dental activities.

For positions at GS–4 and above, candidates must have had 1 year of qualifying experience at the next lower grade in the General Schedule or equivalent experience outside the General Schedule. Qualifying experience at this level is experience in dental assistance to general or specialized dentistry, dental assistant (expanded function) work or any combination of these appropriate to the position being filled.

SUBSTITUTIONS OF EDUCATION AND TRAINING FOR EXPERIENCE

1. For positions at GS–2, completion of a full four-year high school curriculum or high school equivalency is qualifying.

2. For positions at GS–3, the following education and training may be substituted for experience requirements:

—successful completion of a one-year dental assistant program or completion of one year of a dental hygiene program accredited by the American Dental Association's Com-

mission on Accreditation is fully qualifying;
—successful completion of practical nurse training approved by the appropriate State or District of Columbia accrediting body is qualifying;
—completion of education and training other than that outlined above, which is directly related to the routines, procedures, and terminology used in a medical or dental treatment situation may be substituted on a month-for-month basis for the experience requirements. Examples of this training may include, but are not limited to, the U.S. Armed Forces, manpower development, or inservice training programs.

3. For positions at GS–4, the following may be substituted:

—successful completion of a two-year dental assistant program or completion of a two-year dental hygiene program accredited by the American Dental Association's Commission on Accreditation is fully qualifying;
—other training and education which is directly applicable to the performance of dental assistant work may be substituted on a month-for-month basis for the experience requirements. Examples of this training include, the U.S. Armed Forces, manpower development, or inservice training programs.

4. Special Requirements for Dental Assistant (Expanded Function) positions, GS–5 and above.

Candidates for Dental Assistant (Expanded Function) positions must have completed one year of acceptable coursework, preceptorship, or other formal training and/or work assignments specifically designed to equip the candidate with the knowledges and skills required to perform intra-oral procedures involved in the position to be filled, including:

—knowledge of the methods and techniques used in dentistry to perform intra-oral procedures;
—knowledge of the characteristics of a variety of materials and instruments used in performing intra-oral procedures; and
—ability to recognize common dental disorders and conditions such as caries, formations of plaque and calculus, and inflammation of gums.

Examples of acceptable training are:
—courses in a dental hygiene or dental assist-

ant program accredited by the American Dental Association's Commission on Accreditation which are directly related to intra-oral procedures (also referred to as expanded functions) to be performed in the position to be filled;

—U.S. Army's Dental Therapy Assistant Training Program;

—continuing education courses in expanded functions for dental assistants offered by the Indian Health Service of Department of Health, Education, and Welfare;

—other training comparable to the above in private or governmental hospitals, clinics or schools which include formal classroom instruction and clinical training in the knowledges and skills required to perform intra-oral procedures in the position to be filled.

Training may be credited on a month-for-month basis for the experience requirements. Dental Assistant (Expanded Function) positions at GS–6 require one year experience comparable to that of GS–5 level Dental Assistant (Expanded Function).

A written test is required at grade GS–2 and is not to be waived for appointment outside the register, unless authorized by the Office of Personnel Management.

BASIS OF RATING AND RANKING CANDIDATES

Candidates who meet the minimum qualification requirements, including a passing score on the written test, when required, will be rated on a scale of 70 to 100 based on:

For positions at grade GS–1—an evaluation of the candidate's willingness to do simple and repetitive dental aid work, dependability, and ability to work safely.

For positions at grade GS–2—the candidate's score on the written test.

For positions at grades GS–3 and above—an evaluation of the quality and extent of the candidate's experience, education, training or other achievements pertinent to the duties of the position being filled.

In ranking candidates who have met the minimum experience requirements, candidates with dental assistant training should be ranked higher based on the recognition that dental assistant training is more specifically focused on the knowledge, skills, and abilities required by dental assisting work.

PERSONAL CHARACTERISTICS

Dental Assistant and Dental Assistant (Expanded Function) positions involve significant contacts with patients. Candidates must demonstrate the ability to work with patients in a tactful and courteous manner, and relieve fears, and comfort their patients.

SPECIAL PHYSICAL REQUIREMENTS

Usable vision is required and, depending on the essential duties of a specific position, usable hearing and speech may be required.

Dental Hygienist, GS–4/8
Community Health Dental Hygienist, GS–5 and Above

DESCRIPTION OF WORK

Dental Hygienists work in hospitals and outpatient clinics performing oral prophylaxis; applying topical fluorides and desensitizing agents to the teeth; performing examinations of the teeth and surrounding tissues involving the use of diagnostic tests and X-rays; preparing treatment plans for plaque control; instructing individual patients, patient groups, nurses and nursing assistants or other dental hygienists and dental assistants in the techniques and practice of maintaining oral health.

Community Health Dental Hygienists work primarily in nonclinical settings on military installations or in public health program areas planning and carrying out dental health programs to promote public awareness, acceptance, and practice of oral health measures for groups of individuals and communities. Typically, they plan and conduct oral health instructional programs directed toward the needs of various community groups, provide technical advice and assistance to dental personnel on public health matters relating to oral health, make onsite visits to provide policy guidance and insure consistency among areas in accomplishing the objectives of the dental program, conduct surveys and special studies to evaluate the effectiveness of the oral health program and to recommend new or improved methods of oral hygiene, plan and conduct dental inspection programs, develop teaching aids and materials used to improve the oral health of the community, present lectures and demonstrations in new or improved dental techniques and developments, and prepare and compile a variety of records and reports pertaining to the administration of the oral health program.

LICENSURE REQUIREMENTS

Applicants for all grades and specifications must be currently licensed to practice as dental hygienists in a State or territory of the United States or the District of Columbia.

EXPERIENCE REQUIREMENTS FOR CLINICAL DENTAL HYGIENE POSITIONS

For positions at GS–4, no experience is required.

For positions at GS–5, one year of experience as a licensed dental hygienist. This is experience in performing routine oral prophylactic care such as: scaling and polishing the teeth, applying topical flourides and desensitizing agents to the teeth, taking X-rays, sterilizing instruments and instructing patients at chairside in brushing and flossing techniques.

For positions at GS–6, two years of experience as a licensed dental hygienist of which at least one year included duties such as: examining the patient's teeth and surrounding tissues; cleaning, polishing, and applying topical fluorides and other anticariogenic agents to the teeth; treating common abnormalities such as inflammations of the gums; taking and interpreting X-rays for presence of caries and providing oral health care instructions to individuals and groups of patients.

For positions at GS–7, three years of experience as a licensed dental hygienist of which at least one year included duties such as: performing oral prophylaxis in cases of acute gingivitis and periodontal diseases requiring the use of a variety of scalers and ultrasound equipment; performing deep scaling, root planing, and subgingival curettage; taking intraoral impressions, placing temporary fillings; placing and removing rubber dams; planning dental hygiene treatment and series of appointments needed to complete treatment; providing oral hygiene instructions to patients with special problems, and training other hygienists and dental personnel in dental hygiene techniques and procedures.

For positions at GS–8, four years of experience as a licensed dental hygienist of which at least one year included advanced prophylactic and therapeutic hygiene procedures in the treatment of patients with related medical and dental problems. This includes duties such as: performing oral prophylaxis on ambulatory and nonambulatory patients requiring specialized procedures for bedridden patients; preparing dental hygiene treatment plans for patients including assessment of the oral problem, type of oral hygiene care required, and the sequence of appointments needed to complete treatment; presenting lectures and demonstrations to various patient groups such as diabetics and oral cancer patients requiring the use of motivation techniques, dental aids, and educational materials; performing advanced dental hygiene procedures such as root planing and curettage under local anesthesia, polishing and finishing amalgam restorations and inserting temporary fillings in teeth.

EDUCATION AND EXPERIENCE REQUIREMENTS FOR COMMUNITY HEALTH DENTAL HYGIENE POSITIONS

For positions at all grades applicants must meet the basic requirements specified under paragraph A or B below:

A. Successful completion of a full four-year course of study in an accredited college or university leading to a bachelor's degree which must have included or been supplemented by successful completion of a full academic curriculum in dental hygiene accredited by the American Dental Association's Commission on Dental Accreditation.

B. Experience in an amount which, in combination with successful completion of a full academic curriculum in dental hygiene accredited by the American Dental Association's Commission on Dental Accreditation, is sufficient to total at least four years of experience and education. Appropriate experience may be equated to education on a year-for-year basis. To be appropriate, this experience must have demonstrated that the applicant possesses the following:
—ability to plan and direct group activities.
—ability to organize, analyze, and evaluate data; to draw conclusions; and to make decisions or recommendations.
—ability to express ideas and communicate information orally and in writing in a clear, logical, and motivating manner.
—ability to demonstrate and/or present new ideas, techniques, and procedures.
—ability to conduct meetings and present lectures.
—ability to deal effectively with individuals and with groups.

For positions at GS–5, the basic requirements which apply to all grades are fully qualifying.

For positions at GS–7 and above, in addition to the basic requirements, the following amounts of specialized experience are required:

Grade:	Specialized experience (years)
GS–7	1
GS–9	2
GS–11 and above	3

Specialized experience is experience in dental hygiene or in a directly related kind of work. Examples of work which are considered specialized experience include:
—Experience in preparing and conducting educational lectures and demonstrations on dental hygiene.
—Experience in planning and developing public health type programs of broad scope, e.g., for varying age groups and types of audiences.
—Experience in supervising or instructing groups of dental hygienists in the performance of dental hygiene duties.
—Other experience in performing the duties of a community health dental hygienist as described in the "Description of Work" above.

SUBSTITUTION OF EDUCATION FOR EXPERIENCE

For Clinical Dental Hygiene Positions successful completion of a full four-year course of study in an accredited college or university leading to a bachelor's degree in Dental Hygiene or in a directly related field of study such as public health, health education, or education may be substituted in full for the experience required at grade GS–5.

For Community Health Dental Hygiene Positions successful completion of one full academic year of graduate education in dental hygiene or in a directly related field of study such as public health, health education, or education may be substituted in full for the specialized experience required at grade GS–7.

Successful completion of all requirements for a master's or equivalent degree in dental hygiene or in a directly related field of study may be substituted in full for the specialized experience requirements at grade GS–9.

Education may not be substituted for the full experience requirements above the grade GS–9.

QUALITY OF EXPERIENCE

Applicants must demonstrate progressively responsible experience of a scope, quality, and degree such as to have equipped them with the ability to perform duties at the grade level of the position for which the application is made. Typically, this is demonstrated by accomplishment of assignments of the difficulty and responsibility described in the position classification standard used to evaluate positions at the next lower grade in the normal line of promotion to the position being filled.

EMPLOYMENT INTERVIEW

Applicants who meet the minimum experience, training, and other requirements may be requested to appear for an employment interview.

BASIS OF RATING

No written test is required. Applicants will be rated on a scale of 70 to 100 based on an evaluation of the quality and extent of their experience, education, and training or other achievements pertinent to the duties of the positions to be filled. Such ratings will be based upon statements of candidates in their applications, upon qualification inquiries, and upon additional information that may be secured by the examining office.

For all positions, the rating of experience and education may take into account the recency of the experience and education. Extra credit may be given to applicants who show evidence of efforts to keep current in their field.

ACCREDITED SCHOOLS

A listing of accredited schools of dental hygiene may be secured from the American Dental Association, Commission on Dental Accreditation, 211 East Chicago Avenue, Chicago, Illinois 60611.

Pharmacy Aid GS–1/3
Pharmacy Technician GS–4/7

DESCRIPTION OF WORK

Pharmacy technicians perform, under the supervision of a registered pharmacist, a variety of technical support functions in a pharmacy. Pharmacy technicians receive, care for, store, distribute, and bulk compound pharmaceuticals, prepare sterile solutions, and set up prescriptions for a final check by a pharmacist.

EXPERIENCE, EDUCATION, AND TRAINING REQUIREMENTS

GRADE GS–1

For grade GS–1, no written test, experience, training, or education is required. Candidates

must be willing to perform simple routine pharmacy aid work and show evidence of likelihood of success on the job.

Experience requirements

Candidates must have had experience as described below. (Education may be substituted for experience.)

Grade	General experience (years)	Specialized experience (years)	Total experience (years)
GS–1	0	0	0
GS–2	½	0	½
GS–3	1	0	1
GS–4	1½	½	2
GS–5	2	1	3
GS–6	2	2	4
GS–7	2	3	5

General experience

General experience is that which has provided (*a*) a basic knowledge of laboratory procedures and equipment in chemical, biological, or medical laboratories, or (*b*) a background knowledge of the medical environment or hospital or pharmacy procedures.

Specialized experience

This is experience which has provided the knowledges and skills needed to perform pharmacy technician work. The specialized experience must have provided the candidate with a basic knowledge of pharmaceutical nomenclature; characteristics, strengths, and dosage forms of pharmaceuticals; pharmaceutical systems of weights and measures, operation and care of a variety of pharmaceutical equipment; and a variety of procedures and techniques involved in the care, storage, repackaging, bulk compounding, and distribution of pharmaceuticals.

OTHER GRADES

For GS−2 and GS−3, the general experience requirements are broad in intent and do not require any specialized knowledge or skill in pharmacy work.

For GS−4, the six months of specialized experience must have been comparable in difficulty and responsibility to the GS−3 level.

For GS−5, at least one year of the required experience must have been comparable in difficulty and responsibility to the GS−4 level. At least six months of this experience at the GS−4 level must have been specialized experience that included duties such as the care, storage, repackaging, bulk compounding, and distribution of pharmaceuticals.

For GS−6 and GS−7, at least one year of the required specialized experience must have been comparable in difficulty and responsibility to the next lower grade in the Federal service, or two years comparable to the second lower grade in the Federal service.

SUBSTITUTION OF EDUCATION FOR EXPERIENCE

Successfully completed education of acceptable type and quality may be substituted for the experience requirements at the various grade levels, as specified below:

1. Graduation from a full 4-year or senior high school, or possession of a General Education Development High School Equivalency Certificate, may be substituted in full for the experience requirements at the GS−2 level. (High school education, or the General Educational Development High School Equivalency Certificate, may not be substituted for any part of the experience requirements for GS−3 and above.)

2. Successful completion of one academic year of post-high school education that included a course in biology, chemistry, or physics may be substituted for one year of experience and meets in full the experience requirements for GS−3.

3. Successful completion of a course for (*a*) medical technicians, (*b*) hospital corpsmen, (*c*) medical service specialists, or (*d*) hospital training, obtained in a training program given by the Armed Forces or the U.S. Maritime Service under close medical and professional supervision, may be substituted on a month-for-month basis for general experience.

4. Successful completion of pertinent specialized training courses in pharmaceuticals and pharmacy practices while serving in the Armed Forces or in post-high school study may be substituted on a month-for-month basis for up to a total of one year of specialized experience.

5. Successful completion of two academic years of post-high school study in a resident school or institution of pharmacy or pharmacy technology which included course work in the care, storage, distribution, and preparation of pharmaceuticals, and appropriate laboratory work, may be substituted in full for two years of experience required at the GS−4 level (one and one-half years general and one-half year specialized).

6. Successful completion of four years of academic study in pharmacy may be substituted for three years of experience, including one year specialized experience. This meets in full the experience requirements at the GS−5 level.

Appropriate education and training other than that outlined above, such as in "new careers" training programs, manpower development programs, and inservice training programs will be granted credit depending upon its applicability and extent.

Post-high school education or training which is acceptable under these standards may be substituted for part of the required experience on a pro rata basis.

WRITTEN TEST

Candidates for positions at GS–2 and GS–3 must pass the written test of abilities necessary to learn and perform the duties of these positions. The written test may be waived for candidates, who have successfully completed the equivalent of a specialized training program in pharmacy of at least six months.

BASIS OF RATING

Competitors for all positions will be rated on the quality and extent of experience, education, or training in relationship to the duties of the positions. Ranking will be made on the following basis:

For GS–1: An evaluation of the applicant's willingness to do simple and repetitive pharmacy aid work; his dependability; and his ability to work safely.

For GS–2 and GS–3: Written test scores, or an evaluation of experience, education, and training of candidates who attained a passing score on the written test.

For GS–4 and above: An evaluation of experience, education, and training in relationship to the duties of the position.

The information for evaluating experience, education, and training will be taken from the application form and any additional information which may be obtained through reference inquiries to supervisors, teachers, and others.

SELECTIVE PLACEMENT

Some positions may require particular knowledges and skills. For these positions, consideration may be limited to those candidates whose records show that they have the required knowledges and skills.

BASIC SKILLS POSITIONS

Housekeeping Aid, GS–1
Housekeeper, GS–2, 3, 4, 5, 6, 7
Housemother, Matron, Hostess, Cadet Hostess, GS–2, 3, 4, 5, 6, 7

Applicants must have had progressively responsible experience in general housekeeping duties such as dusting, window washing, cleaning, making beds, waxing or polishing floors, or any experience such as work involved in the care, cleaning, maintenance, and servicing of living quarters in homes, lodging houses, hospitals, or other Government establishments; or, being responsible for the discipline and well-being of members of a domiciliary unit, including checking leaves and passes, receiving guests, assisting in recreational activities, orienting new members and giving attention to members of the unit who are sick, answering the telephone and relaying messages. The total experience must have equipped the applicant with a knowledge of cleaning methods, tools, supplies, and equipment used in general housekeeping operations. For positions in grade GS–4 and below with supervisory duties, the applicant's experience must indicate that she possesses supervisory qualifications, preferably demonstrated by supervisory experience. Grades GS–5, 6, and 7 require supervisory experience.

Grade	Total (years)	Supervisory (years)
GS–1	½	None
GS–2	1	None
GS–3	1½	None
GS–4	2	None
GS–5	2½	½
GS–6	3	¾
GS–7	3½	1

Appointment to Housekeeping Aid and to most Housekeeper positions is restricted by law to persons who are entitled to veteran preference, as long as such persons are available. There are, however, Housekeeper positions which are non-custodial in nature and for these positions appointment is not restricted to persons who are entitled to veteran preference.

Messenger, GS–1/3
Messenger (Motor Vehicle Operator), GS–1/3

Appointment is restricted to persons entitled to veterans' preference as long as such persons are available.

DESCRIPTION OF WORK

Messenger work involves the receipt, individual-route sorting, collection or pick-up, and delivery of mail and a variety of other papers, documents, and administrative material processed in a mail unit or messenger room. Messenger positions may also include the performance, as required, of miscellaneous tasks such as operating simple duplicating equipment in an office situation; light manual work such as lifting and emptying mail sacks, moving office machines and equipment, etc.; simple office duties such as checking outgoing material for complete address, noting changes on messenger route, filing alphabetically, date stamping material, etc.; and/or the operation of automotive equipment to facilitate the performance of messenger work.

REQUIREMENTS

For grade GS–1, no written test, experience, training, or education is required. Candidates must be interested in, and willing to perform, routine messenger work, and to show likelihood of success on the job.

Experience which meets the requirements as shown below for grades GS–2 and GS–3 must have been in messenger or general clerical work.

Grade: *Total years*
GS–1 .... None
GS–2 ....   ½
GS–3   1

SUBSTITUTION

The successful completion of a full 4-year senior high school curriculum may be substituted for 6 months of the required experience.

WRITTEN TEST

For grade GS–1, no written test is required. All candidates for competitive appointment at grades GS–2 and GS–3 are required to pass the appropriate written test.

BASIS OF RATING

For GS–1: An evaluation of the candidate's interest in and willingness to perform routine and repetitive messenger work, dependability, and the ability to perform work safely.

For GS–2 and 3: The score on the written test and an evaluation of the extent and quality of experience and education.

REQUIREMENTS FOR MOTOR VEHICLE OPERATION

For those positions requiring the operation of Government-owned automotive vehicles, applicants must either hold or obtain within 30 days of employment, appropriate state permit and U.S. Government motor vehicle operators' identification card.

Park Aid GS–1/3
Park Technician GS–4/9

DESCRIPTION OF WORK

Park Aids and Park Technicians perform technical and practical work supporting the management, conservation, interpretation, development, and use of park areas and resources. Park Aids and Park Technicians carry out various operating tasks involved in law enforcement, traffic control, recreation program operation, campground and picnic area operation, accident prevention, fire control, plant disease and insect control, fish and wildlife surveys, soil and water conservation, preservation of historical structures and objects, and comparable aspects of park operations. The mix of duties depends on the particular needs of areas served.

EXPERIENCE AND TRAINING REQUIRED

Candidates must have had experience as described as follows. (Education may be substituted for experience.)

Grade	General experience (years)	Specialized experience (years)	Total experience (years)
GS–1	None	None	None
GS–2	½	None	½
GS–3	1	None	1
GS–4	1½	½	2
GS–5	2	1	3
GS–6	2	2	4
GS–7	2	3	5
GS–8 and above	2	4	6

General experience

This is experience in park operations or in related fields which provided basic knowledges and skills applicable to general park operations and conservation work.

Specialized experience

This is technical experience gained in actual park operations, or in activities which directly support park, fish and wildlife, recreation management, historic preservation, conservation or park-related work.

QUALITY AND LEVEL OF EXPERIENCE

For eligibility at grade GS–4, the required 6 months of specialized experience must have been comparable in difficulty and responsibility to the GS–3 level in the Federal service.

For eligibility at grade GS–5, at least 1 year of required experience, including 6 months of specialized experience, must have been comparable in difficulty and responsibility to the GS–4 level.

For eligibility at grades GS–6 and above, at least 1 year of the required specialized experience must have been comparable in difficulty and responsibility to the next lower grade in the Federal service; or 2 years must have been comparable to the second lower grade in the Federal service.

For positions at GS–9, at least 1 year of the specialized experience must be directly related to the duties of the specific position to be filled. Placement of technicians in positions at GS–9 must be predicated upon (1) a detailed analysis of the knowledges, abilities, and skills required for the work, and (2) a sound matching of the candidate's knowledges, abilities, and skills to the requirements.

WRITTEN TEST

Candidates for positions at GS–2 and GS–3 must pass a written test of abilities necessary to learn and perform the duties of the positions.

SUBSTITUTION OF EDUCATION FOR EXPERIENCE

Successfully completed education at the high school or higher levels may be substituted for the required experience, as indicated below:

GS–2: Completion of a senior high school curriculum or General Educational Development (GED) high school equivalency certificate may be substituted for the general experience requirement at the GS–2 level. High school education or GED equivalency certificate may not be substituted for any part of the experience requirements at GS–3 and above.

GS–3: Successful completion of at least 1 academic year of post high school education that included at least 12 semester hours credit in any combination of courses listed below may be substituted for 1 year of experience and meets in full the experience requirements at the GS–3 level. Acceptable course work includes any field-oriented natural science, history, archeology, police science, and park and recreation management.

GS–4: Two years of academic study as described for GS–3 above which included or was supplemented by at least 18 semester hours in any combination of the subjects shown for GS–3 above, may be substituted for 2 years of experience including ½ year of specialized experience, and meets in full the experience requirements at the GS–4 level.

GS–5: A full 4-year course of study in an accredited college or university leading to a bachelor's or higher degree which includes at least 24 semester hours in any combination of the subjects described for GS–3 above may be substituted for 3 years of experience. Such substitution meets in full the experience requirements at the GS–5 level, including the 1 year of required specialized experience.

Appropriate education and training other than that outlined above, such as in manpower development programs or military training programs, will be credited depending upon their applicability and extent, generally on a month-for-month basis. Maximum substitution of education for experience is 3 years.

BASIS OF RATING

Competitors for all positions will be rated on a scale of 100. The basis for rating will be as follows:

For grade GS–1: An evaluation of the candidate's willingness to do simple park aid work, his dependability, and his ability to work safely.

For grades GS–2 and GS–3: Written test score.

For grades GS–4 and above: An evaluation of training and experience.

ABILITY IN WORKING WITH THE PUBLIC

Most of these positions require contact with the public to explain programs and procedures, to give general assistance, to interpret the natural, historic, scientific, and/or recreational features of park areas, and to enlist the public's cooperation and support. For such positions candidates must demonstrate that they have the required ability.

ADDITIONAL TECHNICIAN KNOWLEDGES AND SKILLS

Some park technician positions may require specialized technical knowledges and skills in particular phases or types of park work. These include skills in: use of complex audiovisual equipment, fire control practices, wildlife management practices, driving or piloting custom-built land and water conveyances, techniques for mountain or water rescue, use of special recreation equipment, equestrian patrolling, saddling horses and packing supplies and equipment, and comparable activities. For such positions, candidates must show that their experience and training has given them the specific technical knowledges and skills needed to perform the duties of the position for which they are being considered.

INTERVIEW REQUIREMENTS

Candidates may, at the option of the agency, be required to appear for a preemployment interview to evaluate skill in personal relationships for the public contact aspects of park technician work.

REQUIREMENTS FOR MOTOR VEHICLE OPERATION

The duties of these positions normally include driving an automobile or truck. The applicant must, therefore, be a capable driver, and must possess at the time of appointment, or obtain within 30 days, a valid driver's permit for the State or territory in which he lives, or in which he will be principally employed, and a valid U.S. Government operator's permit.

SELECTIVE PLACEMENT

For positions at grades GS–4 and above that require particular knowledges and skills, consideration may be restricted to those candidates whose background indicates that they possess the required knowledges and skills.

GUIDE FOR EVALUATION OF CANDIDATES IN RELATION TO JOB REQUIREMENTS

In evaluating each applicant's experience and training, attention should be given to the following factors:

1. Knowledge of general park operations, conservation, or outdoor recreation programs applicable to parks.
2. Knowledge of history or scientific fields applicable to park work.
3. Specialized technical knowledges and skills of the types described under *Additional Technical Knowledges and Skills* (primarily for GS–5 and above).
4. Ability to make constructive suggestions for modification or improvement of methods, procedures, plans, techniques, equipment or programs.
5. Ability to work independently and plan day-to-day activities.
6. Ability to meet and deal effectively with the park visitors.

The information for evaluating experience and training will be obtained from the application form. Confidential reference inquiries may be sent to supervisors, teachers, and others who can furnish useful information about the candidate's qualifications.

SPECIAL PHYSICAL REQUIREMENTS

Applicants must be physically able to perform efficiently the duties of the positions. Some of the positions require arduous physical exertion under rigorous and unusual environmental conditions, such as travel over rugged, precipitous, slippery, and extremely hazardous terrain at high elevations, carrying packs of heavy equipment. Applicants must be proportioned as to height and weight, and gross disproportion will be cause for rejection. Amputation or serious disabilities of arm, hand, leg, or foot will disqualify an applicant for appointment; however, there may be a few positions suitable for persons with minor handicaps. Vision, with or without glasses, must test at least 20/30 (Snellen) each eye. However, applicants with vision less than 20/30 (Snellen) in one eye will receive consideration if the other eye tests 20/20 (Snellen) with or without glasses. Applicants must be able to distinguish basic colors and must be able to hear the conversational voice, each ear, with or without the use of a hearing aid. Since the duties of the position are exacting, responsible, and require extensive oral communication with the public, applicants must possess emotional and mental stability and unimpaired speech.

THE U.S. POSTAL SERVICE POSITIONS

The United States Postal Service is an independent agency of the Federal Government. As such, employees of the Postal Service are federal employees who enjoy the very generous benefits offered by the government. These benefits include an automatic raise at least once a year, regular cost of living adjustments, liberal paid vacation and sick leave, life insurance, hospitalization, and the opportunity to join a credit union. At the same time, the operation of the Postal Service is businesslike and independent of politics. A postal worker's job is secure even though administrations may change. An examination system is used to fill vacancies. The examination system provides opportunities for those who are able and motivated to enter the Postal Service and to move within it.

Since postal employment is so popular, entry is very competitive. In most areas the Postal Service Entrance Exams are administered only once every three years. The resulting list is used to fill vacancies as they occur in the next three years. An individual who is already employed by the Postal Service, however, may request to take an exam during those intervening years. Any person who has satisfactorily filled a position for a year or more may ask to take the exam for any other position and, if properly qualified, may fill a vacancy ahead of a person whose name is on the regular list. It is even possible to change careers within the Postal Service. If the exam for the precise position that you want will not be administered for some time, it might be worthwhile to take the exam for another position in hopes of entering the Postal Service and then moving from within.

One very common "instant progression" within the Postal Service is that from clerk-carrier, a salary level 5 position, to distribution clerk, machine (also known as letter sorting machine operator), a level 6 position. Anyone who qualifies as a clerk-carrier is automatically offered the opportunity to take the machine exam. The advantages of becoming a letter sorting machine operator include not only higher salary, but also increased employment possibilities. Mechanization is the wave of the future. The field is expanding, and there are far more openings for machine operators than there are for clerks or carriers. Of course, the desirability of the job leads to a greater number of applicants and a still more competitive position for you. This fact should further motivate you to study hard for your exam.

Salaries, hours, and some other working conditions as well are subject to frequent change. The postal workers have a very effective union that bargains for them and gains increasingly better conditions. At the time of your employment, you should make your own inquiry as to salary, hours, and other conditions as they apply to you. Job descriptions and requirements are less subject to change. In the next few pages we quote job descriptions as provided by the government.

Occupations in the Postal Service

The U.S. Postal Service handles billions of pieces of mail a year, including letters, magazines, and parcels. Close to a million workers are required to process and deliver this mail. The vast majority of Postal Service jobs are open to workers with 4 years of high school or less. The work is steady. Some of the jobs, such as mail carrier, offer a good deal of personal freedom. Other jobs, however, are more closely supervised and more routine.

NATURE AND LOCATION OF THE INDUSTRY

Most people are familiar with the duties of the mail carrier and the post office window clerk. Yet few are aware of the many different tasks required in processing mail and of the variety of occupations in the Postal Service.

At all hours of the day and night, a steady stream of letters, packages, magazines, and papers moves through the typical large post office. Mail carriers have collected some of this mail from neighborhood mailboxes; some has been trucked in from surrounding towns or from the airport. When a truck arrives at the post office, mail handlers unload the mail. Postal clerks then sort it according to destination. After being sorted, outgoing mail is loaded into trucks for delivery to the airport or nearby towns. Local mail is left for carriers to deliver the next morning.

To keep buildings and equipment clean and in good working order, the Postal Service employs a variety of service and maintenance workers, including janitors, laborers, truck mechanics, electricians, carpenters, and painters. Some workers specialize in repairing machines that process mail.

Postal inspectors audit the operations of post offices to see that they are run efficiently, that funds are spent properly, and that postal laws and regulations are observed. They also prevent and detect crimes such as theft, forgery, and fraud involving use of the mail.

Postmasters and supervisors are responsible for the day-to-day operation of the post office, for hiring and promoting employees, and for setting up work schedules.

The Postal Service also contracts with private businesses to transport mail. There are more than 12,500 of these "Star" route contracts. Most "Star" route carriers use trucks to haul mail, but in some remote areas horses or boats are used instead.

Almost 85 percent of all postal workers are in jobs directly related to processing and delivering mail. This group includes postal clerks, mail carriers, mail handlers, and truck drivers. Postmasters and supervisors make up nearly 10 percent of total employment, and maintenance workers about 4 percent. The remainder includes such workers as postal inspectors, guards, personnel workers, and secretaries.

The Postal Service operates more than 41,000 installations. Most are post offices, but some serve special purposes such as handling payroll records or supplying equipment.

Although every community receives mail service, employment is concentrated in large metropolitan areas. Post offices in cities such as New York, Chicago, and Los Angeles employ a great number of workers because they not only process huge amounts of mail for their own pop-

ulations, but also serve as mail processing points for the smaller communities that surround them. These large city post offices have sophisticated machines for sorting the mail. In these post offices, distribution clerks who have qualified as machine operators quickly scan addresses and send letters on their way automatically by pushing the proper button. These clerks must be able to read addresses quickly and accurately, must be able to memorize codes and sorting schemes and must demonstrate machine aptitude by their performance on the Number Series part of the exam.

TRAINING, OTHER QUALIFICATIONS, AND ADVANCEMENT

An applicant for a Postal Service job must pass an examination and meet minimum age requirements. Generally, the minimum age is 18 years, but a high school graduate may begin work at 16 years if the job is not hazardous and does not require use of a motor vehicle. Many Postal Service jobs do not require formal education or special training. Applicants for these jobs are hired on the basis of their examination scores.

Applicants should apply at the post office where they wish to work and take the entrance examination for the job they want. Examinations for most jobs include a written test. A physical examination is required as well. Applicants for jobs that require strength and stamina are sometimes given a special test. The names of applicants who pass the examinations are placed on a list in the order of their scores. Separate eligibility lists are maintained for each post office.

Every applicant must pass the exam to find a place on the eligibility list. As compensation for their service, veterans enjoy certain extra consideration in their placement on the list. Five extra points are added to the passing score of an honorably discharged veteran and 10 extra points to the score of a veteran wounded in combat or disabled. Disabled veterans who have a compensable, service-connected disability of 10 percent or more are placed at the top of the eligibility list. When a job opens, the appointing officer chooses one of the top three applicants. Others are left on the list so that they can be considered for future openings.

New employees are trained either on the job by supervisors and other experienced employees or in local training centers. Training ranges from a few days to several months, depending on the job.

Advancement opportunities are available for most postal workers because there is a management commitment to provide career development. Also, employees can get preferred assignments, such as the day shift or a more desirable delivery route, as their seniority increases. When an opening occurs, employees may submit written requests, called "bids,"' for assignment to the vacancy. The bidder who meets the qualifications and has the most seniority gets the job.

In addition, postal workers can advance to better paying positions by learning new skills. Training programs are available for low-skilled workers who wish to become technicians or mechanics.

Applicants for supervisory jobs must pass an examination. Additional requirements for promotion may include training or education, a satisfactory work record, and appropriate personal characteristics such as leadership ability. If the leading candidates are equally qualified, length of service also is considered.

Although opportunities for promotion to supervisory positions in smaller post offices are limited, workers may apply for vacancies in a larger post office and thus increase their chances.

EMPLOYMENT OUTLOOK

Employment of postal clerks is expected to grow slowly. Most openings will result from the need to replace clerks who retire, die, or transfer to other occupations.

Although the amount of mail post offices handle is expected to grow as both population and the number of businesses grow, modernization of post offices and installation of new equipment will increase the amount of mail each clerk can handle. For example, machines which semiautomatically mark destination codes on envelopes are now being tested. These codes can be read by computer-controlled letter-sorting machines which automatically drop each letter into the proper slot for its destination. With this system, clerks read addresses only once, at the time they are coded, instead of several times, as they now do. Eventually this equipment will be installed in all large post offices. Thus, while the total number of postal clerks may not increase, there will be greater need for distribution clerks who operate sorting machines, and job opportunities will open up in more and more cities.

Examination Announcement
Post Office Clerk-Carrier

The Post Office Clerk-Carrier Exam is not a regularly scheduled exam given on the same date all over the country. Rather, the Clerk-Carrier Exam is separately scheduled in each postal geographic area. An area may comprise a number of states or, in densely populated regions, may consist of only a portion of one county. The frequency of administration also varies, though generally the exam is offered every two or three years.

When an exam is about to open in a postal area, the postal examiner for the area sends notices to all the post offices serviced by that area. The examiner also places ads in local newspapers and commercials over local radio stations. State employment offices receive and post copies of the announcement, and Civil Service newspapers carry the information as well.

QUALIFICATION REQUIREMENTS

No experience is required. All applicants will be required to take a written examination designed to test aptitude for learning and performing the duties of the position. The test of literacy and basic clerical stills will consist of four parts:

(A) Address Checking; (B) Memory for Addresses; (C) Number Series; and (D) Following Oral Directions. The test and completion of the forms will require approximately 2 hours and 15 minutes.

DUTIES

Clerks work indoors. Clerks have to handle sacks of mail weighing as much as 70 pounds. They sort mail and distribute it by using a complicated scheme which must be memorized. Some clerks work at a public counter or window doing such jobs as selling stamps and weighing parcels and are personally responsible for all money and stamps. Clerks may be on their feet all day. They also have to stretch, reach, and throw mail. Assignments to preferred positions, such as window clerks, typist and stenographic positions, etc., are filled by open bid and reassignment of the senior qualified clerk.

Carriers have to collect and deliver mail. Some carriers walk, other carriers drive. Carriers must be out in all kinds of weather. Almost all carriers have to carry mail bags on their shoulders; loads weigh as much as 35 pounds. Carriers sometimes have to load and unload sacks of mail weighing as much as 70 pounds.

The duties of newly appointed clerks and carriers are at times interchangeable. As representatives of the Postal Service, they must maintain pleasant and effective public relations with patrons and others, requiring a general familiarity with postal laws, regulations, and procedures commonly used.

Employees may be assigned to work in places exposed to public view. Their appearance influences the general public's confidence and attitude toward the entire Postal Service.

Employees appointed under this standard are, therefore, expected to maintain neat and proper personal attire and grooming appropriate to conducting public business, including the wearing of a uniform when required.

CARRIER POSITIONS REQUIRING DRIVING

Before eligibles may be appointed to carrier positions which require driving, they must demonstrate a Safe Driving record and must pass the Road Test to show they can safely drive a vehicle of the type used on the job.

Eligibles who fail to qualify in the Road Test will not be given the test again in the same group of hires. Those who fail the test a second time will not again be considered as a result of the same examination for appointment to a position that requires driving.

A valid driver's license from the state in which this post office is located must be presented at the time of appointment. Persons who do not have the license will not be appointed but their names will be restored to the register. They may not again be considered for carrier positions until they have obtained the required driver's license. After hire, individuals must also be able to obtain the required type of Government operator's permit.

SPECIAL PHYSICAL REQUIREMENTS

The distant vision for clerk and carrier positions not involving driving duties must test at least 20/30 (Snellen) in one eye, glasses permitted, and applicants generally must be able to hear ordinary conversation with or without a hearing aid, but some clerk positions may be filled by the deaf.

For carrier positions which require driving, applicants must have at least 20/30 (Snellen) in one eye and 20/50 (Snellen) in the other with or without a corrective device for unlimited operation of motor vehicles. Hearing must be at least 15/20 with or without a hearing aid.

A physical examination will be required before appointment.

Examination Announcement
Mail Handler/Mail Processor

QUALIFICATION REQUIREMENTS

No experience is required. All applicants will be required to take a written examination designed to test literacy and basic clerical skills. The four-part exam includes: (A) Address Checking; (B) Memory for Addresses; (C) Number Series; and (D) Following Oral Directions.

The test and completion of the forms will require approximately 2 hours and 15 minutes. Competitors will be rated on a scale of 100. They must score at least 70 on the examination as a whole.

DUTIES

Mail Handler:

Loads, unloads, and moves bulk mail, and performs duties incidental to the movement and processing of mail. Duties may include separation of mail sacks, facing letter mail, canceling stamps on parcel post; operating canceling machines, addressograph, mimeograph; operating fork-lift truck; rewrapping parcels, etc.

Mail Processor:

Operates mail-processing equipment, including bar code sorters and optical bar code readers; acts as minor trouble-shooter for the equipment; collates and bundles processed mail and transfers it from one work area to another; hand-processes mail that cannot be handled by the machines; loads mail into bins and onto trucks; and performs other related tasks.

SPECIAL PHYSICAL REQUIREMENTS

Persons with amputation of arm, leg, or foot should not apply. A physical examination will be required before appointment.

STRENGTH AND STAMINA TEST

Mail Handler:

When eligibles are within reach for appointment they will be required to pass a test of strength and stamina. In this test they will be required to lift, shoulder, and carry two 70-pound sacks — one at a time — 15 feet and load them on a hand truck. They will be required to push that truck to where there are some 40-, 50-, and 60-pound sacks. They will be required to load those sacks onto the truck. They will then have to unload the truck and return the truck to its original location. Eligibles will be notified when and where to report for the test of strength and stamina.

Persons with certain physical conditions will not be permitted to take the test of strength and stamina without prior approval of a physician. These physical conditions are (a) hernia or rupture, (b) back trouble, (c) heart trouble, (d) pregnancy, (e) or any other condition which makes it dangerous to the eligible to lift and carry 70-pound weights. Persons with these physical conditions will be given special instructions at the time they are notified to report for the strength and stamina test.

An eligible being considered for an appointment who fails to qualify on the test will not be tested again in the same group of hires. If he fails the test a second time, his eligibility for the position of mail handler will be cancelled.

Mail Processor:

Physical requirements for mail processors are not as stringent as those for mail handlers because the work is not as strenuous.

Mark-Up Clerk, Automated

DUTIES OF THE JOB

The mark-up clerk, automated, operates an electro-mechanical machine to process mail that is classified as "undeliverable as addressed." In doing this, the mark-up clerk operates the keyboard of a computer terminal to enter and extract data to several databases including change of address, mailer's database, and address-correction file. The mark-up clerk must select the correct program and operating mode for each application, must affix labels to mail either manually or with mechanical devices, and must prepare forms for address-correction services. Other duties may include distribution of processed markups to appropriate separations for further handling, operating of a photocopy machine, and other job-related tasks in support of primary duties.

QUALIFICATION REQUIREMENTS

An applicant for a mark-up clerk position must have had either six months of clerical or office-machine-operating experience or have completed high school or have had a full academic year (36 weeks) of business school. A mark-up clerk must also demonstrate the ability to type 40 wpm for five minutes with no more than 2 errors. The record of experience and training must show ability to use reference materials and manuals; ability to perform effectively under pressure; ability to operate any office equipment appropriate to the position; ability to work with others; and ability to read, understand, and apply certain regulations and procedures commonly used in processing mail undeliverable as addressed.

For appointment, a mark-up clerk must be eighteen years old, or sixteen years old if a high school graduate. An applicant who will reach his or her eighteenth birthday within two years from the date of the exam may participate. A mark-up clerk must be able to read, without strain, printed material the size of typewritten characters and must have 20/40 (Snellen) vision in one eye. Glasses are permitted. In addition, the applicant must pass an examination of literacy and basic clerical skills and a computer administered alpha-numeric typing test.

Rural Carrier

DUTIES OF THE JOB

The work of the rural carrier combines the work of the window clerk and the letter carrier but also has special characteristics of its own. The rural carrier's day begins with sorting and loading the mail for delivery on his or her own route. Then comes a day's drive, which may be over unpaved roads and rough terrain. The rural carrier does most deliveries and pickups of outgoing mail from the car. Occasionally, however, bulky packages must be delivered directly to the homeowner's door. Since rural postal patrons may be far from the nearest post office, the rural carrier sells stamps, weighs and charges for packages to be mailed, and performs most other services performed by window clerks in post offices. At the end of the day, the rural carrier returns to the post office with outgoing mail and money collected in various transactions. The rural carrier must be able to account for the stamps, postcards, and other supplies with which he or she left in the morning and must "balance the books" each day.

A rural carrier enjoys a great deal of independence. No supervisor looks over his or her shoulder. On the other hand, there is no supervisor to turn to for advice on how to handle a new situation that may come up.

QUALIFICATION REQUIREMENTS

The qualifying exam for rural carrier is a four-part test of literacy and basic clerical skills that requires about 2 hours and 15 minutes to administer. The parts of the exam are: (A) Address Checking; (B) Memory for Addresses; (C) Number Series; and (D) Following Oral Directions. The Postal Service sends each applicant a set of sample questions along with the admission card for the exam and the detailed application form. At the test site, the applicant has a chance to try some sample questions before beginning the exam itself.

Since the rural carrier's job requires driving, the minimum age for a rural carrier is eighteen. The rural carrier must have a valid driver's license, good eyesight, and the ability to hear ordinary conversation (glasses and hearing aid are permitted). In addition, the rural carrier must demonstrate physical stamina and ability to withstand the rigors of the job.

Garageman-Driver, Tractor/Trailer Operator, Motor Vehicle Operator

DUTIES OF THE JOB

What all the above job titles have in common is driving various Postal Service vehicles on the highway and within the lots and properties of the Postal Service.

Garagemen are responsible for seeing that each vehicle is in the proper place at the proper time and that each vehicle is roadworthy before it is released. Garagemen must keep accurate records of all activity as it affects each vehicle and must follow through on what movement or maintenance is required.

Tractor/trailer operators drive the huge mail rigs from city to city along the super highways, delivering large quantities of mail as quickly as possible within the bounds of safety. The work of a Postal Service tractor/trailer operator is really no different from the work of a tractor/trailer operator for private industry.

Motor vehicle operators drive the various other Postal Service vehicles as needed, both within and between towns and cities.

QUALIFICATION REQUIREMENTS

The exam for all of these positions is designed to test powers of observation, ability to express oneself, accuracy in record keeping, familiarity with road signs, and ability to follow instructions. The exam is in two parts of 40 questions each. You will have sixty minutes to answer each part. The test requires concentration and careful attention to details. The sample questions that the Postal Service sends to applicants provide a good idea of what to expect from the exam itself.

Since all these positions require driving, applicants must be licensed drivers over the age of eighteen. In addition, applicants must have good eyesight and hearing and be in excellent health and physical condition. A physical exam and strength and stamina tests are part of the hiring process. Candidates must also take training and qualify for federal licensing on the vehicle they are required to drive, and for a state commercial drivers license (CDL).

Postal Police Officer

DUTIES OF THE JOB

A postal police officer is essentially a security guard at post offices and at other postal installations and facilities. The postal police officer may work inside postal buildings or out of doors at loading docks and in parking lots. A postal police officer may be armed.

QUALIFICATION REQUIREMENTS

An applicant for the position of postal police officer must be at least twenty years of age, and, unless a veteran, cannot be appointed until reaching the age of twenty-one years. The postal police officer must be physically able to perform the duties of the job, must have good weight in proportion to height, must have color vision and good distant vision (no weaker than 20/40 in one eye and 20/50 in the other eye correctable to 20/20), and must have keen hearing. Emotional and mental stability are essential for the armed officer, and a psychological interview is part of the qualification process. The candidate must demonstrate the ability to deal with the public in a courteous and tactful manner; to work in stress situations; to collect, assemble, and act on pertinent facts; to prepare clear and accurate records; to deal effectively with individuals and groups; and to express him- or herself in both oral and written communications. A background investigation will be made on all otherwise qualified candidates. In order to be considered, each applicant must pass a written qualifying exam with a score of 70 or better out of a possible 100. The examination tests observation and memory, word knowledge, and the ability to arrange sentences in logical order.

THE ACWA GROUPS

The acronym ACWA stands for Administrative Careers With America. The ACWA exams were introduced with great fanfare in June of 1990. There were six ACWA exams, one for each of the six ACWA occupational groups. The exams were similar in style and level of difficulty; the differences were mainly in actual subject content of the questions.

The Office of Personnel Management administered the ACWA exams and established and maintained registers of eligible job aspirants. Upon request of the various agencies, OPM made available names of eligibles in rank order. The ACWA process was meant to simplify and streamline testing and hiring for many GS-5 to GS-7 positions and to make hiring as unbiased as possible.

The decentralization movement of the mid-1990s led to reorganization of the entire hiring process. OPM remains the overseer of civil service practices, but it is no longer the testing and hiring superagency. Each department, each agency, each bureau announces vacancies as they occur and establishes its own procedures for filling those vacancies. In some instances there is no formal written examination. Other agencies devise their own exams. Still others turn to OPM for assistance of some sort.

The current role of OPM, with respect to testing and hiring, is to serve as a consultant to individual bureaus and agencies. Upon request, OPM will still administer an exam for an individual agency, but more often OPM makes available its bank of exam questions and the agency proceeds on its own. Some agencies have simply adopted the relevant ACWA exam, dropping the ACWA designation. Others have chosen blocks of ACWA questions and merged them with questions borrowed from other OPM exams or with original questions written specifically for the exam.

ACWA no longer exists, but ACWA questions are very much alive. Many positions that fall into the "ACWA groups" test for jobs with ACWA-style questions. In addition, ACWA-style questions sometimes appear on the examinations for positions outside these groups. If your area of interest appears on the following lists, be alert to the possibility of ACWA-style questions on your exam. The name of your exam will not be *ACWA,* but do pay attention to the sample ACWA questions that begin on page 187.

BUSINESS, FINANCE AND MANAGEMENT
OCCUPATIONS

Agricultural Programs*; *Includes*
  Agricultural Marketing
  Agricultural Program Specialist
Business: *Includes*
  Appraising and Assessing
  Bond Sales Promotion
  Budget Analysis
  Building Management
  Financial Administration and Programs
  Food Assistance Program Specialist
  General Business and Industry
  Housing Management
  Public Utilities Specialist
  Realty
  Wage and Hour Law Administration
Communication Specialist*
Contract Specialist*
Financial Institution Examining*
Finance*: *Includes*
  Financial Analysis
  Insurance Examining
  Loan Specialist
Industrial Programs*: *Includes*
  Industrial Property Management
  Industrial Specialist
  Quality Assurance Specialist

Supply: *Includes*
  Distribution Facilities and Storage
    Management
  General Supply
  Inventory Management
  Logistics Management
  Packaging
  Property Disposal
  Supply Cataloging
  Supply Program Management
Trade Specialist*
Transportation*: *Includes*
  Highway Safety Management
  Traffic Management
  Transportation Industry Analysis
  Transportation Operations
  Transportation Specialist
Unemployment Insurance*
An asterisk (*) denotes positions with specific qualification requirements.
Best Opportunities—The options offering the best opportunities for employment are: Business, Contract Specialist, Industrial Programs, and Supply.

BENEFITS REVIEW, TAX AND LEGAL OCCUPATIONS

Claims Examining: *Includes*
  Civil Service Retirement Claims Examining
  Contact Representative
  General Claims Examining
  Passport and Visa Examining
  Unemployment Compensation Claims
    Examining
  Veterans Claims Examining
  Workers' Compensation Claims Examining

Land Law Examining*
Paralegal Specialist
Social Insurance Administration
    (Representative)* and Social
    Insurance Claims Examining
Social Services
Tax Law Specialist*
Tax Technician*

PERSONNEL ADMINISTRATION AND COMPUTER
OCCUPATIONS

Computer Specialists Trainee
Personnel: *Includes*

Contractor Industrial Relations
Employee Development

Employee Relations
Labor-Management Relations Examining
Labor Relations
Manpower Development
Military Personnel Management
Occupational Analysis
Personnel Management
Personnel Staffing
Position Classification

Salary and Wage Administration
Administration: *Includes*
  Administrative Officer
  Miscellaneous Administration and Programs
Program Analysis: *Includes*
  Management Analysis
  Program Analysis
Vocational Rehabilitation*

HEALTH, SAFETY, AND ENVIRONMENTAL OCCUPATIONS

Environmental Protection Specialist
Hospital Housekeeping Management*
Outdoor Recreation Planning*

Public Health Program Specialist
Safety and Occupational Health Management*

LAW ENFORCEMENT AND INVESTIGATION OCCUPATIONS

Alcohol, Tobacco, and Firearms Inspection
Civil Aviation Security Specialists
Criminal Investigator
Customs Inspector
Game Law Enforcement
General Investigator
Immigration Inspector
Internal Revenue Officer

Import Specialist and Security: *Includes*
  Import Specialist
  Intelligence
  Security Administration
Park Ranger*
Public Health Quarantine Inspection*
Securities Compliance Examining*
Wage and Hour Compliance

WRITING AND PUBLIC INFORMATION OCCUPATIONS

Agricultural Market Reporting*
Archives Specialist
General Arts and Information (excluding
  Fine and Applied Arts)

Public Affairs
Technical Information Services*
Technical Writing and Editing*
Writing and Editing

PART THREE

Useful Information About Civil Service Tests

TEST-TAKING TECHNIQUES

1. Give yourself enough time to prepare for the exam. Start studying weeks ahead of time; study every day; don't cram in the last twenty-four hours.
2. Arrive for your exam rested and relaxed. Get a good night's sleep before the exam. Leave home early enough so that you are not flustered by traffic or transit delays.
3. Arrive a bit early so that if you are not assigned a seat you can choose one away from drafts or a flickering light.
4. Wear a watch. Bring identification and admission ticket if one was issued to you.
5. Listen to instructions before the exam begins. Ask questions if there is anything that you do not fully understand.
6. Read directions carefully. Directions which state "Mark (D) if all three names being compared are alike" are very different from directions which state "Mark (D) if none of the three names being compared are alike." Misreading these directions will ruin your score.
7. Read every word of every question. Little words like "not," "most," "all," "every," and "except" can make a big difference.
8. Read all the answer choices before you mark your answer. Don't just choose the first answer that seems correct, read them all to find out which answer is best.
9. Mark your answers by completely blackening the space of your choice. Every answer must be recorded in a space on the answer sheet.
10. Mark only one answer for each question.
11. If you change your mind, erase completely and cleanly. Never cross out an answer.
12. Answer the questions in order. If you are not sure of an answer, eliminate those answers which are obviously wrong and guess from those remaining. Mark the question booklet so that you can return and rethink the guesses if you have time.
13. Check often to be certain that you are marking each question in the right space and that you have not skipped a space by mistake. The answer sheet is scored by a machine. Question 8 must be answered in space 8; question 52 in space 52.
14. Stay awake. Stay alert. Work steadily and carefully using all the time allowed to earn your best possible score.

OPM EXAMINATIONS

The Office of Personnel Management (OPM) administers a wide range of examinations for many different positions in federal government service. Some of these exams are known by their distinctive names. Among these are the Treasury Enforcement Agent Exam (TEA), given to special agent candidates in a number of departments and to Deputy U.S. Marshal candidates, Border Patrol Agent, and Administrative Careers with America (ACWA), the entry exam for a wide variety of administrative, management, and professional careers. Other OPM exams have descriptive titles such as "The Federal Clerical Examination" or are simply known by the job titles for which they test. Some OPM-administered exams are unique to the agencies and positions for which they test. These tailor-made exams tend to draw questions from the whole gamut of OPM exams as appropriate to the specific position. Your best preparation for any unspecified exam is familiarity and competence with all exam question types represented in these pages.

The first examination that follows has no distinctive name; the Office of Personnel Management identifies it only by number, Exam 704. This examination is administered to applicants for a variety of government jobs. Among the positions to which this exam applies are Federal Protective Officer and U.S. Department of the Interior Park Police. It lends questions to other examinations as well. This exam includes five different types of questions. The first, name and number comparisons, checks for detail-mindedness and speed and accuracy of observation and discrimination. The two verbal skills question types, reading comprehension and vocabulary, seek to measure the applicant's ability to understand directions and written materials and to communicate effectively. The last two types of questions, figure analogies and number series, are measures of reasoning, analytical ability, and creative thinking.

The sample questions that follow are the official sample questions distributed by the Office of Personnel Management. Try your hand at these questions to evaluate your skill with them and your chances for success on this exam. We have supplied a full set of explanations of the correct answers to help you understand the rationale behind the questions and to lead your thinking processes so that you can answer such questions on your own.

The structure of a recent full-length exam was as follows:

Part I: Name and Number Comparisons
           8 minutes; 50 questions
           Questions were arranged in order of increasing difficulty so that
               towards the end of the section number groups consisted of 8
               and 9 digits.

Part II: Vocabulary and Reading Comprehension
           25 minutes; 30 questions
           15 vocabulary questions; 15 reading questions

Part III: Symbol Reasoning
20 minutes; 20 questions
Questions were based on curves and angles, on sizes of symbols, and on location of symbols within symbols rather than on quality of lines as in the sample questions.

Part IV: Numerical Sequence
20 minutes; 24 questions

ANSWER SHEET: SAMPLE QUESTIONS: OPM EXAM 704

1 Ⓐ Ⓑ Ⓒ Ⓓ Ⓔ	13 Ⓐ Ⓑ Ⓒ Ⓓ Ⓔ	25 Ⓐ Ⓑ Ⓒ Ⓓ Ⓔ	37 Ⓐ Ⓑ Ⓒ Ⓓ Ⓔ
2 Ⓐ Ⓑ Ⓒ Ⓓ Ⓔ	14 Ⓐ Ⓑ Ⓒ Ⓓ Ⓔ	26 Ⓐ Ⓑ Ⓒ Ⓓ Ⓔ	38 Ⓐ Ⓑ Ⓒ Ⓓ Ⓔ
3 Ⓐ Ⓑ Ⓒ Ⓓ Ⓔ	15 Ⓐ Ⓑ Ⓒ Ⓓ Ⓔ	27 Ⓐ Ⓑ Ⓒ Ⓓ Ⓔ	39 Ⓐ Ⓑ Ⓒ Ⓓ Ⓔ
4 Ⓐ Ⓑ Ⓒ Ⓓ Ⓔ	16 Ⓐ Ⓑ Ⓒ Ⓓ Ⓔ	28 Ⓐ Ⓑ Ⓒ Ⓓ Ⓔ	40 Ⓐ Ⓑ Ⓒ Ⓓ Ⓔ
5 Ⓐ Ⓑ Ⓒ Ⓓ Ⓔ	17 Ⓐ Ⓑ Ⓒ Ⓓ Ⓔ	29 Ⓐ Ⓑ Ⓒ Ⓓ Ⓔ	41 Ⓐ Ⓑ Ⓒ Ⓓ Ⓔ
6 Ⓐ Ⓑ Ⓒ Ⓓ Ⓔ	18 Ⓐ Ⓑ Ⓒ Ⓓ Ⓔ	30 Ⓐ Ⓑ Ⓒ Ⓓ Ⓔ	42 Ⓐ Ⓑ Ⓒ Ⓓ Ⓔ
7 Ⓐ Ⓑ Ⓒ Ⓓ Ⓔ	19 Ⓐ Ⓑ Ⓒ Ⓓ Ⓔ	31 Ⓐ Ⓑ Ⓒ Ⓓ Ⓔ	43 Ⓐ Ⓑ Ⓒ Ⓓ Ⓔ
8 Ⓐ Ⓑ Ⓒ Ⓓ Ⓔ	20 Ⓐ Ⓑ Ⓒ Ⓓ Ⓔ	32 Ⓐ Ⓑ Ⓒ Ⓓ Ⓔ	44 Ⓐ Ⓑ Ⓒ Ⓓ Ⓔ
9 Ⓐ Ⓑ Ⓒ Ⓓ Ⓔ	21 Ⓐ Ⓑ Ⓒ Ⓓ Ⓔ	33 Ⓐ Ⓑ Ⓒ Ⓓ Ⓔ	45 Ⓐ Ⓑ Ⓒ Ⓓ Ⓔ
10 Ⓐ Ⓑ Ⓒ Ⓓ Ⓔ	22 Ⓐ Ⓑ Ⓒ Ⓓ Ⓔ	34 Ⓐ Ⓑ Ⓒ Ⓓ Ⓔ	46 Ⓐ Ⓑ Ⓒ Ⓓ Ⓔ
11 Ⓐ Ⓑ Ⓒ Ⓓ Ⓔ	23 Ⓐ Ⓑ Ⓒ Ⓓ Ⓔ	35 Ⓐ Ⓑ Ⓒ Ⓓ Ⓔ	47 Ⓐ Ⓑ Ⓒ Ⓓ Ⓔ
12 Ⓐ Ⓑ Ⓒ Ⓓ Ⓔ	24 Ⓐ Ⓑ Ⓒ Ⓓ Ⓔ	36 Ⓐ Ⓑ Ⓒ Ⓓ Ⓔ	48 Ⓐ Ⓑ Ⓒ Ⓓ Ⓔ

SAMPLE QUESTIONS: OPM EXAM 704

Each question has several suggested answers lettered A, B, C, etc. Decide which one is the best answer to the question. Then, on the sample answer sheet, find the answer space that is numbered the same as the number of the question and darken completely the circle that is lettered the same as the letter of your answer. Compare your answers with those given. Then study the explanations of the correct answers which follow the correct answer key.

DIRECTIONS: Sample questions 1 through 20 require name and number comparisons. In each line across the page there are three names or numbers that are very similar. Compare the three names or numbers and decide which ones are exactly alike. On your sample answer sheet, mark the answer

    A   if ALL THREE names or numbers are exactly ALIKE
    B   if only the FIRST and SECOND names or numbers are exactly ALIKE
    C   if only the FIRST and THIRD names or numbers are exactly ALIKE
    D   if only the SECOND and THIRD names or numbers are exactly ALIKE
    E   if ALL THREE names or numbers are DIFFERENT

#			
1.	Davis Hazen	David Hozen	David Hazen
2.	Lois Appel	Lois Appel	Lois Apfel
3.	June Allan	Jane Allan	Jane Allan
4.	Emily Neal Rouse	Emily Neal Rowse	Emily Neal Rowse
5.	H. Merritt Audubon	H. Merriott Audubon	H. Merritt Audubon
6.	6219354	6219354	6219354
7.	2312793	2312793	2312793
8.	1065407	1065407	1065047
9.	3457988	3457986	3457986
10.	4695682	4695862	4695682
11.	Francis Ransdell	Frances Ramsdell	Francis Ramsdell
12.	Cornelius Detwiler	Cornelius Detwiler	Cornelius Detwiler
13.	Stricklund Kanedy	Stricklund Kanedy	Stricklund Kanedy
14.	Joy Harlor Witner	Joy Harloe Witner	Joy Harloe Witner
15.	R. M. O. Uberroth	R. M. O. Uberroth	R. N. O. Uberroth
16.	2395890	2395890	2395890
17.	1926341	1926347	1926314
18.	5261383	5261383	5261338
19.	8125690	8126690	8125609
20.	6177396	6177936	6177396

Sample questions 21 through 30 require verbal skills.

DIRECTIONS: Reading. In questions 21 through 25, read the paragraph carefully and base your answer on the material given.

21. Probably few people realize, as they drive on a concrete road, that steel is used to keep the surface flat and even, in spite of the weight of buses and trucks. Steel bars, deeply embedded in the concrete, provide sinews to take the stresses so that they cannot crack the slab or make it wavy.

    The paragraph best supports the statement that a concrete road
    (A) is expensive to build.
    (B) usually cracks under heavy weights.
    (C) is used exclusively for heavy traffic.
    (D) is reinforced with other material.

22. The likelihood of America's exhausting its natural resources seems to be growing less. All kinds of waste are being reworked and new uses are constantly being found for almost everything. We are getting more use out of our goods and are making many new byproducts out of what was formerly thrown away.

    The paragraph best supports the statement that we seem to be in less danger of exhausting our resources because
    (A) economy is found to lie in the use of substitutes.
    (B) more service is obtained from a given amount of material.
    (C) we are allowing time for nature to restore them.
    (D) supply and demand are better controlled.

23. Through advertising, manufacturers exercise a high degree of control over consumers' desires. However, the manufacturer assumes enormous risks in attempting to predict what consumers will want and in producing goods in quantity and distributing them in advance of final selection by the consumers.

    The paragraph best supports the statement that manufacturers
    (A) can eliminate the risk of overproduction by advertising.
    (B) distribute goods directly to the consumers.
    (C) must depend upon the final consumers for the success of their undertakings.
    (D) can predict with great accuracy the success of any product they put on the market.

24. What constitutes skill in any line of work is not always easy to determine; economy of time must be carefully distinguished from economy of energy, as the quickest method may require the greatest expenditure of muscular effort and may not be essential or at all desirable.

    The paragraph best supports the statement that
    (A) the most efficiently executed task is not always the one done in the shortest time.
    (B) energy and time cannot both be conserved in performing a single task.
    (C) a task is well done when it is performed in the shortest time.

(D) skill in performing a task should not be acquired at the expense of time.

25. In the relations of people to nature, the procuring of food and shelter is fundamental. With the migration of people to various climates, ever new adjustments to the food supply and to the climate became necessary.

The paragraph best supports the statement that the means by which people supply their material needs are
(A) accidental.
(B) varied.
(C) limited.
(D) inadequate.

DIRECTIONS: Vocabulary. For questions 26 through 30 choose the one of the four suggested answers that means most nearly the same as the word in *italics*.

26. *Flexible* means most nearly
    (A) breakable   (C) pliable
    (B) flammable   (D) weak

27. *Option* means most nearly
    (A) use   (C) value
    (B) choice   (D) blame

28. To *verify* means most nearly to
    (A) examine   (C) confirm
    (B) explain   (D) guarantee

29. *Previous* means most nearly
    (A) abandoned   (C) timely
    (B) former   (D) younger

30. *Respiration* means most nearly
    (A) recovery   (C) pulsation
    (B) breathing   (D) sweating

DIRECTIONS: Each of these reasoning questions, 31 through 35, consists of two sets of symbols. Find the one rule that explains the similarity of the symbols within each set and also explains the difference between the two sets. Among the five suggested answers, find the symbol that can best be substituted for the question mark in the second set. In all these questions you will find details that have nothing to do with the principle of the question: to find the similarity between the symbols within a set and the difference between the sets.

SET 1   SET 2

31.

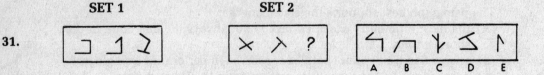

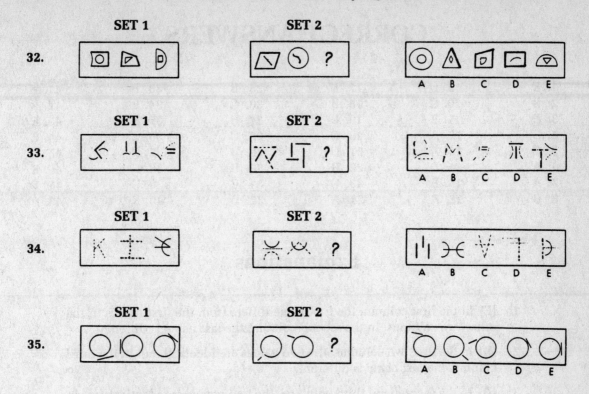

DIRECTIONS: Questions 36 through 48 require number reasoning skills. In each question there is at the left a series of numbers which follow some definite order and, at the right, five sets of two numbers each. You are to look at the numbers in the series at the left and find out what order they follow. Then, from the suggested answers at the right, select the set that gives the next two numbers in the series.

36. 12 10 13 10 14 10 15 . . . . (A) 15 10 (B) 10 15 (C) 10 16 (D) 10 10 (E) 15 16

37. 9 2 9 4 9 6 9 . . . . (A) 9 9 (B) 9 8 (C) 8 10 (D) 10 8 (E) 8 9

38. 1 2 5 6 9 10 13 . . . . (A) 15 17 (B) 14 15 (C) 14 16 (D) 15 16 (E) 14 17

39. 1 2 3 2 2 3 3 2 3 . . . . (A) 2 3 (B) 3 2 (C) 3 4 (D) 4 2 (E) 4 3

40. 9 10 12 15 19 24 30 . . . . . . (A) 35 40 (B) 36 42 (C) 30 36 (D) 30 37 (E) 37 45

41. 35 34 31 30 27 26 23 . . . . (A) 22 19 (B) 22 20 (C) 23 22 (D) 20 19 (E) 20 17

42. 16 21 19 24 22 27 25 . . . . (A) 28 30 (B) 30 28 (C) 29 24 (D) 30 27 (E) 26 29

43. 48 44 40 36 32 28 24 . . . . (A) 22 20 (B) 24 22 (C) 23 22 (D) 20 18 (E) 20 16

44. 20 30 39 47 54 60 65 . . . . (A) 70 75 (B) 68 70 (C) 69 72 (D) 66 67 (E) 68 71

45. 10 13 13 16 16 19 19 . . . . (A) 19 19 (B) 19 22 (C) 22 22 (D) 22 25 (E) 22 24

46. 2 4 25 8 16 25 32 . . . . (A) 32 35 (B) 25 64 (C) 48 25 (D) 25 48 (E) 64 25

47. 38 15 32 17 27 19 23 . . . . (A) 20 20 (B) 21 26 (C) 20 21 (D) 21 20 (E) 21 25

48. 80 12 40 17 20 22 10 . . . . (A) 25 15 (B) 15 25 (C) 24 5 (D) 25 5 (E) 27 5

CORRECT ANSWERS

1. E	9. D	17. E	25. B	33. B	41. A
2. B	10. C	18. B	26. C	34. E	42. B
3. D	11. E	19. E	27. B	35. B	43. E
4. D	12. A	20. C	28. C	36. C	44. C
5. C	13. A	21. D	29. B	37. E	45. C
6. A	14. D	22. B	30. B	38. E	46. E
7. A	15. B	23. C	31. E	39. D	47. D
8. B	16. A	24. A	32. D	40. E	48. E

Explanations

1. **(E)** In the first column, the first name differs from the first names in the other two columns. In the second column, the last name is different.

2. **(B)** In the first two columns, the two names are identical, but in the third column, the last name is different.

3. **(D)** In the second and third columns, the two names are identical, but in the first column, the first name is different.

4. **(D)** In the second and third columns, the names are identical, but in the first column, the last name is different.

5. **(C)** In all three columns, the initial and last names are identical, but in the second column, the middle name differs from the middle name in the first and third columns.

6. **(A)** All three numbers are identical.

7. **(A)** All three numbers are identical.

8. **(B)** In the first two columns, the last three digits are "407," but in the third column, they are "047."

9. **(D)** The number in the first column ends with "88," while the other two columns end with "86."

10. **(C)** Again the difference occurs in the ending of the numbers. The numbers in the first and third columns end with "682," while the number in the second column ends with "862."

11. **(E)** In the first column, the last name differs from the last name in the other two columns. In the second column, the first name differs from that in the other two.

12. **(A)** All three names are identical.

13. **(A)** All three names are identical.

14. **(D)** The only difference is that in the first column the middle name differs from that in the other two columns.

15. **(B)** The names in the first two columns are identical, but in the third column, the second initial is different.

16. **(A)** All three numbers are identical.

17. **(E)** All the numbers differ from each other. In the first column, the last two digits are "41"; in the second column they are "47"; and in the third, "14."

18. **(B)** The first two columns end with "83," while the third ends with "38."

19. **(E)** There are differences in central digits and in final digits. The "66" in the middle of the number in the second column differs from the "56" in the middle of the other two. The "09" at the end of the number in the third column differs from the "90" at the end of the other two.

20. **(C)** The number in the second column ends with "936," while the numbers in the first and third columns end with "396."

21. **(D)** The steel bars which keep the concrete road from cracking are reinforcing it.

22. **(B)** The effect of recycling is to make greater use of resources so that we do not need to constantly deplete fresh resources.

23. **(C)** If consumers don't buy, the manufacturers are stuck with excess stock.

24. **(A)** Many considerations must enter into an assessment of efficiency. Time, effort, energy and money are all factors.

25. **(B)** The ability of people to adjust and adapt to changing climates and to changing circumstances implies that human beings are capable of varied responses and behaviors.

26. **(C)** *Flexible*, the opposite of rigid or stiff, means *easily bent*, *adjustable*, or *pliable*.

27. **(B)** An *option* is a *choice*.

28. **(C)** To *verify* is to *check the accuracy of* or to *confirm*.

29. **(B)** *Previous* means *occurring before in time or order*, hence *former*.

30. **(B)** *Respiration is breathing*.

31. **(E)** The simplest general rule that guides this question is that all the symbols are made up of lines that touch each other. In the first set, each of the symbols consists of three lines that touch. The second set contains symbols consisting of two lines that touch. Only choice (E) fulfills this requirement.

32. **(D)** The general rule governing this question is that all symbols are made up to two figures, one inside the other. The first set consists of a closed figure inside the outer figure. In the second set, there is a single line inside the outer figure. Only choice (D) conforms to this rule. Note that the shapes of the figures are irrelevant to the question.

33. **(B)** The general rule is that all symbols are made up of four lines. In the first set, all symbols consist of both straight and curved lines. In the second set the symbols are made up of straight lines only. Of the choices, only (B) is made up of only straight lines. Whether or not lines within a symbol touch is irrelevant to the question.

34. **(E)** Each symbol is made up of three lines. In set 1, the lines which compose each symbol are of like quality, that is, solid, broken, or dotted. In set 2, the lines composing each symbol are not of the same quality. Of the choices, only (E) consists of straight and dotted lines. All the other choices are of figures made up of lines of the same quality. The shapes of the lines are irrelevant.

35. **(B)** All symbols consist of a circle and a line. In the first set, the line is tangent to the circle. In the second set, the line is perpendicular or nearly perpendicular to the circle. Choice (B) best fits this requirement.

36. **(C)** The series is a simple +1 series with the number <u>10</u> inserted after each step of the series.

37. **(E)** This is a simple +2 series with the number <u>9</u> appearing before each member of the series.

38. **(E)** Read aloud (softly): 1   2⟍   ⟋5   6⟍   ⟋9   10⟍   ⟋13
                          whisper   ⟍3   4⟋   ⟍7   8⟋   ⟍11   12⟋

    The next number to read aloud is <u>14</u>, to be followed by a whispered <u>15</u>, <u>16</u>, and then aloud again <u>17</u>. Sometimes the ear is more perceptive than the eye.

39. **(D)** In this series a rhythm emerges when you accent the first number in each group: <u>1</u> 2 3; <u>2</u> 2 3; <u>3</u> 2 3. Try grouping and sounding out before you begin to search for more complicated patterns.

    Many number series questions can be solved by writing the direction and amount of change between numbers in the space above and between each member of the series.

40. **(E)**
    $$\begin{array}{ccccccccc} & +1 & +2 & +3 & +4 & +5 & +6 & +7 & +8 \\ 9 & 10 & 12 & 15 & 19 & 24 & 30 & 37 & 45 \end{array}$$

41. **(A)**
    $$\begin{array}{ccccccccc} & -1 & -3 & -1 & -3 & -1 & -3 & -1 & -3 \\ 35 & 34 & 31 & 30 & 27 & 26 & 23 & 22 & 19 \end{array}$$

42. **(B)**
    $$\begin{array}{ccccccccc} & +5 & -2 & +5 & -2 & +5 & -2 & +5 & -2 \\ 16 & 21 & 19 & 24 & 22 & 27 & 25 & 30 & 28 \end{array}$$

43. **(E)**
    $$\begin{array}{ccccccccc} & -4 & -4 & -4 & -4 & -4 & -4 & -4 & -4 \\ 48 & 44 & 40 & 36 & 32 & 28 & 24 & 20 & 16 \end{array}$$

44. **(C)**
    $$\begin{array}{ccccccccc} & +10 & +9 & +8 & +7 & +6 & +5 & +4 & +3 \\ 20 & 30 & 39 & 47 & 54 & 60 & 65 & 69 & 72 \end{array}$$

    Some arithmetical series may be interrupted by a particular number that appears periodically or by a repetition of numbers according to a pattern. In marking the progression of these series, write "r" in the space between repeated numbers and circle extraneous numbers that are repeated periodically.

When choosing your answer you must be alert to the point at which the pattern was interrupted. Do not further repeat a number that has already been repeated; do not forget to repeat before continuing the arithmetical pattern if repetition is called for at this point in the series.

45. **(C)** $10 \overset{+3}{} 13 \overset{r}{} 13 \overset{+3}{} 16 \overset{r}{} 16 \overset{+3}{} 19 \overset{r}{} 19 \overset{+3}{} 22 \overset{r}{} 22$

46. **(E)** $2 \overset{\times 2}{} 4 \overset{\times 2}{} \textcircled{25} \; 8 \overset{\times 2}{} 16 \overset{\times 2}{} \textcircled{25} \; 32 \overset{\times 2}{} 64 \overset{\times 2}{} \textcircled{25}$

Some number series questions encompass two alternating series. Each of the two series which alternate will follow a pattern, but they may not necessarily follow the same pattern. Diagram one series above the row of numbers and the other below in order to determine the next two numbers.

47. **(D)**
$$
\begin{array}{ccccccccc}
 & & -6 & & -5 & & -4 & & -3 \\
38 & 15 & 32 & 17 & 27 & 19 & 23 & 21 & 20 \\
 & & +2 & & +2 & & +2 & & \\
\end{array}
$$

48. **(E)**
$$
\begin{array}{ccccccccc}
 & & \div 2 & & \div 2 & & \div 2 & & \div 2 \\
80 & 12 & 40 & 17 & 20 & 22 & 10 & 27 & 5 \\
 & & +5 & & +5 & & +5 & & \\
\end{array}
$$

SAMPLE QUESTIONS: THE TEA EXAM

The Treasury Enforcement Agent Exam (TEA) is given to candidates for the positions of Internal Security Inspector with the IRS; Secret Service Special Agent; Customs Special Agent; Bureau of Alcohol, Tobacco, and Firearms Special Agent; IRS Special Agent with the Criminal Investigation Division; Deputy U.S. Marshal; and a number of other positions as well. If you are a candidate for any of these positions, give careful attention to the official sample questions which follow. Even if you are applying for a local or state law enforcement position, you should give serious attention to all federal exam questions. Some of the same types of questions are likely to appear on whatever exam you must take.

The Treasury Enforcement Agent Exam (TEA) is divided into three parts: Part A, verbal reasoning; Part B, arithmetic reasoning; and Part C, problems for investigation. The official sample questions that follow are similar to the questions you will find in the actual test in terms of difficulty and form.

PART A—VERBAL REASONING QUESTIONS

In each of these questions you will be given a paragraph which contains all the information necessary to infer the correct answer. Use **only** the information provided in the paragraph. Do not speculate or make assumptions that go beyond this information. Also, assume that all information given in the paragraph is true, even if it conflicts with some fact known to you. Only one correct answer can be validly inferred from the information contained in the paragraph.

Pay special attention to negated verbs (for example, "are *not*") and negative prefixes (for example, "*in*complete" or "*dis*organized"). Also pay special attention to quantifiers, such as "all," "none," and "some." For example, from a paragraph in which it is stated that "it is not true that all contracts are legal," one can validly infer that "some contracts are not legal," or that "some contracts are illegal," or that "some illegal things are contracts," but one **cannot** validly infer that "no contracts are legal," or that "some contracts are legal." Similarly, from a paragraph that states "all contracts are legal" and "all contracts are two-sided agreements," one can infer that "some two-sided agreements are legal," but one **cannot** validly infer that "all two-sided agreements are legal."

Bear in mind that in some tests, universal quantifiers such as "all" and "none" often give away incorrect response choices. That is **not** the case in this test. Some correct answers will refer to "all" or "none" of the members of a group.

Be sure to distinguish between essential information and unessential, peripheral information. That is to say, in a real test question, the example above ("all contracts are legal" and "all contracts are two-sided agreements") would appear in a longer, full-fledged paragraph. It would be up to you to separate the essential information from its context and then to realize that a response choice that states "some two-sided agreements are legal" represents a valid inference and hence the correct answer.

Sample questions 1 and 2 are examples of the reading questions on the test.

1. Impressions made by the ridges on the ends of the fingers and thumbs are useful means of identification, since no two persons have the same pattern of ridges. If finger patterns from fingerprints are not decipherable, then they cannot be classified by general shape and contour or by pattern type. If they cannot be classified by these characteristics, then it is impossible to identify the person to whom the fingerprints belong.

The paragraph best supports the statement that

(A) if it is impossible to identify the person to whom fingerprints belong, then the fingerprints are not decipherable.
(B) if finger patterns from fingerprints are not decipherable, then it is impossible to identify the person to whom the fingerprints belong
(C) if fingerprints are decipherable, then it is impossible to identify the person to whom they belong
(D) if fingerprints can be classified by general shape and contour or by pattern type, then they are not decipherable
(E) if it is possible to identify the person to whom fingerprints belong, then the fingerprints cannot be classified by general shape and contour or pattern

The correct answer is response B. The essential information from which the answer can be inferred is contained in the second and third sentences. These sentences state that "if finger patterns from fingerprints are not decipherable, then they cannot be classified by general shape and contour or by pattern type. If they cannot be classified by these characteristics, then it is impossible to identify the person to whom they belong." Since response B refers to a condition in which finger patterns from fingerprints are not decipherable, we know that, in that circumstance, they cannot be classified by general shape and contour or by pattern type. From the paragraph, we can infer that since they cannot be classified by these characteristics, then it is impossible to identify the person to whom the fingerprints belong.

Response A cannot be inferred because the paragraph does not give information about all the circumstances under which it is impossible to identify the person to whom the fingerprints belong. It may be that the person is not identifiable for reasons other than the decipherability of the person's fingerprints.

Response C is incorrect because the paragraph does not provide enough information to conclude whether or not it would be possible to identify the person to whom the fingerprints belong from the mere fact of the decipherability of the fingerprints.

Response D is wrong because it contradicts the information in the second sentence of the paragraph. From that sentence, it can be concluded that if fingerprints can be classified by general shape and contour or by pattern type, then they are decipherable.

Response E is incorrect for a similar reason; it contradicts the information presented in the third sentence of the paragraph.

2. Law enforcement agencies use scientific techniques to identify suspects or to establish guilt. One obvious application of such techniques is the examination of a crime scene. Some substances found at a crime scene yield valuable clues under microscopic examination. Clothing fibers, dirt particles, and even pollen grains may reveal important information to the careful investigator. Nothing can be overlooked because all substances found at a crime scene are potential sources of evidence.

The paragraph best supports the statement that

(A) all substances that yield valuable clues under microscopic examination are substances found at a crime scene

(B) some potential sources of evidence are substances that yield valuable clues under microscopic examination

(C) some substances found at a crime scene are not potential sources of evidence

(D) no potential sources of evidence are substances found at a crime scene

(E) some substances that yield valuable clues under microscopic examination are not substances found at a crime scene

The correct answer is response B. The essential information from which the answer can be inferred is contained in the third and fifth sentences. The third sentence tells us that "some substances found at a crime scene yield valuable clues under microscopic examination." The fifth sentence explains that "...all substances found at a crime scene are potential sources of evidence." Therefore, we can conclude that "some potential sources of evidence are substances that yield valuable clues under microscopic examination."

Response A cannot be inferred because the paragraph does not support the statement that all substances which yield valuable clues are found exclusively at a crime scene. It may be that valuable clues could be found elsewhere.

Responses C and D are incorrect because they contradict the fifth sentence of the paragraph which clearly states that "all substances found at a crime scene are potential sources of evidence."

Response E is incorrect because the paragraph provides no information about the value of substances found somewhere other than at the crime scene.

PART B—ARITHMETIC REASONING QUESTIONS

In this part you will have to solve problems formulated in both verbal and numeric form. You will have to analyze a paragraph in order to set up the problem, and then solve it. If the exact answer is not given as one of the response choices, you should select response E, "none of these." Sample questions 3 and 4 are examples of the arithmetic reasoning questions. The use of calculators will NOT be permitted during the actual testing; therefore, they should not be used to solve these sample questions.

3. A police department purchases badges at $16 each for all the graduates of the police training academy. The last training class graduated 10 new officers. What is the total amount of money the department will spend for badges for these new officers?

(A) $70
(B) $116
(C) $160
(D) $180
(E) none of these

The correct response is C. It can be obtained by computing the following:

$$16 \times 10 = 160$$

The badges are priced at $16 each. The department must purchase 10 of them for the new officers. Multiplying the price of one badge ($16) by the number of graduates (10) gives the total price for all of the badges.

Responses A, B, and D are the result of erroneous computations.

4. An investigator rented a car for six days and was charged $450. The car rental company charged $35 per day plus $.30 per mile driven. How many miles did the investigator drive the car?

(A) 800
(B) 900
(C) 1,290
(D) 1,500
(E) none of these

The correct answer is A. It can be obtained by computing the following:

$$6(35) + .30X = 450$$

The investigator rented the car for six days at $35 per day, which is $210; $210 subtracted from the total charge of $450 leaves $240, the portion of the total charge which was expended for the miles driven. This amount divided by the charge per mile ($240/.30) gives the number of miles (800) driven by the investigator.

Responses B, C, and D are the result of erroneous computations.

PART C—PROBLEMS FOR INVESTIGATION

In this part you will be presented with a paragraph and several related statements. Sample questions 5 through 9 are based on the following paragraph and statements. Read them carefully and then answer questions 5 through 9.

On October 30th, the Belton First National Bank discovered that the $3,000 it had received that morning from the Greenville First National Bank was in counterfeit 10, 20, and 50 dollar bills. The genuine $3,000 had been counted by Greenville First National bank clerk, Iris Stewart, the preceding afternoon. They were packed in eight black leather satchels and stored in the bank vault overnight. Greenville First National clerk, Brian Caruthers, accompanied carriers James Clark and Howard O'Keefe to Belton in an armored truck. Belton First National clerk, Cynthia Randall, discovered the counterfeit bills when she examined the serial numbers of the bills.

During the course of the investigation, the following statements were made.

(1) Gerald Hathaway, clerk of the Greenville bank, told investigators that he had found the bank office open when he arrived to work on the morning of October 30th. The only articles which appeared to be missing were eight black leather satchels of the type used to transport large sums of money.

(2) Jon Perkins, head teller of the Greenville bank, told investigators that he did not check the contents of the black leather satchels after locking them in the vault around 4:30 p.m., on October 29th.

(3) Henry Green, janitor of the Greenville bank, said that he noticed Jon Perkins leaving the bank office around 5:30 p.m., one-half hour after the bank closed on October 29th. He said that Perkins locked the door.

(4) A scrap of cloth, identical to the material of the carriers' uniforms, was found caught in the seal of one of the black leather satchels delivered to Belton.

(5) Brian Caruthers, clerk, said he saw James Clark and Howard O'Keefe talking in a secretive manner in the armored truck.

(6) Thomas Stillman, Greenville bank executive, identified the eight black leather satchels containing the counterfeit money which arrived at the Belton First National Bank, as the eight satchels which had disappeared from the bank office. He had noticed a slight difference in the linings of the satchels.

(7) Virginia Fowler, bank accountant, noticed two 10 dollar bills with the same serial numbers as the lost bills in a bank deposit from Ferdinand's Restaurant of Greenville.

(8) Vincent Johnson, manager of Ferdinand's Restaurant, told police that Iris Stewart frequently dined there with her boyfriend.

5. Which one of the following statements best indicates that satchels containing the counterfeit bills were substituted for satchels containing genuine bills while they were being transported from Greenville to Belton?

(A) statement (1)
(B) statement (3)
(C) statement (4)
(D) statement (5)
(E) statement (7)

The correct answer is (C). The armor carriers had the greatest opportunity to substitute counterfeit bills for real ones during the transportation procedure. The scrap of material from an armor carrier's uniform caught in the seal of one of the satchels strongly links the carriers to the crime.

6. Which one of the following statements best links the information given in statement (1) with the substitution of the counterfeit bills?

(A) statement (2)
(B) statement (3)
(C) statement (4)
(D) statement (5)
(E) statement (6)

The correct answer is (E). Statement (1) establishes that eight satchels were missing from Greenville Bank. Statement (6) identifies the satchels which arrived at the Belton Bank as the missing satchels.

7. Which one of the following statements along with statement (7) best indicates that the substitution of the counterfeit bills casts suspicion on at least one employee of the Greenville bank?

(A) statement (1)
(B) statement (2)
(C) statement (3)
(D) statement (5)
(E) statement (8)

The correct answer is (E). Statement (7) establishes that two stolen 10-dollar bills were spent at Ferdinand's Restaurant. Statement (8) identifies a bank employee as a frequent diner at Ferdinand's Restaurant. This statement "casts suspicion" on the bank employee but does not prove complicity.

8. Which one of the following statements would least likely be used in proving a case?

(A) statement (1)
(B) statement (3)
(C) statement (4)
(D) statement (5)
(E) statement (7)

The correct answer is (D). The fact that the bank clerk saw the armor carriers talking secretively may cast some suspicion but would not be useful in proving the case. Men who work together may very likely exchange private jokes or share personal information.

9. Which one of the following statements best indicates that the substitution of the counterfeit bills could have taken place before the satchels left the Greenville bank?

(A) statement (1)
(B) statement (2)
(C) statement (3)
(D) statement (4)
(E) statement (7)

The correct answer is (B). The satchels were locked in the vault at 4:30 p.m. on one day and not delivered until the following morning. Since we learn in statement (2) that the satchels were not checked after they were locked into the vault, the exchange could have taken place in the Greenville Bank.

SAMPLE QUESTIONS: BORDER PATROL AGENT EXAM

Applicants for the position of Border Patrol Agent must pass an OPM exam and qualify in the Spanish language. If the candidate feels comfortable speaking and understanding Spanish, he or she may choose to take an oral examination at the time of the interview for the position. If the candidate does not know any Spanish or if he or she is not certain of passing the oral exam, the candidate may elect to take a written multiple-choice test of ability to learn a foreign language. The multiple-choice language aptitude test must be requested and taken at the same time as the OPM exam. The candidate cannot choose the language aptitude exam after failing the oral Spanish exam at interview.

The following are official sample questions for the Border Patrol Agent Exam. This exam is administered by the Office of Personnel Management to candidates for other positions as well. The exam is a 65-question multiple-choice exam. It is divided into four parts, each of which is separately timed. The structure of the exam is as follows:

	Number of Questions	Timing (minutes)
Part A		25
Vocabulary	15	
Reading Comprehension	15	
Part B		
English usage (Grammar)	15	7
Part C		
General Knowledge and Judgment	10	10
Part D		
Logical Reasoning	10	15
Total	65	57

When the exam is scored, you will receive credit for every correct answer but suffer no penalty for a wrong answer. That means it is best to answer every question. A space left blank cannot raise your score, but even a wild guess could possibly help you. Choose the correct answer if you can. If not, eliminate obviously wrong answers and choose intelligently from the remaining choices, or make a wild stab if you must. The official instructions which will be read to you in the examination room state: "It will be to your advantage to answer every question in this test that you can, since your score will be number of right answers only. If you don't know the answer to a question, make the best guess you can. You may write in the test booklet if you need to."

These official sample questions are just samples. They will give you a good idea of the kinds of questions that you must answer.

DIRECTIONS: Each question has five suggested answers, lettered A, B, C, D, and E. Decide which one is the best answer to the question. Then darken completely the space corresponding to the letter that is the same as the letter of your answer. Keep your mark within the space. If you have to erase a mark, be sure to erase it completely. Mark only one answer for each question.

Sample Answer Sheet

1. Ⓐ Ⓑ Ⓒ Ⓓ Ⓔ	4. Ⓐ Ⓑ Ⓒ Ⓓ Ⓔ	7. Ⓐ Ⓑ Ⓒ Ⓓ Ⓔ	10. Ⓐ Ⓑ Ⓒ Ⓓ Ⓔ	13. Ⓐ Ⓑ Ⓒ Ⓓ Ⓔ
2. Ⓐ Ⓑ Ⓒ Ⓓ Ⓔ	5. Ⓐ Ⓑ Ⓒ Ⓓ Ⓔ	8. Ⓐ Ⓑ Ⓒ Ⓓ Ⓔ	11. Ⓐ Ⓑ Ⓒ Ⓓ Ⓔ	14. Ⓐ Ⓑ Ⓒ Ⓓ Ⓔ
3. Ⓐ Ⓑ Ⓒ Ⓓ Ⓔ	6. Ⓐ Ⓑ Ⓒ Ⓓ Ⓔ	9. Ⓐ Ⓑ Ⓒ Ⓓ Ⓔ	12. Ⓐ Ⓑ Ⓒ Ⓓ Ⓔ	15. Ⓐ Ⓑ Ⓒ Ⓓ Ⓔ

Sample Questions 1 through 3. In each of the sample questions below, select the one of the five suggested answers that is closest in meaning to the word in *italics.* Then darken the proper space on the sample answer sheet.

1. The new training program is much better than any of the *previous* ones. *Previous* means most nearly

    (A) abandoned
    (B) former
    (C) unused
    (D) recent
    (E) ineffective

2. The officer made several phone calls in an attempt to *verify* the report. To *verify* means most nearly to

    (A) examine
    (B) explain
    (C) confirm
    (D) believe
    (E) improve

3. The driver's only *option* was to turn right at the intersection. *Option* means most nearly

    (A) use
    (B) direction
    (C) hope
    (D) choice
    (E) opportunity

Sample Questions 4 through 6. In each of the next three sample questions, select the one of the five suggested answers that is best supported by the paragraph. Then darken the proper space on the sample answer sheet.

4. Just as the procedure of a collection department must be clear cut and definite, the steps being taken with the sureness of a skilled chess player, so the various paragraphs of a collection letter must show clear organization, giving evidence of a mind that, from the beginning, has had a specific end in view.

The paragraph best supports the statement that a collection letter should always

(A) show a spirit of sportsmanship
(B) be divided into several paragraphs
(C) be brief, but courteous
(D) be carefully planned
(E) be written by the head of the collection department

5. To prevent industrial accidents it is not only necessary that safety devices be used to guard exposed machinery, but also that mechanics be instructed in safety rules which they must follow for their own protection and that the lighting in the plant be adequate.

The paragraph best supports the statement that industrial accidents

(A) may be due to ignorance
(B) are always avoidable
(C) usually result from unsafe machinery
(D) cannot be entirely overcome
(E) usually result from inadequate lighting

6. Through advertising, manufacturers exercise a high degree of control over consumers' desires. However, the manufacturer assumes enormous risks in attempting to predict what consumers will want and in producing goods in quantity and distributing them in advance of final selection by the consumers.

The paragraph best supports the statement that manufacturers

(A) can eliminate the risk of overproduction by advertising
(B) distribute goods directly to the consumers
(C) must depend on the final consumers for the success of their undertakings
(D) can predict with great accuracy the success of any product they put on the market
(E) are more concerned with advertising than with the production of goods

Sample Questions 7 through 9. Each of the next three sample questions contains five sentences. Decide which one of the five sentences would be most suitable in a formal letter or report with respect to grammar and usage. Then darken the proper space on the sample answer sheet.

7. (A) The officer should of answered courteously the questions asked by the callers.
(B) The officer must answer courteously the questions of all them callers.
(C) The officer must answer courteously the questions what are asked by the callers.
(D) There would have been no trouble if the officer had have always answered courteously.
(E) The officer should answer courteously the questions of all callers.

8. (A) There are less mistakes in his work since he took the training course.
(B) The training course being completed, he makes very few mistakes in his work.
(C) Since he has completed the training course, he makes few mistakes in his work.

(D) After taking the training course, his work was found to contain hardly any mistakes.

(E) After he completed the training course, he seldom ever made any mistakes in his work.

9. (A) If properly addressed, the letter will reach my supervisor and I.
(B) The letter had been addressed to myself and my supervisor.
(C) I believe the letter was addressed to either my supervisor or I.
(D) My supervisor's name, as well as mine, was on the letter.
(E) My supervisor and me will receive the letter if it is probably addressed.

Sample Questions 10 through 12. In each of these sample questions, use your judgment and general knowledge to select the *best* or *most important* answer from the five suggested answers. Then darken the proper space on the sample answer sheet.

10. From the standpoint of the prisoners, the *chief* advantage to be derived from a properly administered parole system is the

(A) freedom from fear of being returned to prison
(B) opportunity to adjust themselves to release from imprisonment
(C) removal of the temptation to commit crime
(D) reduced cost of supervising prisoners
(E) opportunity to save whatever they are able to earn

11. An officer of the law may arrest a person without a warrant upon reasonable suspicion that the person has committed a felony. The *chief* purpose of this rule is to

(A) prevent the person's escape while his or her guilt is being investigated
(B) prevent the person from committing more crimes immediately
(C) give the person a chance to confess
(D) permit observation of the person's behavior
(E) increase the rate of arrest in proportion to the number of crimes committed

12. Acquaintance with all types of ammunition commonly in use is extremely valuable to the worker in crime detection *chiefly* because

(A) all criminals possess this knowledge
(B) a broad background is desirable for success in investigative work
(C) the worker's safety is thus insured in time of danger
(D) the worker can thus eventually become a specialist in this line
(E) such knowledge often simplifies the problem of investigation

Sample Questions 13 through 15. Each of these sample questions consists of five related events followed by five suggested orders in which the events could have occurred. Each suggested order represents the sequence in which the five sentences should be read, i.e., 3-5-1-2-4 indicates that the third sentence should be read first, the fifth sentence second, the first sentence third, etc. Select the one of the five suggested orders, lettered A, B, C, D, and E, in which the events most probably happened. Then darken the proper space on the sample answer sheet.

13. 1. The maid discovered the body and called the police.
    2. The police found Mary at the home of her sister.
    3. A man was shot while swimming in his private pool.
    4. A gun was found in Mary's pocketbook and was identified as the murder weapon.
    5. The police questioned the maid and discovered that the victim had had a heated argument with his wife, Mary, the night before.

    (A) 1-3-5-4-2
    (B) 3-5-1-4-2
    (C) 3-1-5-2-4
    (D) 1-5-2-4-3
    (E) 3-1-2-4-5

14. 1. In addition to the paper, a printing press and a stack of freshly printed $10 bills were found in Mr. Hayes' basement.
    2. A detective saw Mr. Hayes leave a printing shop with a large package.
    3. Mr. Hayes was arrested for counterfeiting and taken to the station.
    4. The owner of the shop said Mr. Hayes had bought very high quality paper.
    5. Mr. Hayes was under surveillance as a suspect in a counterfeiting case.

    (A) 2-4-1-5-3
    (B) 5-2-4-1-3
    (C) 3-2-4-1-5
    (D) 2-5-1-4-3
    (E) 5-2-3-4-1

15. 1. The inspector realized that Ms. Smith was wearing a wig and had her searched.
    2. The inspector decided to search Ms. Smith's luggage.
    3. Although the inspector could not place the face, he knew that Ms. Smith looked familiar.
    4. Narcotics were found sewn to the crown of Ms. Smith's wig.
    5. The inspector found nothing in Ms. Smith's luggage, but her passport photograph revealed her identity as a suspected smuggler.

    (a) 2-5-3-1-4
    (b) 3-1-4-2-5
    (c) 1-4-2-5-3
    (d) 3-2-5-1-4
    (e) 2-1-3-5-4

The correct answers are:

1. B	4. D	7. E	10. B	13. C
2. C	5. A	8. C	11. A	14. B
3. D	6. C	9. D	12. E	15. D

EXPLANATIONS OF ANSWERS TO BORDER PATROL AGENT EXAM

1. (B) *Previous* means coming or occurring before something else.
2. (C) To *verify* means to prove or to determine the truth or correctness of something.
3. (D) *Option* means something that may be or is chosen.
4. (D) The correct answer, D, is supported by the paragraph's statement that a collection letter should show clear organization and be written with a specific end in view. There is nothing in the paragraph to support alternatives A or E. Although the paragraph does imply that collection letters may contain several paragraphs (alternative B), it does not state that they should *always* be so divided. Also, the paragraph says nothing about the length or tone of a collection letter (alternative C), but only refers to the letter's clarity of thought and organization.
5. (A) The correct answer, A, is supported by the paragraph's statement that instructing mechanics in safety rules can help prevent industrial accidents, which implies that in some cases accidents may be due to ignorance of these rules. The paragraph does not support the statements that, in actual practice, industrial accidents are either *always* avoidable (alternative B) or that they cannot be entirely overcome (alternative D); it merely states the requirements of successful accident prevention. Although the paragraph does imply that industrial accidents can be caused by unsafe machinery (alternative C) and inadequate lighting (alternative E), it does not support the statements that such accidents *usually* result from these causes.
6. (C) The correct answer, C, is supported by the paragraph's statement that although advertising gives manufacturers considerable control over the consumers' demands for their products, there are still big risks involved in producing and distributing their goods in advance of the consumers' final selection, which implies that manufacturers' ultimate success depends on the consumers. The paragraph's statement that there are such risks, in spite of advertising, contradicts alternatives A and D; nor is there any support for the statements that manufacturers distribute goods *directly* to consumers (alternative B) or that they are more concerned with advertising than production (alternative E).
7. (E) Alternative A is incorrect because the word *have* should have been used instead of the word *of.* Alternative B is incorrect because the word *those* should have been used instead of the word *them.* Alternative C is incorrect because the word *that* should have been used instead of the word *what.* Alternative D is incorrect because the phrase *had have* is incorrect grammar; only the word *had* should have been used.
8. (C) Alternative A is incorrect because the word *fewer* should have been used instead of the word *less.* Alternative B is incorrect because poor word usage makes it seem as if *he* refers to the *training course.* Alternative D is incorrect because the word *few* should have been used instead of the phrase *hardly any.* Alternative E is incorrect because it is poor usage for the word *ever* to follow the word *seldom.*
9. (D) In alternative A, "my supervisor and me" is the object of the verb. In alternative C, "my supervisor and me" is the object of the preposition. In alternative B, the word *myself* should be replaced with the word *me.* In alternative E, "my supervisor and I" is the subject of the sentence.
10. (B) The *chief* advantage of a properly administered parole system from the prisoners' standpoint is the opportunity it provides them for information and assistance concerning their reentry into society. A parole system can-

not guarantee that released prisoners will never return to prison in the future (alternative A), that they will not be tempted to commit crime (alternative C), or that they will have the opportunity to save whatever they earn (alternative E), since these possibilities are largely in the hands of the prisoners themselves. While alternative D may be a result of the parole system, it is not the chief advantage from the standpoint of the prisoners.

11. (A) The *chief* purpose of arresting a person suspected of committing a felony is to insure that the suspect does not escape while further investigation takes place. While there may be some truth in all of the other alternatives, none of them can be considered to be the primary reason for this rule.

12. (E) The *chief* advantage of familiarity with all types of ammunition for the worker in crime detection lies in the fact that such knowledge can be a valuable aid in discovering and following up clues during the process of investigation. Alternatives A and C are untrue, and while alternatives B and D may be true in some cases, neither one is the most important reason why acquaintance with ammunition is valuable to the worker in crime detection.

13. (C) The most logical order of the five events is that first the man was shot (3); second, his body was discovered by the maid and the police were called (1); third, the police questioned the maid and learned of the couple's argument of the previous night (5); fourth, the police found Mary at her sister's home (2); and fifth, a gun was found in Mary's pocketbook and identified as the murder weapon (4). The answer is not A because the maid could not have discovered the body (1) before the man was shot (3). The answer is not B because the police could not have questioned the maid (5) before she called them (1). The answer is not D because the first four events could not have taken place before the man was shot (3). The answer is not E because the police could not have looked for Mary (2) before learning from the maid that she was the victim's wife (5).

14. (B) The most logical order of the five events is that first Mr. Hayes was under surveillance (5); second, a detective saw him leave a printing shop with a large package (2); third, the shop owner said he had bought high quality paper (4); fourth, a printing press and freshly printed bills were found in Mr. Hayes' basement along with the paper (1); and fifth, he was arrested for counterfeiting (3). The answer is not A or D because the detective would not have seen Mr. Hayes leave the printing shop (2) if he had not been under surveillance (5). The answer is not C or E because Mr. Hayes could not have been arrested for counterfeiting (3) before any evidence was discovered (1).

15. (D) The most logical order of the five events is that first the inspector saw that Ms. Smith looked familiar (3); second, he decided to search her luggage (2); third, he found nothing in her luggage but identified her from her passport photograph as a suspected smuggler (5); fourth, he realized that she was wearing a wig and had her searched (1); and fifth, narcotics were found in her wig (4). The answer is not A because the inspector would not have decided to search Ms. Smith's luggage (2) unless his suspicions were aroused by the fact that she looked familiar (3). The answer is not B, C, or E because the inspector would not have realized Ms. Smith was wearing a wig (1) before seeing her passport photograph (5).

If you choose to take the language aptitude exam, you will take this exam after a break on the same day as you take the OPM exam just described above. The language aptitude exam is an Artificial Language exam. You must demonstrate your ability to learn a foreign language by manipulating vocabulary and grammar in an artificial language.

You will be presented with a booklet describing the artificial language. The booklet will include two vocabulary lists. One list, presented alphabetically by English word, gives the English word and its artificial language equivalent [Example: alien = huskovy]. The other list is alphabetized by artificial language and gives the English equivalent of each artificial language word [Example: friggar = to work]. The booklet includes a glossary of grammatical terms. Grammatical terms have the same meaning in both English and the artificial language. [Example: An adjective is a word that describes a noun.] Finally, the booklet sets out grammar rules for the artificial language. [Example: The feminine singular of a noun, pronoun, and adjective is formed by adding the suffix *ver* to the masculine singular form.]

The exam contains four different types of questions, 50 questions in all. The parts are *not* separately timed. You are allowed 1 hour and 45 minutes to study the accompanying booklet and to answer the questions. The artificial language test is a test of your ability to reason and to manipulate the vocabulary and grammar of a foreign language. It is not a memory test. It does not test your ability to remember vocabulary or language. You may keep the booklet open in front of you and refer to it frequently as you answer the questions. You do not need to memorize any information.

The Office of Personnel Management does not provide official sample questions for the Artificial Language test. The exam description below can give you a feeling for the phrasing and style of questions, but without a vocabulary and grammar list, you cannot even attempt to answer these unofficial sample questions.

The first part consists of questions 1 to 20. In this part you must identify correctly translated words. For example: You may be given an English sentence such as "He injured the man," followed by a sentence in the artificial language such as "Yer Zelet wir huskoy." You must then mark (A) if only #1 is translated correctly, (B) if only #2 is correct, (C) if only #3 is correct, (D) if two or more are correct, and (E) if none are correct.

The second part consists of questions 21 to 30. In this part you must choose which of five choices correctly translates an underlined word or group of words from English into the artificial language. [Example: There is the lost boy. (A) bex kapkoy, (B) wir kapvoy, (C) bex kapvoy, (D) wir kapkoy, (E) bex kapyok.]

The third part, questions 31 to 42, puts a slightly different spin on translation into the artificial language. You are given an incomplete sentence in the artificial language and must complete it with the correctly translated English word, being conscious not only of the vocabulary word but also the grammatical form. [Example: Synet bex avekoy (man). (A) ekapiko, (B) ekapiver, (C) kopiak, (D) ekapiak, (E) pokiver.]

The fourth part, questions 43 to 50, requires you to correct a sentence in the artificial language. You must change the form of the italicized word or words in the sentence according to instructions given in parentheses. [Example: Yer *bongar* wir broukon (present tense). (A) bongaro, (B) bonagar, (C) bongarara, (D) bongo, (E) bongit.]

FEDERAL CLERICAL JOBS

Jobs in over 60 different clerical fields are filled using the Federal Clerical Examination. These jobs, like many other jobs in the Federal Government, are in the General Schedule (or GS), which assigns different "grades" to jobs which have different levels of responsibility or require different levels of experience or education.

There are jobs at various grade levels in each clerical field. Generally, all you need to qualify for jobs at the entry grades is to have graduated from high school (or some previous job experience). Some of the occupations at the entry level also require specific skills, such as typing or shorthand.

As you gain experience, you become eligible for promotion to higher level, more specialized clerical and administrative jobs. You can also enter the Federal Government for the first time at these higher grade levels if you already have the specialized experience or additional education these jobs require.

Except for the clerk-stenographer, the entry level for clerical jobs is GS-2, and initial hires are usually made at either GS-2 or GS-3. The entry level for clerk-stenographers is GS-3, and initial hires are usually made at GS-3 or GS-4. Appointment at the higher grade levels is made for applicants who have appropriate experience or education above the high school level. Experience from summer jobs and part-time jobs is often appropriate. Therefore, many applicants are eligible for entry at the higher grades without additional education.

Following are descriptions of some of the jobs in the clerical field.

Clerk-Typist

Most hiring at the entry level in the clerical field is done for clerk-typist positions, which combine clerical work with typing duties. Thousands of these clerk-typist positions are filled each year, particularly in areas where a number of Federal agencies are located. Vacancies are constantly occurring in these positions as employees are promoted to higher-graded positions, transfer to other jobs, or leave for other reasons.

Clerk-Stenographer

Clerk-stenographer jobs combine clerical tasks with both dictation and typing duties. There are usually many job openings in areas where there are large concentrations of Federal employees, and many opportunities for movement into higher grades.

Office Automation Clerk

Office automation clerks and assistants operate personal computers to perform word processing tasks, desktop publishing, database management, financial spreadsheets, electronic bulletin boards, etc. This work can also be carried out on mainframe computers through telecommunications equipment. This occupation is new, and office automation clerks are taking the place of clerk-typists in many organizations.

Data Transcriber

The job title "data transcriber" covers positions which involve the input or recording of different types of data into data processing files. Several thousand entry-level data transcribers are usually hired each year, and the number of jobs in the field is increasing as more use is made of automated systems.

Clerk

The title "clerk" covers many specific positions in which typing, stenographic, or data entry skills either are not required or are not an important part of the job. (In a few cases, one of these skills is important, in which case it is included in the job title.) Opportunities at the entry level in these fields are more limited than for typist, stenographer, and data transcriber jobs because more of these positions require specialized experience or training. However, entry-level opportunities do exist in some fields, as described below.

There are thousands of general clerks, such as mail and file clerks and miscellaneous clerks, who perform a variety of typical office and record-keeping tasks. Most of these jobs are filled at the lower entry levels. There are also many entry-level openings for sales store checkers. These clerks work in a variety of store-like situations, usually on military bases or in agency supply stores.

There are a variety of clerical jobs, such as the calculating machine operator, which involve the use of some type of office machine. Many of these jobs are filled at the entry level, although they often require special skills and training and have additional selection requirements specific to each job. There are several hundred of these office machine operator types of jobs.

Jobs in the following fields are usually above the entry level. However, some entry-level jobs are available. There are many jobs in the personnel field, supporting the professional personnel staff. There are good opportunities for advancement to technical and administrative jobs in this field. There are opportunities in the fields of supply, transportation, and stock control. Most of these positions exist in military and supply agencies. Finally, there are clerical positions in accounting, payroll, and fiscal work. For example, payroll clerks keep records and do other work related to issuing paychecks, and cash processing clerks handle and track cash disbursements.

SKILL REQUIREMENTS

When a job requires typing skill, you must be able to type accurately at 40 words per minute. When dictation skill is required, you must be able to transcribe dictation accurately at 80 words per minute. GS-2 data transcribers must be able to type accurately at 20 words per minute, and GS-3 and 4 data transcribers must be able to type accurately at 25 words per minute. Stenographer applicants may use any system of taking and transcribing dictation they wish.

The Federal Clerical Examination consists of two separately timed sections, a Verbal Tasks Test and a Clerical Tasks Test.

The Verbal Tasks Test

WHAT THE TEST IS ABOUT

The Verbal Tasks Test includes questions in such areas as spelling, meaning, and relationship of words; recognition of sentences which are grammatically correct; and reading, understanding, and using written material.

These test tasks relate to a variety of job tasks, such as proofreading and correcting typed copy, using instruction manuals, organizing new files of related materials, and carrying out written instructions.

There are 85 questions — 25 on word meaning, 20 on word relationships, 20 on spelling, 10 on grammar, and 10 on reading. There are a few questions of each type on each page of the test. For each question, you will select the best answer from among a set of suggested answers.

Word meaning questions consist of one given word followed by four different words labeled A, B, C, and D. You are to select the word which has the closest meaning to the word given in the question. It may help if you remember you are looking for the best match among the choices given, but not necessarily a perfect match.

Answering these questions depends upon your knowledge of vocabulary, but there are some steps you can take if you do not recognize the correct answer immediately.

- If you have a general idea about what the given word means, but are having trouble choosing an answer, try using the word in a short sentence. Then, substitute each of the answer choices in the same sentence to see which one seems best to fit the sentence.

- Try to break the given word into parts to see if the suffix (ending) or the prefix (beginning) of the word gives a clue about its meaning.

The reading questions consist of a paragraph followed by four statements. You read the paragraph first and then select the one statement which is based on information given in the paragraph.

- Do not worry if you are unfamiliar with the subject discussed in the paragraph. You do not need to have any knowledge about the subject of the paragraph since the answer to the question is always given in the paragraph itself.

- Do not worry about whether the correct statement, or any of the incorrect statements, are true. The important thing is that the correct answer is the *only* statement which says the same thing as is said in the paragraph. Some of the other statements may be true, but they are not based on the content of the paragraph.

- To select the correct statement, first eliminate choices which clearly conflict with the paragraph. Then, if you still have two or more choices, look for the specific section of the paragraph which covers the information given in each one of the choices.

- Compare the facts given carefully, until you can eliminate the remaining incorrect choices.

Grammar questions give four versions of a single sentence. Each sentence tries to express the same thought, but only one of them is *grammatically* correct.

- Most of the incorrect sentences are obviously poorly constructed.

- Others have such errors as using singular verbs with plural nouns.

- In the more difficult questions, you must pay attention to smaller details, like the misuse of punctuation, which can make a sentence very difficult to understand.

To answer these questions, first eliminate the sentences you are sure are incorrect. Then compare the remaining ones until you can choose one as being more correct than the others.

- It is possible that one sentence will seem to be correct because it uses the same informal grammar that people often use when talking. However, this type of sentence structure is not suitable for writing.

Spelling questions give three spellings of a common word, labeled A, B, and C. Each question also offers the option of "none of these" as choice D. You must decide which one of the three given spellings is correct, or that none of them is correct.

- Sometimes it helps to answer these questions by looking away from the given choices and writing the word yourself on the margin of your test booklet. Then check to see if the spelling you believe is correct is given as one of the choices.

Word relationship questions give two words which are related in some way, and then give the first word of a second word relationship which you are to complete. You are given four choices of words to complete that relationship. The correct choice is the word which completes that relationship in the way most similar to the relationship in the first pair of words.

To answer these questions, look at the first pair of words and decide what the relationship between the words is. Then choose the answer that best completes that relationship for the second pair of words.

- Remember that the correct answer is chosen because it completes an analogous relationship, not because it is on the same subject as the first pair of words.

The Clerical Tasks Test

WHAT THE TEST IS ABOUT

The Clerical Tasks Test is a test of speed and accuracy on four clerical tasks. There are 120 questions given with a short time limit. The test contains 30 questions on name and number checking, 30 on arranging names in correct alphabetical order, 30 on simple arithmetic, and 30 on inspecting groups of letters and numbers. The questions are arranged in groups or cycles of five questions of each type.

The Clerical Tasks Test is planned as a test of speed in carrying out these relatively simple clerical tasks. This means you should work quickly through the test. However, the test is also planned to measure accuracy, and there is a penalty for wrong answers in the total test score. This means you need to be careful as you work and that wild guessing is not a good idea. However, do not be so concerned about accuracy that you do the test more slowly than you should. Remember that both speed and accuracy are important to achieve a good score.

The different question types in this test appear on each page of the test. You may find it easier to answer all questions of one type that appear in the test rather than switching from one question type to another. This is perfectly acceptable, but extra caution should be taken to mark your answers in the right place on the answer sheet.

Memorizing the answer choices for name and number checking questions may be helpful in increasing your speed. In these questions, you are to compare three names or numbers and decide which ones are exactly alike. You then select your answer from a set of choices which describe whether all of them, some of them, or none of them are alike. These choices are labeled A, B, C, D, and E and are repeated on each page of the test booklet.

- These choices remain the same for all questions of this type in the test so if you memorize these choices you will not have to refer constantly back to them before choosing your answers.

For the alphabetizing questions, remember that the most important rule for putting the names in order is to consider each letter in the complete last name in strict alphabetical order, exactly as it appears.

- This is true even when the name includes more than one capital letter (as in DeLong), or involves prefixes which are often spelled differently in different names (as in McDuff and MacDuff).

- Ignore punctuation, such as apostrophes and hyphens, that appear in a name (as in O'Hara).

When two last names are identical in every way, then alphabetize according to the first and second names given, following the same rules.

The key to the arithmetic questions is to avoid careless errors. Remember that the correct answer may not be included as one of the given alternatives. In this case you mark choice E on the answer sheet.

- Answers will always be exact (no decimal places), so if the answer you get is not exact, work the problem again.

There are several different ways of approaching the letter and number inspection questions. You should use the method that works best for you.

One method is to work from the answer choices to the questions. Look at each answer choice and, one at a time, compare each letter or number it contains with the question until you can accept or reject it. Here is how you would use this method to answer the following set of sample questions.

There is one set of suggested answers for the next group of sample questions. Do not try to memorize these answers, because there will be a different set on each page in the test.

To find the answer to a question, find which suggested answer contains numbers and letters all of which appear in the question. If no suggested answer fits, mark E for that question.

1.	8	N	K	9	G	T	4	6			A = 7, 9, G, K
2.	T	9	7	Z	6	L	3	K	Suggested	B = 8, 9, T, Z
3.	Z	7	G	K	3	9	8	N	Answers	C = 6, 7, K, Z
4.	3	K	9	4	6	G	Z	L		D = 6, 8, G, T
5.	Z	N	7	3	8	K	T	9		E = none of these

- Start by looking at the first number given in choice A, which is a 7.

- Quickly scan question 1 for this number. Since it does not include a 7, choice A can be rejected.

- Next consider the first number in choice B, which is an 8. Scanning question 1 confirms that an 8 is present. Moving on to the next number in choice B (a 9), scanning of the question confirms its presence also, as well as the next letter in choice B (a T). There is no Z, however, so choice B is then rejected.

- Using the same process of elimination for choice C, no number 7 is found, and this choice is rejected.

- One by one, all of the letters and numbers in choice D are found, so choice D is marked as correct on the separate answer sheet.

- If all the letters and numbers in choice D had not been found in question 1, then choice **E,** "none of these," would have been marked as the correct answer.

You may be able to save time using this method by scanning for two of the letters or numbers given at one time.

Another method is to look at the particular question and quickly and lightly memorize all the numbers and letters it contains. Then, glance at each choice to select one which is a good possibility based on your memory.

- Carefully double-check this choice with each of the numbers and letters given in the question.

- If you use this method, be sure to spend only a few seconds memorizing the numbers and letters in the question, or you will waste too much time on one question.

Whichever method you choose, remember that any of the answer choices given may be used to answer more than one of the five questions included in the set on each page. Also, note that the letters and numbers given in the answer choices and questions do not have to be in the same order.

Answer Sheet for Federal Clerical Examination

VERBAL TASKS TEST

1. Ⓐ Ⓑ Ⓒ Ⓓ Ⓔ   5. Ⓐ Ⓑ Ⓒ Ⓓ Ⓔ   9. Ⓐ Ⓑ Ⓒ Ⓓ Ⓔ   13. Ⓐ Ⓑ Ⓒ Ⓓ Ⓔ

2. Ⓐ Ⓑ Ⓒ Ⓓ Ⓔ   6. Ⓐ Ⓑ Ⓒ Ⓓ Ⓔ   10. Ⓐ Ⓑ Ⓒ Ⓓ Ⓔ   14. Ⓐ Ⓑ Ⓒ Ⓓ Ⓔ

3. Ⓐ Ⓑ Ⓒ Ⓓ Ⓔ   7. Ⓐ Ⓑ Ⓒ Ⓓ Ⓔ   11. Ⓐ Ⓑ Ⓒ Ⓓ Ⓔ   15. Ⓐ Ⓑ Ⓒ Ⓓ Ⓔ

4. Ⓐ Ⓑ Ⓒ Ⓓ Ⓔ   8. Ⓐ Ⓑ Ⓒ Ⓓ Ⓔ   12. Ⓐ Ⓑ Ⓒ Ⓓ Ⓔ   16. Ⓐ Ⓑ Ⓒ Ⓓ Ⓔ

                                                                           17. Ⓐ Ⓑ Ⓒ Ⓓ Ⓔ

The total raw score on this test consists of the total number of questions that are answered correctly. There is no penalty for wrong answers or correction made for guessing. However, no credit is given for any question with more than one answer marked.

My raw score _____

CLERICAL TASKS TEST

1. Ⓐ Ⓑ Ⓒ Ⓓ Ⓔ   6. Ⓐ Ⓑ Ⓒ Ⓓ Ⓔ   11. Ⓐ Ⓑ Ⓒ Ⓓ Ⓔ   16. Ⓐ Ⓑ Ⓒ Ⓓ Ⓔ

2. Ⓐ Ⓑ Ⓒ Ⓓ Ⓔ   7. Ⓐ Ⓑ Ⓒ Ⓓ Ⓔ   12. Ⓐ Ⓑ Ⓒ Ⓓ Ⓔ   17. Ⓐ Ⓑ Ⓒ Ⓓ Ⓔ

3. Ⓐ Ⓑ Ⓒ Ⓓ Ⓔ   8. Ⓐ Ⓑ Ⓒ Ⓓ Ⓔ   13. Ⓐ Ⓑ Ⓒ Ⓓ Ⓔ   18. Ⓐ Ⓑ Ⓒ Ⓓ Ⓔ

4. Ⓐ Ⓑ Ⓒ Ⓓ Ⓔ   9. Ⓐ Ⓑ Ⓒ Ⓓ Ⓔ   14. Ⓐ Ⓑ Ⓒ Ⓓ Ⓔ   19. Ⓐ Ⓑ Ⓒ Ⓓ Ⓔ

5. Ⓐ Ⓑ Ⓒ Ⓓ Ⓔ   10. Ⓐ Ⓑ Ⓒ Ⓓ Ⓔ   15. Ⓐ Ⓑ Ⓒ Ⓓ Ⓔ   20. Ⓐ Ⓑ Ⓒ Ⓓ Ⓔ

On this test there is a penalty for wrong answers. The total raw score on the test is the number of right answers minus one-fourth of the number of wrong answers. (Fractions of one-half or less are dropped.) First count the number of correct answers you have made. Do not count as correct any questions with more than one answer marked. Then count the number of incorrect answers. Omits are not counted as wrong answers, but double responses do count as wrong. Multiply the total number of incorrect answers by one-fourth. Subtract this number from the total number correct to get the test total score.

Number Right	minus	Number Wrong ($\div 4$)	equals	Raw Score
_____	−	_____	=	_____

SAMPLE QUESTIONS: FEDERAL CLERICAL EXAMINATION

Verbal Tasks Test

Directions: Read each question carefully. Select the best answer and darken the proper space on the answer sheet.

1. To *counteract* means most nearly to
   - (A) undermine
   - (B) censure
   - (C) preserve
   - (D) neutralize

2. *Deferred* means most nearly
   - (A) reversed
   - (B) delayed
   - (C) considered
   - (D) forbidden

3. *Feasible* means most nearly
   - (A) capable
   - (B) justifiable
   - (C) practicable
   - (D) beneficial

4. To *encounter* means most nearly to
   - (A) meet
   - (B) recall
   - (C) overcome
   - (D) retreat

5. *Innate* means most nearly
   - (A) eternal
   - (B) well-developed
   - (C) native
   - (D) prospective

6. STUDENT is related to TEACHER as DISCIPLE is related to
   - (A) follower
   - (B) master
   - (C) principal
   - (D) pupil

7. LECTURE is related to AUDITORIUM as EXPERIMENT is related to
   - (A) scientist
   - (B) chemistry
   - (C) laboratory
   - (D) discovery

8. BODY is related to FOOD as ENGINE is related to
   - (A) wheels
   - (B) fuel
   - (C) motion
   - (D) smoke

9. SCHOOL is related to EDUCATION as THEATER is related to
(A) management   (C) recreation
(B) stage   (D) preparation

10. (A) Most all these statements have been supported by persons who are reliable and can be depended upon.
(B) The persons which have guaranteed these statements are reliable.
(C) Reliable persons guarantee the facts with regards to the truth of these statements.
(D) These statements can be depended on, for their truth has been guaranteed by reliable persons.

11. (A) The success of the book pleased both the publisher and authors.
(B) Both the publisher and they was pleased with the success of the book.
(C) Neither they or their publisher was disappointed with the success of the book.
(D) Their publisher was as pleased as they with the success of the book.

12. (A) extercate   (C) extricate
(B) extracate   (D) none of these

13. (A) hereditory   (C) hereditairy
(B) hereditary   (D) none of these

14. (A) auspiceous   (C) auspicious
(B) auspiseous   (D) none of these

15. (A) sequance   (C) sequense
(B) sequence   (D) none of these

16. The prevention of accidents makes it necessary not only that safety devices be used to guard exposed machinery but also that mechanics be instructed in safety rules which they must follow for their own protection, and that the lighting in the plant be adequate.

The paragraph best supports the statement that industrial accidents

(A) may be due to ignorance
(B) are always avoidable
(C) usually result from inadequate machinery
(D) cannot be entirely overcome

17. The English language is peculiarly rich in synonyms, and there is scarcely a language spoken that has not some representative in English speech. The spirit of the Anglo-Saxon race has subjugated these various elements to one idiom, making not a patchwork, but a composite language.

The paragraph best supports the statement that the English language

(A) has few idiomatic expressions
(B) is difficult to translate
(C) is used universally
(D) has absorbed words from other languages

Clerical Tasks Test

In questions 1 through 5, compare the three names or numbers, and mark the answer:

A if ALL THREE names or numbers are exactly ALIKE
B if only the FIRST and SECOND names or numbers are exactly ALIKE
C if only the FIRST and THIRD names or numbers are exactly ALIKE
D if only the SECOND and THIRD names or numbers are exactly ALIKE
E if ALL THREE names or numbers are DIFFERENT

1. 5261383	5261383	5261338
2. 8125690	8126690	8125609
3. W. E. Johnston	W. E. Johnson	W. E. Johnson
4. Vergil L. Muller	Vergil L. Muller	Vergil L. Muller
5. Atherton R. Warde	Asheton R. Warde	Atherton P. Warde

In questions 6 through 10, find the correct place for the name in the box.

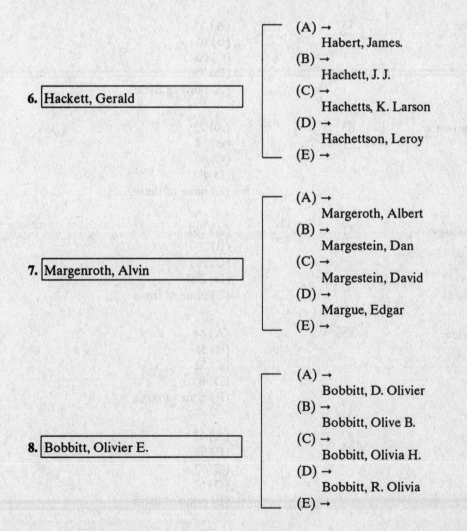

6. | Hackett, Gerald |

(A) →
    Habert, James.
(B) →
    Hachett, J. J.
(C) →
    Hachetts, K. Larson
(D) →
    Hachettson, Leroy
(E) →

7. | Margenroth, Alvin |

(A) →
    Margeroth, Albert
(B) →
    Margestein, Dan
(C) →
    Margestein, David
(D) →
    Margue, Edgar
(E) →

8. | Bobbitt, Olivier E. |

(A) →
    Bobbitt, D. Olivier
(B) →
    Bobbitt, Olive B.
(C) →
    Bobbitt, Olivia H.
(D) →
    Bobbitt, R. Olivia
(E) →

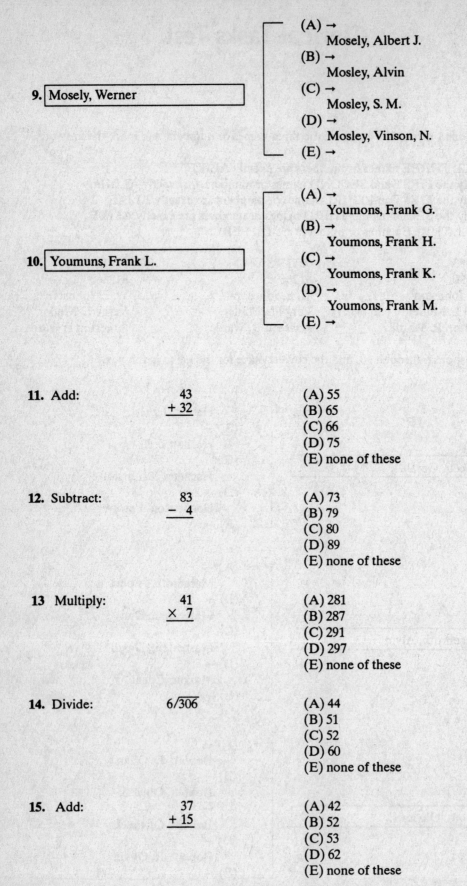

9. Mosely, Werner

(A) →
   Mosely, Albert J.
(B) →
   Mosley, Alvin
(C) →
   Mosley, S. M.
(D) →
   Mosley, Vinson, N.
(E) →

10. Youmuns, Frank L.

(A) →
   Youmons, Frank G.
(B) →
   Youmons, Frank H.
(C) →
   Youmons, Frank K.
(D) →
   Youmons, Frank M.
(E) →

11. Add:
   43
   + 32

(A) 55
(B) 65
(C) 66
(D) 75
(E) none of these

12. Subtract:
   83
   − 4

(A) 73
(B) 79
(C) 80
(D) 89
(E) none of these

13 Multiply:
   41
   × 7

(A) 281
(B) 287
(C) 291
(D) 297
(E) none of these

14. Divide:
   6/306

(A) 44
(B) 51
(C) 52
(D) 60
(E) none of these

15. Add:
   37
   + 15

(A) 42
(B) 52
(C) 53
(D) 62
(E) none of these

For each question below, find which one of the suggested answers appears in that question.

16.	6	2	5	K	4	P	T	G			A = 4, 5, K, T
17.	L	4	7	2	T	6	V	K	Suggested		B = 4, 7, G, K
18.	3	5	4	L	9	V	T	G	Answers		C = 2, 5, G, L
19.	G	4	K	7	L	3	5	Z			D = 2, 7, L, T
20.	4	K	2	9	N	5	T	G			E = none of these

CORRECT ANSWERS

Verbal Tasks Test

1. D	6. B	10. D	14. C
2. B	7. C	11. D	15. B
3. C	8. B	12. C	16. A
4. A	9. C	13. B	17. D
5. C			

Clerical Tasks Test

1. B	6. E	11. D	16. A
2. E	7. A	12. B	17. D
3. D	8. D	13. B	18. E
4. A	9. B	14. B	19. B
5. E	10. E	15. B	20. A

EXPLANATIONS—VERBAL TASKS TEST

1. **(D)** To COUNTERACT is to *act directly against* or to *neutralize*. My father's vote for the Republican candidate always counteracts my mother's vote for the Democrat.

2. **(B)** DEFERRED means *postponed* or *delayed*. Because I had no money in the bank, I deferred paying my taxes until the due date.

3. **(C)** FEASIBLE means *possible* or *practicable*. It is not feasible for the 92-year-old woman to travel abroad.

4. **(A)** To ENCOUNTER is to *come upon* or to *meet*. If you encounter my brother at the ball game, please give my regards.

5. **(C)** INNATE means *existing naturally* or *native*. Some people argue that the maternal instinct is learned rather than innate.

6. **(B)** The DISCIPLE learns from a MASTER as a STUDENT learns from a TEACHER.

7. **(C)** In this analogy of place, an EXPERIMENT occurs in a LABORATORY as a LECTURE occurs in an AUDITORIUM.

8. **(B)** FUEL powers the ENGINE as FOOD powers the BODY.

9. **(C)** RECREATION occurs in the THEATER as EDUCATION occurs in a SCHOOL.

10. **(D)** Choice A might state either "most" or "all" but not both; choice B should read "persons who"; choice C should read "with regard to. . . ."

11. **(D)** Choice A is incorrect because *both* can refer to only two, but the publisher and authors implies at least three; choice B requires the plural verb "were"; choice C requires the correlative construction "neither . . . nor."

12. **(C)** The correct spelling is *extricate*.

13. **(B)** The correct spelling is *hereditary*.

14. **(C)** The correct spelling is *auspicious*.

15. **(B)** The correct spelling is *sequence*.

16. **(A)** If instruction in safety rules will help to prevent accidents, some accidents must occur because of ignorance.

17. **(D)** The language that has some representative in English speech has had some of its words absorbed into English.

EXPLANATIONS—CLERICAL TASKS TEST

1. **(B)** The last two digits of the third number are reversed.

2. **(E)** The middle digit of the second number is "6" while that of the first and third numbers is "5." The last two digits of the third number are reversed.

3. **(D)** The surname of the second and third names is "Johnson"; the surname of the first name is "Johnston."

4. **(A)** All three names are exactly alike.

5. **(E)** The middle initial of the third name differs from the other two. "Asheton" of the second name differs from "Atherton" of the other two.

6. **(E)** Hachettson; Hackett

7. **(A)** Margenroth; Mageroth

8. **(D)** Bobbitt, Olivia H.; Bobbitt, Olivier E.; Bobbitt, R. Olivia

9. **(B)** Mosely, Albert J.; Mosely, Werner; Mosley, Alvin

10. **(E)** Youmons; Youmuns

11. **(D)**
$$\begin{array}{r} 43 \\ +32 \\ \hline 75 \end{array}$$

12. **(B)**
$$\begin{array}{r} 83 \\ -\ 4 \\ \hline 79 \end{array}$$

13. **(B)**
$$\begin{array}{r} 41 \\ \times\ 7 \\ \hline 287 \end{array}$$

14. **(B)**
$$6\overline{)306} \quad 51$$

15. **(B)**
$$\begin{array}{r} 37 \\ +15 \\ \hline 52 \end{array}$$

16. **(A)** 6 2 **5** K **4** P T G.

17. **(D)** L **4** 7 **2** T 6 V K. The answer cannot be (A) because question 17 contains no **5**; it cannot be (B) or (C) because question 17 contains no **G**.

18. **(E)** The answer cannot be (A) or (B) because question 18 contains no **K**; it cannot be (C) or (D) because question 18 contains no **2**.

19. **(B)** G **4** K **7** L 3 **5** Z. The answer cannot be (A) because question 19 contains no **T**.

20 **(A)** **4** K 2 9 N **5** T G.

THE TYPING TEST

Assuming that you already know how to type, the best preparation for any typing test is typing. You may choose any material at all and practice copying it line for line, exactly as you see it. As on the actual typing test, spell, capitalize, punctuate, and begin and end lines exactly as they appear on the page being copied. Do NOT stop to erase or to correct. An error is an error, even if it has been corrected. And corrections take up valuable time. If you make an error, just continue, hoping to compensate for your inaccuracy with superior speed. On the actual typing exam, a basic speed is required, but then accuracy counts more than speed. Try to balance yourself so as to meet speed requirements while maintaining a very high level of accuracy.

The following is a typical test exercise, though NOT the actual test exercise that you will be given. Follow instructions exactly, and practice. Words-per-minute points are marked on the test exercise for your guidance. Try to keep your typing error-free; if you make errors, try to increase your speed. Use an accurate signal timer or have a friend or relative time you.

Space, paragraph, spell, punctuate, capitalize, and begin and end each line precisely as shown in the exercise.

You will have exactly five minutes in which to make repeated copies of the test exercise itself on the paper that will be given to you. Each time you complete the exercise, simply double-space once and begin again. If you fill up one side of the paper, turn it over and continue typing on the other side. Keep on typing until told to stop.

Keep in mind that you must meet minimum standards in both speed and accuracy and that, above these standards, accuracy is twice as important as speed. Make no erasures, insertions, or other corrections in this plain-copy test. Since errors are penalized whether or not they are erased or otherwise "corrected," it is best to keep on typing even though you detect an error.

TEST EXERCISE

	1st typing of exercise	2nd typing of exercise
Because they have often learned to know types of archi-	_____	52 wpm
tecture by decoration, casual observers sometimes fail to	_____	54
realize that the significant part of a structure is not the	_____	56
ornamentation but the body itself. Architecture, because	_____	59
of its close contact with human lives, is peculiarly and	_____	61
intimately governed by climate. For instance, a home built	_____	64
for comfort in the cold and snow of the northern areas of	_____	66
this country would be unbearably warm in a country with	_____	68
weather such as that of Cuba. A Cuban house, with its open	_____	71
court, would prove impossible to heat in a northern winter.	_____	73
Since the purpose of architecture is the construction of	_____	76
shelters in which human beings may carry on their numerous	_____	78
activities, the designer must consider not only climatic con-	_____	80
ditions, but also the function of a building. Thus, although	_____	_____
the climate of a certain locality requires that an auditorium	_____	_____
and a hospital have several features in common, the purposes	_____	_____
for which they will be used demand some difference in struc-	40 wpm	
ture. For centuries builders have first complied with these	42	_____
two requirements and later added whatever ornamentation they	44	_____
wished. Logically, we should see as mere additions, not as	47	_____
basic parts, the details by which we identify architecture.	49	

EACH TIME YOU REACH THIS POINT, DOUBLE-SPACE ONCE AND BEGIN AGAIN.

STENOGRAPHY

Only stenographer competitors take a stenography test. The sample below shows the length of material dictated. Have someone dictate the passage to you so that you can see how well prepared you are to take dictation at 80 words per minute. Take notes on your own paper.

Directions to person dictating: This practice dictation should be dictated at the rate of 80 words a minute. Do not dictate the punctuation except for periods, but dictate with the expression the punctuation indicates. Use a watch with a second hand to enable you to read the exercises at the proper speed.

Exactly on a minute start dictating.

Finish reading each two lines at the number of seconds indicated below.

I realize that this practice dictation is not a part of the examination	10
proper and is not to be scored. (Period) The work of preventing and correcting	20
physical defects in children is becoming more effective as a result of change	30
in the attitude of many parents. (Period) In order to bring about this change,	40
parents have been invited to visit the schools when their children are being examined	50
and to discuss the treatment necessary for the correction of defects. (Period)	1 min.
There is a distinct value in having a parent see that his or her child is not the	10
only one who needs attention. (Period) Otherwise a few parents might feel that they	20
were being criticized by having the defects of their children singled out for medical	30
treatment. (Period) The special classes that have been set up have shown the value of	40
the scientific knowledge that has been applied in the treatment of children. (Period)	50
In these classes the children have been taught to exercise by a trained teacher	2 min.
under medical supervision. (Period) The hours of the school day have been divided	10
between school work and physical activity that helps not only to correct their defects	20
but also to improve their general physical condition. (Period) This method of treatment	30
has been found to be very effective except for those who have severe medical	40
defects. (Period) Most parents now see how desirable it is to have these classes	50
that have been set up in the regular school system to meet special needs. (Period)	3 min.

After dictating the practice, pause for 15 seconds to permit competitor to complete notetaking.

SAMPLE DICTATION TRANSCRIPT SHEET

The transcript below is part of the material that was dictated to you for practice, except that many of the words have been left out. From your notes, you are to tell what the missing words are. Proceed as follows:

Compare your notes with the transcript and, when you come to a blank in the transcript, decide what word (or words) belongs there. For example, you will find that the word "practice" belongs in blank number 1. Look at the word list to see whether you can find the same word there. Notice what letter (A, B, C, or D) is printed beside it, and write that letter in the blank. For example, the word "practice" is listed followed by the letter B. We have already written B in blank number 1 to show you how you are to record your choice. Now decide what belongs in each of the other blanks. (You may also write the word or words, or the shorthand for them, if you wish.) The same word may belong in more than one blank. If the exact answer is not listed, write E in the blank.

ALPHABETIC WORD LIST

Write *E* if the answer is NOT listed.

about—B	paper—B
against—C	parents—B
attitude—A	part—C
being—D	physical—D
childhood—B	portion—D
children—A	practical—A
correcting—C	practice—B
doctors—B	preliminary—D
effective—D	preventing—B
efficient—A	procedure—A
examination—A	proper—C
examining—C	reason for—A
for—B	result—B
health—B	result of—C
mothers—C	schools—C
never—C	to be—C
not—D	to prevent—A

TRANSCRIPT

I realize that this ___B___ dictation is ____

      1   2

a ____ of the ____ ____ and is ____ ____
    3   4   5   6   7

scored.

The work ____ and ____ ____ defects
          8   9   10

in ____ is becoming more ____ as a ____
    11   12   13

a change in the ____ of many ____ .
                  14   15

ALPHABETIC WORD LIST

Write *E* if the answer is NOT listed.

all—A	reducing—A
at—C	satisfied—D
bring—A	say—C
collection—B	see—B
correction—C	soon—C
discuss—C	their—D
during—D	to discover—A
friend—A	to discuss—D
indicated—C	to endorse—C
insisted—D	to visit—B
is—B	treatments—A
is not—A	understand—D
know—A	undertake—B
knows—D	virtue—D
needed—B	visit—A
promote—B	volume—B
recognizing—D	young—C

TRANSCRIPT (Continued)

In order to ____ ____ this change,
    16   17

parents have been invited ____ the
                        18

schools when ____ children are being
            19

examined and ____ the ____ necessary for
            20   21

the ____ of defects. There is a distinct
    22

____ in having a parent ____ that his or her
23   24

child ____ the only one who needs
     25

attention. . . . (The rest of the sample

dictation is not transcribed here.)

(For the next sentences there would be another word list, if the entire sample dictation were transcribed.)

You will be given an answer sheet like the sample below, on which your answers can be scored by machine. Each number on the answer sheet stands for the blank with the same number in the transcript. Darken the space with the letter that is the same as the letter you wrote in the transcript. If you have not finished writing letters in the blanks in the transcript, or if you wish to make sure you have lettered them correctly, you may continue to use your notes after you begin marking the answer sheet.

Answer Sheet for Sample Dictation

1. Ⓐ Ⓑ Ⓒ Ⓓ Ⓔ	8. Ⓐ Ⓑ Ⓒ Ⓓ Ⓔ	14. Ⓐ Ⓑ Ⓒ Ⓓ Ⓔ	20. Ⓐ Ⓑ Ⓒ Ⓓ Ⓔ
2. Ⓐ Ⓑ Ⓒ Ⓓ Ⓔ	9. Ⓐ Ⓑ Ⓒ Ⓓ Ⓔ	15. Ⓐ Ⓑ Ⓒ Ⓓ Ⓔ	21. Ⓐ Ⓑ Ⓒ Ⓓ Ⓔ
3. Ⓐ Ⓑ Ⓒ Ⓓ Ⓔ	10. Ⓐ Ⓑ Ⓒ Ⓓ Ⓔ	16. Ⓐ Ⓑ Ⓒ Ⓓ Ⓔ	22. Ⓐ Ⓑ Ⓒ Ⓓ Ⓔ
4. Ⓐ Ⓑ Ⓒ Ⓓ Ⓔ	11. Ⓐ Ⓑ Ⓒ Ⓓ Ⓔ	17. Ⓐ Ⓑ Ⓒ Ⓓ Ⓔ	23. Ⓐ Ⓑ Ⓒ Ⓓ Ⓔ
5. Ⓐ Ⓑ Ⓒ Ⓓ Ⓔ	12. Ⓐ Ⓑ Ⓒ Ⓓ Ⓔ	18. Ⓐ Ⓑ Ⓒ Ⓓ Ⓔ	24. Ⓐ Ⓑ Ⓒ Ⓓ Ⓔ
6. Ⓐ Ⓑ Ⓒ Ⓓ Ⓔ	13. Ⓐ Ⓑ Ⓒ Ⓓ Ⓔ	19. Ⓐ Ⓑ Ⓒ Ⓓ Ⓔ	25. Ⓐ Ⓑ Ⓒ Ⓓ Ⓔ
7. Ⓐ Ⓑ Ⓒ Ⓓ Ⓔ			

The correct answers for the sample dictation are:

1. B	8. B	14. A	20. D
2. D	9. C	15. B	21. E
3. C	10. D	16. A	22. C
4. A	11. A	17. E	23. E
5. C	12. D	18. B	24. B
6. D	13. C	19. D	25. A
7. C			

Compare your answers with the correct answers. If one of your answers does not agree with the correct answer, again compare your notes with the samples and make certain you understand the instructions.

Your notes should show that the word "bring" goes in blank 16, and "about" in blank 17. But "about" is *not in the list;* so E should be your answer for question 17.

The two words, "to visit—B," are needed for 18, and the one word "visit—A," would be an incorrect answer.

For the actual test you will use a separate answer sheet. As scoring will be done by an electric machine, it is important that you follow directions carefully. Make a heavy mark for each answer. If you have to change your mark for any question, be sure to erase the first mark completely (do not merely cross it out) before making another.

Correctly Filled Transcript for Sample Dictation

Check your notes against the dictation; check your notes against the alphabetic list of words and the transcript sheet; check the transcript against your answer grid. Identify your errors.

I realize that this ___B___ dictation is ___D___
                   1   2

a ___C___ of the ___A___ ___C___ and is ___D___ ___C___
    3   4   5   6   7

scored.

The work ___B___ and ___C___ ___D___ defects
             8   9   10

in ___A___ is becoming more ___D___ as a ___C___
   11   12   13

a change in the ___A___ of many ___B___ .
              14   15

In order to ___A___ ___E___ this change,
            16   17

parents have been invited ___B___ the
                         18

schools when ___D___ children are being
              19

examined and ___D___ the ___E___ necessary for
             20   21

the ___C___ of defects. There is a distinct
     22

___E___ in having a parent ___B___ that his or her
23   24

child ___A___ the only one who needs
     25

attention. . . . (The rest of the sample

dictation is not transcribed here.)

MISCELLANEOUS OPM QUESTIONS

The following questions represent a sample of OPM questions drawn from a variety of specialized exams.

Directions: For each question, circle the letter of the answer you choose.

Mechanical and Nonverbal Tests

SYMBOL SERIES

Questions 1 and 2 consist of a series of five symbols at the left and five other symbols labeled A, B, C, D, and E at the right.

In each question, first study the series of symbols at the left; then from the symbols at the right, labeled A, B, C, D, and E, select the one which continues the series most completely.

1.

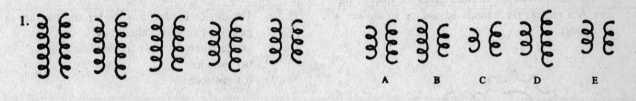

Each symbol in the series at the left has two coils. The symbols differ from one another in the number of loops that each coil has. In the first symbol, each coil has five loops; in the second, the left-hand one has four and the right-hand one has five; in the third, each coil has four. In this series, first the left-hand coil loses a loop and then the right-hand coil loses one.

Since the fifth symbol has three loops in each coil, the next symbol in this series must have two loops in the left-hand coil and three in the right-hand coil. Since symbol A is the only one which has two loops in the left-hand coil and three in the right-hand coil, A is the answer.

2.

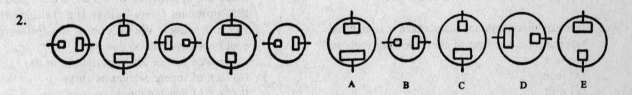

Question 2 is harder. The first five symbols show an alternation from small to large to small; and a quarter-turn in a counterclockwise direction each time. The answer should be a large circle, therefore (which eliminates B from the alternatives), with the larger rectangle at the bottom of the circle (which eliminates D and E). A second look at A shows that the rectangles within it are larger than any of the rectangles in the other circles; this change has no basis in the series. Thus C is left as the correct answer.

TOOLS AND MECHANICAL PRINCIPLES

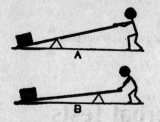

1. In which, if either, of the figures shown above can the man lift more weight?
   (A) A
   (B) B
   (C) The men in figures A and B can lift equal weights.
   (D) The man who can lift more weight cannot be determined.

   The position of the fulcrum gives the man in figure A a greater mechanical advantage so answer A is correct.

2. In the gears shown above, as gear X turns in a counterclockwise direction, gear Y turns
   (A) clockwise at the same speed
   (B) clockwise at a faster speed
   (C) counterclockwise at a slower speed
   (D) counterclockwise at the same speed

3. In order to smooth and standardize a straight or tapered hole, the best of the following tools to use is a
   (A) reamer
   (B) drill
   (C) tap
   (D) cold chisel
   (E) compass saw

4. The tool illustrated above is a
   (A) counterbore
   (B) tap
   (C) center punch
   (D) rose countersink
   (E) pin punch

5. Which one of the following frequencies is most commonly used in the United States in alternating-current lighting circuits?
   (A) 10 cycles   (D) 60 cycles
   (B) 25 cycles   (E) 110 cycles
   (C) 40 cycles

6. The device used to mix the air and the fuel in a gasoline engine is called the
   (A) carburetor   (D) manifold
   (B) cylinder   (E) valve
   (C) distributor

7. Which one of the following would cause excessive backlash in the rear axle assembly?
   (A) bent rear axle shaft
   (B) chipped differential gears
   (C) improper lubrication
   (D) worn differential gears and thrust washers
   (E) ring gear adjusted too close to pinion

8. As a driver brought his truck into a long curve to the left at 40 miles per hour, he made a moderate application of his air brakes, and at that point he felt a pull to the right on the steering wheel. Which one of the following could *not* have caused that pull?
   (A) sudden loss of air from right front tire
   (B) lack of superelevation on curve
   (C) lack of adequate tread on front tires
   (D) unbalanced adjustment of brakes

ANSWER KEY

1. A	3. A	5. D	7. D
2. B	4. C	6. A	8. C

GRAPH AND METER READING

The following questions can be answered by reading the bar graph at the right.

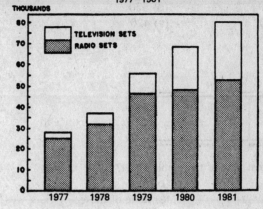

OUTPUT OF RADIO SETS AND TELEVISION SETS BY FACTORY "K"
1977–1981

1. In the year in which the total output of the factory was the least, the percentage of that output which consisted of television sets was approximately
   (A) 10%   (D) 30%
   (B) 20%   (E) 40%
   (C) 25%

2. In which year did the production of television sets total approximately 20,000?
   (A) 1977   (D) 1980
   (B) 1978   (E) 1981
   (C) 1979

3. The position of the pointer on the meter scale is nearest to
   (A) 2.6   (C) 3.2
   (B) 3.1   (D) 3.3

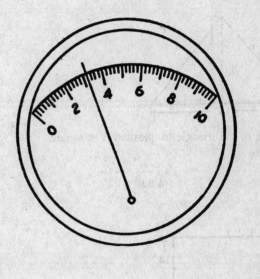

An examination of the meter scale shows, first, that only the even numbers are given on the dial. Between each pair of numbers are 10 small subdivisions. The position of the odd numbers is indicated by the slightly longer subdivision mark. Since there are five subdivisions between the positions of two successive whole numbers, each subdivision indicates 1/5 or .2.

The pointer in the example is closest to one subdivision beyond 3; the correct reading of the meter would 3 + 1/5, or 3.2

For a reading of 3.1, the pointer would be midway between the mark corresponding to 3 and the mark corresponding to 3.2.

ANSWER KEY

1. A   2. D   3. C

SHOP ARITHMETIC

1. When 100, 125, 75, and 20 are added the answer is
   (A) 220
   (D) 320
   (B) 270
   (E) 420
   (C) 325

2.

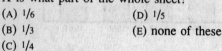

   X is what part of the whole sheet?
   (A) 1/6
   (D) 1/5
   (B) 1/3
   (E) none of these
   (C) 1/4

3.

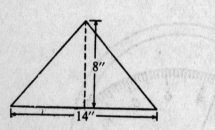

   The area of the triangle in question 3 in square inches is
   (A) 56
   (D) 22
   (B) 112
   (E) 448
   (C) 122

4.

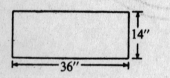

   What is the greatest number of pieces 9" × 2" that could be cut from the given sheet of metal?
   (A) 18
   (D) 80
   (B) 21
   (E) 28
   (C) 26

5.

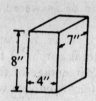

   The volume of the rectangular solid in cubic inches is
   (A) 224
   (D) 56
   (B) 28
   (E) 32
   (C) 896

6. 1/2 of 1/4 is
   (A) 1/12
   (D) 1/4
   (B) 1/8
   (E) 8
   (C) 1/2

7. A circular saw cuts 8 boards per minute. If there are 1,440 boards to be cut, the number of *hours* required to cut these boards is
   (A) 2 1/3
   (D) 3 2/3
   (B) 2 2/3
   (E) 3
   (C) 4

8. A drawing of a certain building is 10 inches by 15 inches. On this drawing 1 inch represents 5 feet. If the same drawing had been made 20 inches by 30 inches, 1 inch on the drawing would represent
   (A) 7 1/2 feet
   (D) 3 1/3 feet
   (B) 5 feet
   (E) 2 1/2 feet
   (C) 10 feet

9. During his first 8-hour day, an apprentice earned 40 percent as much as a master mechanic. If the master mechanic earned $112.00, what was the apprentice's average *hourly* earning?
   (A) $6.40
   (D) $4.48
   (B) $9.60
   (E) none of these
   (C) $6.72

10. An opening 6 yards long and 3 feet wide is to be covered by sheathing. Enough lumber is available to cover two-thirds of the area of the opening. How many square feet will remain uncovered?
    (A) 2
    (D) 12
    (B) 4
    (E) none of these
    (C) 6

ANSWER KEY

1. D	3. A	5. A	7. E	9. E
2. C	4. E	6. B	8. E	10. E

Knowledge Tests for Professional and Semiprofessional Positions

STATISTICS

1. If 4 is added to every observation in a sample, the mean is
   (A) increased by 4
   (B) increased by 4 times the number of observations
   (C) increased by 4 divided by the number of observations
   (D) decreased by 4
   (E) not affected

2. A distribution for which one of the following variables would constitute a discrete series?
   (A) weight of eighth-grade pupils
   (B) width of the visual field
   (C) "items right" score on a history test
   (D) auditory reaction time
   (E) age at marriage of 850 musicians

3. Of the following measures, which one is the most stable under conditions of random sampling?
   (A) mode
   (B) median
   (C) arithmetic mean
   (D) harmonic mean
   (E) geometric mean

4. The standard deviation is a measure of which one of the following characteristics of a population?
   (A) skewness
   (B) symmetry
   (C) normality
   (D) randomness
   (E) variability

ANSWER KEY

1. A	3. C
2. C	4. E

ACCOUNTING

1. An operating mining company properly charged $1,200 to expense to reflect the wear and tear on its equipment. The corresponding credit should have been made to
   (A) reserve for contingent liability
   (B) reserve for depletion
   (C) reserve for depreciation
   (D) surplus reserve
   (E) earned surplus

2. The Jones Company had a merchandise inventory of $24,625 on January 1, 1950. During the year the company purchased $60,000 worth of goods, sales were $85,065, and the cost of goods sold was $28,060. The inventory on December 31, 1950, was
   (A) $28,065.00
   (B) $28,500.00
   (C) $49,690.00
   (D) $57,005.00
   (E) none of these

ANSWER KEY

1. C	2. E

WEATHER FORECASTING

1. Particles of dust, smoke, or microbes often cause the air to be
   - (A) hazy
   - (B) clear
   - (C) humid
   - (D) dry
   - (E) cold

2. Helium, neon, krypton, and xenon are
   - (A) never found in the atmosphere
   - (B) found in place of hydrogen in the upper atmosphere
   - (C) found in the atmosphere in very small quantities
   - (D) found in the Arctic region in largest proportion
   - (E) found only over the ocean

3. The air is warmed to the greatest extent by
   - (A) the sun's rays directly
   - (B) only conduction from the earth
   - (C) hot vapors
   - (D) dust particles
   - (E) both convection and conduction from the earth

ANSWER KEY

1. A   2. C   3. E

SAFETY

1. An electrical detonator is
   - (A) an instrument used to measure electrical energy
   - (B) a part of an electrical signaling apparatus
   - (C) a device used for detecting sound
   - (D) a device used to fire explosives
   - (E) a part of an electric-light bulb

2. Most authorities in the field of safety planning agree that the ultimate success of any safety program depends on the
   - (A) individual worker
   - (B) foreman
   - (C) management
   - (D) state government
   - (E) safety instructor

ANSWER KEY

1. D   2. A

MATHEMATICS

1. The product of $(3m - n)$ and $3m$ is
   - (A) $9m^2 - 3mn$
   - (B) $9m^2 - mn$
   - (C) $9m - 3n$
   - (D) $9m^2 - n^2$
   - (E) $3m^2 - 3mn$

2. Find the total differential of $(x^2 + y^2)^{1/2}$.
   - (A) $x(x^2 + y^2) - 1/2$
   - (B) $y(x^2 + y^2) - 1/2$
   - (C) $xdx + ydy$
   - (D) $\dfrac{xdx}{\sqrt{x^2 + y^2}} + \dfrac{ydy}{\sqrt{x^2 + y^2}}$
   - (E) $xdx - ydy$

3. The length l of a spiral spring supporting a pan is increased c centimeters for x grams of weight placed on the pan. What is the length of the spring if w grams are placed on the pan?
   - (A) $lc + \dfrac{x}{w}$
   - (B) $l + \dfrac{w}{cw}$
   - (C) $l + \dfrac{cw}{x}$
   - (D) $\dfrac{l + cw}{x}$
   - (E) $\dfrac{l + cx}{w}$

ANSWER KEY

1. A   2. D   3. C

ENGINEERING AND OTHER PHYSICAL SCIENCES

1. A plane figure consists of a square 10 inches on a side and an isosceles triangle whose base is the left edge of the square and whose altitude dropped from the vertex opposite the 10-inch base of the triangle common to the square is 6 inches. Approximately how far in inches from the left side of the square is the center of gravity of the whole figure located?
   - (A) 2.92
   - (B) 3.15
   - (C) 3.38
   - (D) 3.75
   - (E) 4.28

2. The stiffness of a rectangular beam varies
   - (A) as the depth
   - (B) inversely as the depth
   - (C) as the square of the depth
   - (D) as the cube of the depth
   - (E) inversely as the cube of the depth

3. At atmospheric pressure, steam at 100° C. is passed into 400 grams of water at 10° C. until the temperature of the water rises to 40° C. It is then found that the weight of the water has increased to 420 grams due to the condensing steam. The heat of vaporization of steam in calories per gram at 100° C. is
   - (A) 60
   - (B) 300
   - (C) 540
   - (D) 600
   - (E) none of these

4. The addition of HCl to a solution of sodium acetate causes
   - (A) the precipitation of sodium chloride
   - (B) a decrease in the concentration of acetate ion
   - (C) an increase in the concentration of sodium ion
   - (D) an increase in the concentration of hydroxide ion
   - (E) no change in the concentration of hydroxide ion

ANSWER KEY

1. C   2. D   3. C   4. B

PSYCHOLOGY

1. In experiments on the localization of sound in space, the sounds which can be most accurately located by the hearer are those sounds originating at points
   (A) in the plane equidistant from the two ears of the hearer
   (B) in front of the hearer
   (C) above and below the hearer
   (D) to the left and to the right of the hearer
   (E) behind the hearer

2. In the field of measurement of interests, the Preference Record is associated with the name of
   (A) Remmers
   (B) Kuder
   (C) Bingham
   (D) Viteles
   (E) Bell

ANSWER KEY

1. D   2. B

ADMINISTRATION

1. A number of national organizations require the approval of the headquarters office on all actions originating in the field offices, instead of following the alternate procedure of delegating authority for such actions. This requirement of headquarters' review and approval is frequently unsatisfactory to the headquarters office itself. In general, the most frequent reason for the *dissatisfaction* in the headquarters office is that
   (A) headquarters may lack the information necessary for approving these cases
   (B) field offices resent the review
   (C) the review causes delay
   (D) it is felt that authority should be commensurate with responsibility
   (E) clearance through a large number of divisions is required in most headquarters offices

ANSWER KEY

1. A

OCCUPATIONAL ANALYSIS

1. In the machine shop of a manufacturing firm, a job with the title of Foreman has the following duties:

"Installs cutting tools in various types of semiautomatic machinery. Adjusts the guides, stops, working tables of machines, and other controls to handle the size of stock to be machined. Operates and adjusts machine until accurate production (based on blueprint specifications, patterns, or templates) has been achieved. Checks production with precision gages, often to tolerances of 0.0005 inch. Turns machine over to regular operator when it is producing satisfactorily."

Which of the following would be the most descriptive title for this job?
(A) cutting-machine mechanic
(B) dimensional checker
(C) job setter
(D) machinist
(E) tool and die maker

ANSWER KEY

1. C

PUBLIC AFFAIRS

1. The most important way in which geographic factors influence rural community structure is by
   (A) influencing the size of the farms and thus the density of the population
   (B) influencing the birth rate
   (C) dictating the habits of the people
   (D) influencing the temperament of the people in such a way as to make them cooperative or non-cooperative
   (E) being the most important determinants of community boundaries

ANSWER KEY

1. A

SUPERVISION

1. In general, the most important advantage of good employee morale is that it results in
   (A) high production
   (B) decreased work for the supervisor
   (C) increased ease in rating workers' efficiency
   (D) high standing for the supervisor with management
   (E) less desire for wage increases among employees

2. Which one of the following types of information would be most useful to a supervisor in determining which employee should lose his job in case lay-offs are necessary?
   (A) length of service with the supervisor
   (B) marital status
   (C) education
   (D) age
   (E) job performance rating

3. A supervisor is planning a discussion with his workers as part of a training course. To which one of the following factors should he give the most attention?
   (A) preparing in advance questions that will promote the discussion of important matters
   (B) getting as many workers as possible to attend the meeting
   (C) inviting only those workers who do not hesitate to speak in a group
   (D) making certain that the meeting will not drag out too long
   (E) selecting about six workers to make speeches which they will prepare in advance

4. A group of employees has recently been hired to perform simple, routine tasks. The use of which one of the following statements in the training of the group would be most likely, in general, to create interest in this work?

(A) emphasis upon the pleasant working conditions and special services which the company offers its employees

(B) explanation of the inspection system by which all work is reviewed in order to make certain that it conforms with requirements.

(C) demonstration that the work is extremely simple and therefore there can be no excuse for failure to perform it properly

(D) a frank statement that the work is monotonous but must be done even if it is not interesting

(E) explanation of the relationship and the importance of the work to the total work of the organization

Answer Key

1. A		3. A	
2. E		4. E	

SAMPLE QUESTIONS: ACWA

The questions selected as sample questions for the written test are similar to the questions you will find in the actual test in terms of difficulty and form. In general, the test questions deal with topics related to Government business which you would be likely to encounter.

PART A: VOCABULARY AND READING

The total time alloted for Part A is 50 minutes. Part A will consist of fifteen vocabulary questions and twenty reading questions. It should take you about 5 minutes to answer the vocabulary questions, which would leave you 45 minutes for the reading questions. Do not spend much more than five minutes on the vocabulary questions, since this would cut into the time you have for answering the reading questions. However, if you finish Part A before the allotted time is over, you should review your answers in both the Vocabulary and the Reading sections, especially any answers about which you were uncertain.

VOCABULARY QUESTIONS

Federal jobs require you to communicate well both in written and spoken language. Consequently, a good vocabulary is important for successful job performance. The following questions present a key word and five suggested answers. Your task is to find the suggested answer that is closest in meaning to the key word. Wrong answers may have some connection with the word, but their meanings will be essentially different from that of the key word. Sample questions 1 and 2 are examples of the vocabulary questions in the test.

1. To *collaborate* means most nearly to work

   (A) rapidly
   (B) together
   (C) independently

   (D) overtime
   (E) carefully

The word *collaborate* means to work with another, especially on a project of mutual interest. Therefore, response B, *together*, is the best answer. Responses A, D, and E are clearly unrelated to the meaning of *collaborate,* and response C, *independently*, is opposite in meaning.

2. *Altruistic* means most nearly

   (A) unselfish
   (B) extended
   (C) unimaginative

   (D) organized
   (E) appealing

To be *altruistic* means to be concerned for or devoted to the welfare of others. Therefore, response A, *unselfish*, is an excellent synonym. Response B could be viewed as slightly related, since *altruistic* people often extend themselves to help others. However, the basic meaning of *extended*—stretched out—is completely different from the meaning of *altruistic.* Responses C and D are clearly unrelated to the meaning of *altruistic.* A vague connection exists between *altruistic* and response E, *appealing. Altruistic* people often make appeals on behalf of those less fortunate than themselves. Simultaneously, the generosity of *altruistic* people often makes them very *appealing* to other people. Although this vague connection exists between *altruistic* and *appealing*, they do not share a similar meaning.

READING QUESTIONS

In each of these questions you will be given a paragraph which contains all the information necessary to infer the correct answer. Use **only** the information provided in the paragraph. Do not speculate or make assumptions that go beyond this information. Also, assume that all information given in the paragraph is true, even if it conflicts with some fact known to you. Only one correct answer can be validly inferred from the information contained in the paragraph.

Pay special attention to negated verbs (for example, "are *not*") and negative prefixes (for example, "*in*complete" or "*dis*organized"). Also pay special attention to quantifiers, such as "all," "none," and "some." For example, from a paragraph in which it is stated that "it is not true that all contracts are legal" one can validly infer that "some contracts are not legal," or that "some contracts are illegal," or that "some illegal things are contracts," but one **cannot** validly infer that "no contracts are legal," or that "some contracts are legal." Similarly, from a paragraph that states "all contracts are legal" and "all contracts are two-sided agreements," one can infer that "some two-sided agreements are legal," but one **cannot** validly infer that "all two-sided agreements are legal."

Bear in mind that in some tests, universal quantifiers such as "all" and "none" often give away incorrect response choices. That is **not** the case in this test. Some correct answers will refer to "all" or "none" of the members of a group.

Be sure to distinguish between essential information and unessential, peripheral information. That is to say, in a real test question, the example above ("all contracts are legal" and "all contracts are two-sided agreements") would appear in a longer, full-fledged paragraph. It would be up to you to separate the essential information from its context, and then to realize that a response choice that states "some two-sided agreements are legal" represents a valid inference and hence the correct answer.

Sample questions 3 and 4 are examples of the reading questions in the text.

3. Personnel administration begins with the process of defining the quantities of people needed to do the job. Therefore, people must be recruited, selected, trained, directed, rewarded, transferred, promoted, and perhaps released or retired. However, it is not true that all organizations are structured so that workers can be dealt with as individuals. In some organizations, employees are represented by unions, and managers bargain directly only with these associations.

The paragraph best supports the statement that

(A) no organizations are structured so that workers cannot be dealt with as individuals

(B) some working environments other than organizations are structured so that workers can be dealt with as individuals

(C) all organizations are structured so that employees are represented by unions

(D) no organizations are structured so that managers bargain with unions

(E) some organizations are not structured so that workers can be dealt with as individuals

- The correct answer is response E. This conclusion can be derived from information contained in the third sentence of the paragraph, which states that *it is not true that all organizations are structured so that workers can be dealt with as individuals.* From this statement, it can be inferred that *some organizations are not structured so that workers can be dealt with as individuals.*

- Response A is incorrect because it contradicts the information in the third and fourth sentences of the paragraph. With its double negation, response A is in effect saying that all organizations are structured so that workers can be dealt with as individuals. This flatly contradicts the third sentence and also contradicts the fourth sentence, which says that *in some organizations, employees are represented by unions, and managers bargain with these associations.*

- Response B is not supported by the paragraph because the paragraph gives no information about working environments other than organizations.

- Response C is not supported by the paragraph because the paragraph says only that employees are represented by unions in *some* organizations. One cannot generalize from this to say that employees are represented by unions in *all* organizations.

- Response D is incorrect because it contradicts the fourth sentence, which says that managers bargain with unions in some organizations.

Note that in this question, the correct answer follows basically from one sentence in the paragraph—the third sentence. The rest of the paragraph presents additional information about personnel administration which is relevant to the discussion, but not necessary to make the inference. Part of your task in the Reading section is to *understand* what you read, and then to *discern* what conclusions follow logically from statements in the paragraph. Consequently, in this test, you will find some questions in which it is necessary to use all or most of the statements presented in the paragraph, while in others, such as this one, only one statement is needed to infer the correct answer.

4. Many kinds of computer programming languages have been developed over the years. Initially, programmers had to write instructions in machine language. If a computer programming language is a machine language, then it is a code which can be read directly by a computer. Most high-level computer programming languages, such as Fortran and Cobol, use strings of common English phrases which communicate with the computer only after being converted or translated into a machine code.

The paragraph best supports the statement that

(A) all high-level computer programming languages use strings of common English phrases which are converted to a machine code

(B) if a computer programming language is a machine language, then it is not a code which can be read directly by a computer

(C) if a computer programming language is a code which can be read directly by a computer, then it is not a machine language

(D) if a computer programming language is not a code which can be read directly by a computer, then it is not a machine language

(E) if a computer programming language is not a machine language, then it is a code which can be read directly by a computer

- The correct answer is response D. The answer can be derived from the information presented in the third sentence. That sentence states that *if a computer programming language is a machine language, then it is a code which can be read directly by a computer.* From this statement it can be seen that all machine languages are codes which can be read directly by a computer, and that if a computer programming language is not such a code, then it is not a machine language.

- Response A goes beyond the information presented in the paragraph, which states only that *most* high-level computer programming languages use strings of common English phrases.
- Response B represents a complete contradiction of the third sentence of the paragraph.
- Response C contradicts the paragraph. We know from the paragraph that at least some coded languages which can be read directly by a computer are machine languages.
- Response E is incorrect because the paragraph does not say whether or not computer languages that are *not* machine languages are codes which can be read directly by a computer.

PART B: TABULAR COMPLETION AND ARITHMETIC REASONING

The total time allotted to Part B is 50 minutes. Part B will consist of ten tabular completion questions and fifteen arithmetic reasoning questions. It should take you no more than 15 minutes to answer the tabular completion questions, which would leave you 35 minutes for the arithmetic reasoning questions. Some problems in Part B may be solved by more than one method. When this is the case, use whatever method is fastest and easiest for you. Keep in mind, however, that each question has only **one** correct answer. If you finish Part B before the allotted time is over, you should review your answers in both the Tabular Completion and Arithmetic Reasoning sections, especially any answers about which you were uncertain. *The use of calculators will NOT be permitted during the actual test; therefore, they should not be used to solve these sample questions.*

TABULAR COMPLETION QUESTIONS

These questions are based on information presented in tables. Only *two* sample questions of this type appear below, although, in the actual test, you will have to find *five* unknown values in each table. You must calculate these unknown values by using the known values given in the table. In some questions, the exact answer will not be given as one of the response choices. In such cases, you should select response E, "none of these." Sample questions 5 and 6, which are based on the accompanying table, are examples of the tabular completion questions in this test.

FEDERAL BUDGET RECEIPTS OUTLAYS, AND DEBT
FISCAL YEARS 1981-1985
(In millions of dollars)

ITEM	FISCAL YEAR				
	1981	1982	1983	1984	1985
Total Receipts	I	298,060	355,559	399,561	463,302
Federal funds....................	187,505	201,099	241,312	270,490	316,366
Trust funds......................	116,683	131,750	150,560	165,569	186,988
Interfund transactions..........	−25,098	−34,789	−36,313	−36,498	−40,052
Total Outlays	324,244	364,473	400,507	448,368	490,997
Federal funds....................	240,080	269,921	295,757	331,991	362,396
Trust funds.....................	109,262	II	141,063	152,875	168,653
Interfund transactions..........	−25,098	−34,789	−36,313	−36,498	−40,052
Total Surplus or Deficit (−).......	−45,154	−66,413	−44,948	−48,807	V
Federal funds....................	−52,576	−68,822	−54,444	−61,501	−40,030
Trust funds.....................	7,422	2,409	9,496	12,694	12,336
Gross Federal Debt	544,131	631,866	III	780,425	833,751
Held by Government agencies ...	147,225	151,566	157,295	169,477	189,162
Held by the public..............	396,906	480,300	551,843	610,948	644,589
Federal Reserve System	84,993	94,714	105,004	IV	115,594
Other	311,913	385,586	446,839	495,468	528,995

Hypothetical data.

5. What is the value of I in millions of dollars?

(A)   91,585
(B)   162,407
(C)   279,090
(D)   304,188
(E)   none of these

The correct answer is C. It can be calculated by adding the Receipt values for *Federal funds, Trust funds,* and *Interfund transactions.* Numerically, 187,505 + 116,683 + (−25,098) = 279,090.

6. What is the value of II in millions of dollars?

(A)   329,684
(B)   129,341
(C)   94,552
(D) −101,202
(E)   none of these

The correct answer is B. It can be calculated by subtracting the Outlay values for *Federal funds* and *Interfund transactions* from the value for *Total Outlays.* Numerically, 364,473 − (269,921) − (−34,789) = 129,341.

ARITHMETIC REASONING QUESTIONS

In this part of the test you will have to solve problems formulated in both verbal and numeric form. You will have to analyze a paragraph in order to set up the problem, and then solve it. If the exact answer is not given as one of the response choices, you should select response E, "none of these." Sample questions 7 and 8 are examples of the arithmetic reasoning questions in this test.

7. An interagency task force has representatives from three different agencies. Half of the task force members represent Agency A, one-third represent Agency B, and three represent Agency C. How many people are on the task force?

   (A) 12
   (B) 15
   (C) 18
   (D) 24
   (E) none of these

The correct answer is response C. It can be obtained by computing the following:

$$1/2 \, X + 1/3 \, X + 3 = X$$

X is equal to the total number of task force members; $1/2 \, X$ represents the number from Agency A; $1/3 \, X$ represents the number from Agency B; and 3 is the number from Agency C. The first two terms on the left side of the equation can be combined by computing their lowest common denominator, which is 6. Therefore:

$$1/2 \, X = 3/6 \, X \text{ and } 1/3 \, X = 2/6 \, X$$

The sum of $3/6 \, X$ and $2/6 \, X$ is $5/6 \, X$, which, when subtracted from X (or $6/6 \, X$), yields the results:

$$1/6 \, X = 3 \text{ and } X = 18$$

Responses A, B, and D are the result of erroneous computations.

8. It has been established in recent productivity studies that, on the average, it takes a filing clerk 2 hours and 12 minutes to fill four drawers of a filing cabinet. At this rate, how long would it take two clerks to fill 16 drawers?

   (A) 4 hrs.
   (B) 4 hrs., 20 min.
   (C) 8 hrs.
   (D) 8 hrs., 40 min.
   (E) none of these

The answer is E. The correct answer is not given as one of the response choices. The answer can be obtained by first converting 12 minutes to .2 hour, and then setting up a simple proportion:

$$2.2/4 = X/16$$

Solving this proportion, we obtain $4X = 35.2$; $X = 8.8$. This, however, is the number of hours that it would take one filing clerk to do the job. If two clerks are filling the 16 drawers, the job would be completed in half that time or in 4.4 hours, which is 4 hours, 24 minutes.

Responses A, B, C, and D are the result of erroneous computations.

SAMPLE QUESTIONS: POSTAL EXAMS

After many years of administering a different postal examination for each individual job title or for a small cluster of job titles, the postal service has determined that it is more efficient and equally effective to administer the same exam for large groups of postal occupations that require related skills and abilities.

Accordingly, the same examination is now administered for the following job titles:

Clerk-Carrier
Mail Handler
Mail Processor
Distribution Clerk, Machine
Mark-up Clerk
Flat Sorting Machine Operator
Rural Carrier

The following are official test instructions and official sample questions distributed by the postal service to candidates for all of these jobs.

TEST INSTRUCTIONS

During the test session, it will be your responsibility to pay close attention to what the examiner has to say and to follow all instructions. One of the purposes of the test is to see how quickly and accurately you can work. Therefore, each part of the test will be carefully timed. You will not **START** until you are told to do so. Also, when you are told to **STOP,** you must immediately **STOP** answering the questions. When you are told to work on a particular part of the examination, regardless of which part, you are to work on that part **ONLY. If you finish a part before time is called, you may review your answers for that part, but you will not go on or back to any other part. Failure to follow ANY** directions given to you by the examiner may be grounds for disqualification. Instructions read by the examiner are intended to ensure that each applicant has the same fair and objective opportunity to compete in the examination.

The following questions are like the ones that will be on the test. Study these carefully. This will give you practice with the different kinds of questions and show you how to mark your answers.

Part A: Address Checking

In this part of the test, you will have to decide whether two addresses are alike or different. If the two addresses are exactly *Alike* in every way, darken circle A for the question. If the two addresses are *Different* in any way, darken circle D for the question.

Mark your answers to these sample questions on the Sample Answer Grid at the right.

1...2134 S 20th St   2134 S 20th St

Since the two addresses are exactly alike, mark A for question 1 on the Sample Answer Grid.

2...4608 N Warnock St   4806 N Warnock St

3...1202 W Girard Dr   1202 W Girard Rd

4...Chappaqua NY 10514   Chappaqua NY 10514

5...2207 Markland Ave   2207 Markham Ave

The correct answers to questions 2 to 5 are: 2D, 3D, 4A, and 5D.

Sample Answer Grid
1 Ⓐ Ⓓ
2 Ⓐ Ⓓ
3 Ⓐ Ⓓ
4 Ⓐ Ⓓ
5 Ⓐ Ⓓ

Your score on Part A of the actual test will be based on the number of wrong answers as well as on the number of right answers. Part A is scored right answers minus wrong answers. Random guessing should not help your score. For the Part A test, you will have six minutes to answer as many of the 95 questions as you can. It will be to your advantage to work as quickly and as accurately as possible. You will not be expected to be able to answer all the questions in the time allowed.

Part B: Memory for Addresses

In this part of the test, you will have to memorize the locations (A, B, C, D, or E) of 25 addresses shown in five boxes, like those below. For example, "Sardis" is in Box C, "6800-6999 Table" is in Box B, etc. (The addresses in the actual test will be different.)

A	B	C	D	E
4700-5999 Table	6800-6999 Table	5600-6499 Table	6500-6799 Table	4400-4699 Table
Lismore	Kelford	Joel	Tatum	Ruskin
5600-6499 West	6500-6799 West	6800-6999 West	4400-4699 West	4700-5599 West
Hesper	Musella	Sardis	Porter	Nathan
4400-4699 Blake	5600-6499 Blake	6500-6799 Blake	4700-5599 Blake	6800-6999 Blake

Study the locations of the addresses for five minutes. As you study, silently repeat these to yourself. Then cover the boxes and try to answer the questions below. Mark your answers for each question by darkening the circle as was done for questions 1 and 2.

1. Musella
2. 4700-5599 Blake
3. 4700-5599 Table
4. Tatum

5. 4400-4699 Blake
6. Hesper
7. Kelford
8. Nathan

9. 6500-6799 Blake
10. Joel
11. 4400-4699 Blake
12. 6500-6799 West

13. Porter
14. 6800-6999 Blake

Sample Answer Grid
1 Ⓐ ● Ⓒ Ⓓ Ⓔ   5 Ⓐ Ⓑ Ⓒ Ⓓ Ⓔ   9 Ⓐ Ⓑ Ⓒ Ⓓ Ⓔ   13 Ⓐ Ⓑ Ⓒ Ⓓ Ⓔ
2 Ⓐ Ⓑ Ⓒ ● Ⓔ   6 Ⓐ Ⓑ Ⓒ Ⓓ Ⓔ   10 Ⓐ Ⓑ Ⓒ Ⓓ Ⓔ   14 Ⓐ Ⓑ Ⓒ Ⓓ Ⓔ
3 Ⓐ Ⓑ Ⓒ Ⓓ Ⓔ   7 Ⓐ Ⓑ Ⓒ Ⓓ Ⓔ   11 Ⓐ Ⓑ Ⓒ Ⓓ Ⓔ
4 Ⓐ Ⓑ Ⓒ Ⓓ Ⓔ   8 Ⓐ Ⓑ Ⓒ Ⓓ Ⓔ   12 Ⓐ Ⓑ Ⓒ Ⓓ Ⓔ

The correct answers for questions 3 to 14 are: 3A, 4D, 5A, 6A, 7B, 8E, 9C, 10C, 11A, 12B, 13D, and 14E.

During the examination, you will have three practice exercises to help you memorize the location of addresses shown in five boxes. After the practice exercises, the actual test will be given. Part B is scored right answers minus one-fourth of the wrong answers. Random guessing should not help your score. But, if you can eliminate one or more alternatives, it is to your advantage to guess. For the Part B test, you will have five minutes to answer as many of the 88 questions as you can. It will be to your advantage to work as quickly and as accurately as you can. You will not be expected to be able to answer all the questions in the time allowed.

Part C: Number Series

For each *Number Series* question there is at the left a series of numbers which follow some definite order and at the right five sets of two numbers each. You are to look at the numbers in the series at the left and find out what order they follow. Then decide what the next two numbers in that series would be if the same order were continued. Mark your answers on the Sample Answer Grid.

1. 1 2 3 4 5 6 7 . . . . (A) 1 2   (B) 5 6   (C) 8 9   (D) 4 5   (E) 7 8

The numbers in this series are increasing by 1. If the series were continued for two more numbers, it would read: 1 2 3 4 5 6 7 8 9. Therefore the correct answer is 8 and 9 and you should have darkened C for question 1.

2. 15 14 13 12 11 10 9 . . . . . (A) 2 1   (B) 17 16   (C) 8 9   (D) 8 7   (E) 9 8

The numbers in this series are decreasing by 1. If the series were continued for two more numbers, it would read: 15 14 13 12 11 10 9 8 7. Therefore the correct answer is 8 and 7 and you should have darkened D for question 2.

3. 20 20 21 21 22 22 23 . . . . (A) 23 23   (B) 23 24   (C) 19 19   (D) 22 23   (E) 21 22

Each number in this series is repeated and then increased by 1. If the series were continued for two more numbers, it would read: 20 20 21 21 22 22 23 23 24. Therefore the correct answer is 23 and 24 and you should have darkened B for question 3.

4. 17 3 17 4 17 5 17 . . . . (A) 6 17   (B) 6 7   (C) 17 6   (D) 5 6   (E) 17 7

This series is the number 17 separated by numbers increasing by 1, beginning with the number 3. If the series were continued for two more numbers, it would read: 17 3 17 4 17 5 17 6 17. Therefore the correct answer is 6 and 17 and you should have darkened A for question 4.

5. 1 2 4 5 7 8 10 . . . . (A) 11 12   (B) 12 14   (C) 10 13   (D) 12 13   (E) 11 13

The numbers in this series are increasing first by 1 (plus 1) and then by 2 (plus 2). If the series were continued for two more numbers, it would read: 1 2 4 5 7 8 10 (plus 1) *11* and (plus 2) *13*. Therefore the correct answer is 11 and 13 and you should have darkened E for question 5.

Now read and work sample questions 6 through 10 and mark your answers on the Sample Answer Grid.

6. 21 21 20 20 19 19 18 . . . (A) 18 18   (B) 18 17   (C) 17 18   (D) 17 17   (E) 18 19

7. 1 22 1 23 1 24 1 . . . . (A) 26 1   (B) 25 26   (C) 25 1   (D) 1 26   (E) 1 25

8. 1 20 3 19 5 18 7 . . . . (A) 8 9   (B) 8 17   (C) 17 10   (D) 17 9   (E) 9 18

9. 4 7 10 13 16 19 22 . . . . . (A) 23 26   (B) 25 27   (C) 25 26   (D) 25 28   (E) 24 27

10. 30 2 28 4 26 6 24 . . . . . . (A) 23 9   (B) 26 8   (C) 8 9   (D) 26 22   (E) 8 22

Sample Answer Grid

6 Ⓐ Ⓑ ©Ⓒ Ⓓ Ⓔ **8** Ⓐ Ⓑ Ⓒ Ⓓ Ⓔ **9** Ⓐ Ⓑ Ⓒ Ⓓ Ⓔ **10** Ⓐ Ⓑ Ⓒ Ⓓ Ⓔ
7 Ⓐ Ⓑ Ⓒ Ⓓ Ⓔ

The correct answers to sample questions 6 to 10 are: 6B, 7C, 8D, 9D, and 10E. Explanations follow.

6. Each number in the series repeats itself and then decreases by 1 or minus 1; *21* (repeat) *21* (minus 1) *20* (repeat) *20* (minus 1) *19* (repeat) *19* (minus 1) *18* (repeat) *?* (minus 1) *?*

7. The number 1 is separated by numbers which begin with 22 and increase by 1; *1 22 1* (increase 22 by 1) *23 1* (increase 23 by 1) *24 1* (increase 24 by 1) *?*

8. This is best explained by two alternating series—one series starts with 1 and increases by 2 or plus 2; the other series starts with 20 and decreases by 1 or minus 1.

1	*3*	*5*	*7*	*?*
^	^	^	^	
20	*19*	*18*	*?*	

9. This series of numbers increases by 3 (plus 3) beginning with the first number— *4 7 10 13 16 19 22 ? ?*

10. Look for two alternating series—one series starts with 30 and decreases by 2 (minus 2); the other series starts with 2 and increases by 2 (plus 2).

Now try questions 11 to 15.

11. 5 6 20 7 8 19 9 . . . . (A) 10 18 (B) 18 17 (C) 10 17 (D) 18 19 (E) 10 11

12. 4 6 9 11 14 16 19 . . . . . . (A) 21 24 (B) 22 25 (C) 20 22 (D) 21 23 (E) 22 24

13. 8 8 1 10 10 3 12 . . . . (A) 13 13 (B) 12 5 (C) 12 4 (D) 13 5 (E) 4 12

14. 10 12 50 15 17 50 20 . . . (A) 50 21 (B) 21 50 (C) 50 22 (D) 22 50 (E) 22 24

15. 20 21 23 24 27 28
32 33 38 39 . . . . (A) 45 46 (B) 45 52 (C) 44 45 (D) 44 49 (E) 40 46

Sample Answer Grid

11 Ⓐ Ⓑ Ⓒ Ⓓ Ⓔ **13** Ⓐ Ⓑ Ⓒ Ⓓ Ⓔ **14** Ⓐ Ⓑ Ⓒ Ⓓ Ⓔ **15** Ⓐ Ⓑ Ⓒ Ⓓ Ⓔ
12 Ⓐ Ⓑ Ⓒ Ⓓ Ⓔ

The correct answers to the sample questions above are: 11A, 12A, 13B, 14D, and 15A.

It will be to your advantage to answer every question in Part C that you can, since your score on this part of the test will be based on the number of questions that you answer correctly. Answer first those questions which are easiest for you. For the Part C test, you will have 20 minutes to answer as many of the 24 questions as you can.

Instructions to be read for Part D. **(The words in parentheses should NOT be read aloud.)**

You are to follow the instructions that I shall read to you. I cannot repeat them.

Look at the samples. Sample 1 has a number and a line beside it. On the line write A as in ace. **(Pause 2 seconds.)** Now on the Sample Answer Grid, find number 5 **(pause 2 seconds)** and darken the letter you just wrote on the line. **(Pause 2 seconds.)**

Look at Sample 2. **(Pause slightly.)** Draw a line under the third number. **(Pause 2 seconds.)** Now look on the Sample Answer Grid, find the number under which you just drew a line and darken B as in boy. **(Pause 5 seconds.)**

Look at the letters in Sample 3. **(Pause slightly.)** Draw a line under the third letter in the line. **(Pause 2 seconds.)** Now on your Sample Answer Grid, find number 9 **(pause 2 seconds)** and darken the letter under which you drew a line. **(Pause 5 seconds.)**

Look at the five circles in Sample 4. **(Pause slightly.)** Each circle has a number and a line in it. Write D as in dog on the line in the last circle. **(Pause 2 seconds.)** Now on the Sample Answer Grid, darken the number-letter combination that is in the circle you just wrote in. **(Pause 5 seconds.)**

Look at Sample 5. **(Pause slightly.)** There are two circles and two boxes of different sizes with numbers in them. **(Pause slightly.)** If 4 is more than 2 and if 5 is less than 3, write A as in ace in the smaller circle. **(Pause slightly.)** Otherwise write C as in car in the larger box. **(Pause 2 seconds.)** Now on the Sample Answer Grid, darken the number-letter combination in the box or circle in which you just wrote. **(Pause 5 seconds.)**

Now look at the Sample Answer Grid. **(Pause slightly.)** You should have darkened 4B, 5A, 9A, 10D, and 12C on the Sample Answer Grid. **(If the person preparing to take the examination made any mistakes, try to help him or her see why he or she made wrong marks.)**

Part D: Following Oral Directions

In this part of the test, you will be told to follow directions by writing in a test booklet and then on an answer sheet. The test booklet will have lines of material like the following five samples:

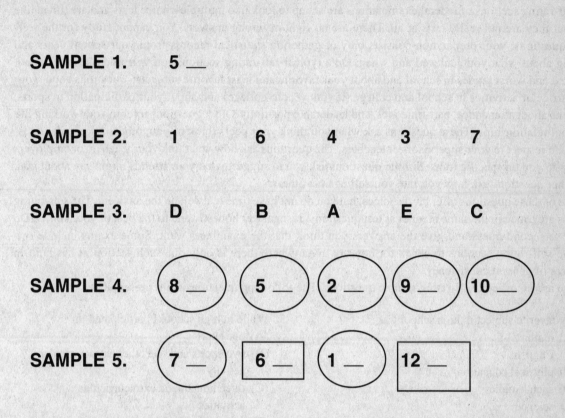

SAMPLE 1. 5 __

SAMPLE 2. 1 6 4 3 7

SAMPLE 3. D B A E C

SAMPLE 4. 8 __ 5 __ 2 __ 9 __ 10 __

SAMPLE 5. 7 __ 6 __ 1 __ 12 __

To practice this part of the test, tear out the page of instructions to be read. Then have somebody read the instructions to you and you follow the instructions. When he or she tells you to darken the space on the Sample Answer Grid, use the one on this page.

Your score for Part D will be based on the number of questions that you answer correctly. Therefore, if you are not sure of an answer, it will be to your advantage to guess. Part D will take about 25 minutes.

Sample Answer Grid		
1 Ⓐ Ⓑ Ⓒ Ⓓ Ⓔ	5 Ⓐ Ⓑ Ⓒ Ⓓ Ⓔ	9 Ⓐ Ⓑ Ⓒ Ⓓ Ⓔ
2 Ⓐ Ⓑ Ⓒ Ⓓ Ⓔ	6 Ⓐ Ⓑ Ⓒ Ⓓ Ⓔ	10 Ⓐ Ⓑ Ⓒ Ⓓ Ⓔ
3 Ⓐ Ⓑ Ⓒ Ⓓ Ⓔ	7 Ⓐ Ⓑ Ⓒ Ⓓ Ⓔ	11 Ⓐ Ⓑ Ⓒ Ⓓ Ⓔ
4 Ⓐ Ⓑ Ⓒ Ⓓ Ⓔ	8 Ⓐ Ⓑ Ⓒ Ⓓ Ⓔ	12 Ⓐ Ⓑ Ⓒ Ⓓ Ⓔ

SELF-RATING QUESTIONS

The self-rating sections of federal examinations are set up to look like multiple-choice tests and are timed like tests, but they are not really tests at all. There are no right or wrong answers. You cannot study for the self-rating questions; your preparation consists only of gathering statistical records from your school years and thinking about what you achieved and when. On a typical self-rating section, you will find questions about your best and worst grades in school and about your favorite and least favorite subjects; questions about your extracurricular activities in school and college (if you went to college) and about your participation in sports; questions about attendance, part-time jobs, and leadership positions. Other questions refer to your working life or school relationships. These questions ask what you think your peers think of you; others ask similar questions with respect to your supervisors or teachers. The questions ask how you think your teachers or employers might rate you on specific traits. Similar questions ask you to suggest what your friends might say about you. Still other questions ask how you rate yourself against others.

Some of these questions offer hard choices, but you do not have time to dwell on the answers. The self-rating sections are timed in the same manner as test questions. Just answer honestly and to the best of your ability. Do not try to second-guess and give the answers you think that the examiners want. Some exams include two separate self-rating sections to check for honesty. Even where there is only one such section, it has built-in measures of general consistency.

There are no official self-rating sample questions. The following questions are representative.

1. My favorite subject in high school was
   (A) math
   (B) English
   (C) physical education
   (D) social studies
   (E) science

2. My GPA upon graduation from high school (on a 4.0 scale) was
   (A) lower than 2.51
   (B) 2.51 to 2.80
   (C) 2.81 to 3.25
   (D) 3.26 to 3.60
   (E) higher than 3.60

3. In my second year of high school I was absent
   (A) never
   (B) not more than 3 days
   (C) 4 to 10 days
   (D) more often than 10 days
   (E) do not recall

4. My best grades in high school were in
   (A) art
   (B) math
   (C) English
   (D) social studies
   (E) music

5. While in high school I participated in
   (A) one sport
   (B) two sports and one other extracurricular activity
   (C) three nonathletic extracurricular activities
   (D) no extracurricular activities
   (E) other than the above

6. During my senior year in high school I held a paying job
   (A) 0 hours a week
   (B) 1 to 5 hours a week
   (C) 6 to 10 hours a week
   (D) 11 to 16 hours a week
   (E) more than 16 hours a week

7. The number of semesters in which I failed a course in high school was
   (A) none
   (B) one
   (C) two or three
   (D) four or five
   (E) more than five

8. In high school I did volunteer work
   (A) more than 10 hours a week
   (B) 5 to 10 hours a week on a regular basis
   (C) sporadically
   (D) seldom
   (E) not at all

If you did not go to college, skip questions 9–20. Go to question 21.

9. My general area of concentration in college was
   (A) performing arts
   (B) humanities
   (C) social sciences
   (D) business
   (E) none of the above

10. At graduation from college, my age was
    (A) under 20
    (B) 20
    (C) 21 to 24
    (D) 25 to 29
    (E) 30 or over

11. My standing in my graduating class was in the
    (A) bottom third
    (B) middle third
    (C) top third
    (D) top quarter
    (E) top 10 percent

12. In college, I was elected to a major office in a class or in a club or organization
    (A) more than six times
    (B) four or five times
    (C) two or three times
    (D) once
    (E) never

13. In comparison to my peers, I cut classes
    (A) much less often than most
    (B) somewhat less often than most
    (C) just about the same as most
    (D) somewhat more often than most
    (E) much more often than most

14. The campus activities in which I participated most were
    (A) social service
    (B) political
    (C) literary
    (D) did not participate in campus activities
    (E) did not participate in any of these activities

15. My name appeared on the dean's list
    (A) never
    (B) once or twice
    (C) in three or more terms
    (D) in more terms than it did not appear
    (E) do not remember

16. The volunteer work I did while in college was predominantly
    (A) health-care related
    (B) religious
    (C) political
    (D) educational
    (E) did not volunteer

17. While a college student, I spent most of my summers
    (A) in summer school
    (B) earning money
    (C) traveling
    (D) in service activities
    (E) resting

18. My college education was financed
    (A) entirely by my parents
    (B) by my parents and my own earnings
    (C) by scholarships, loans, and my own earnings
    (D) by my parents and loans
    (E) by a combination of sources not listed above

19. In the college classroom I was considered
    (A) a listener
    (B) an occasional contributor
    (C) an average participant
    (D) a frequent contributor
    (E) a leader

20. The person on campus whom I most admired was
    (A) another student
    (B) an athletic coach
    (C) a teacher
    (D) an administrator
    (E) a journalist

21. My peers would probably describe me as
    (A) analytical
    (B) glib
    (C) organized
    (D) funny
    (E) helpful

22. According to my supervisors (or teachers), my greatest asset is my
    (A) ability to communicate orally
    (B) written expression
    (C) ability to motivate others
    (D) organization of time
    (E) friendly personality

23. In the past two years, I have applied for
    (A) no jobs other than this one
    (B) one other job
    (C) two to four other jobs
    (D) five to eight other jobs
    (E) more than eight jobs

24. In the past year, I read strictly for pleasure
    (A) no books
    (B) one book
    (C) two books
    (D) three to six books
    (E) more than six books

25. When I read for pleasure, I read mostly
    (A) history
    (B) fiction
    (C) poetry
    (D) biography
    (E) current events

26. My peers would say of me that, when they ask me a question, I am
    (A) helpful
    (B) brusque
    (C) condescending
    (D) generous
    (E) patient

27. My supervisors (or teachers) would say that my area of least competence is
    (A) analytical ability
    (B) written communication
    (C) attention to detail
    (D) public speaking
    (E) self-control

28. In the past two years, the number of full-time (35 hours or more) jobs I have held is
    (A) none
    (B) one
    (C) two or three
    (D) four
    (E) five or more

29. Compared to my peers, my supervisors (or teachers) would rank my dependability
    (A) much better than average
    (B) somewhat better than average
    (C) about average
    (D) somewhat less than average
    (E) much less than average

30. In my opinion, the most important of the following attributes in an employee is
    (A) discretion
    (B) loyalty
    (C) open-mindedness
    (D) courtesy
    (E) competence

31. My peers would say that the word that describes me least is
    (A) sociable
    (B) reserved
    (C) impatient
    (D) judgmental
    (E) independent

32. My attendance record over the past year has been
    (A) not as good as I would like it to be
    (B) not as good as my supervisors (or teachers) would like it to be
    (C) a source of embarrassment
    (D) satisfactory
    (E) a source of pride

There are no "right" answers to these questions, so there is no answer key.